AF348497

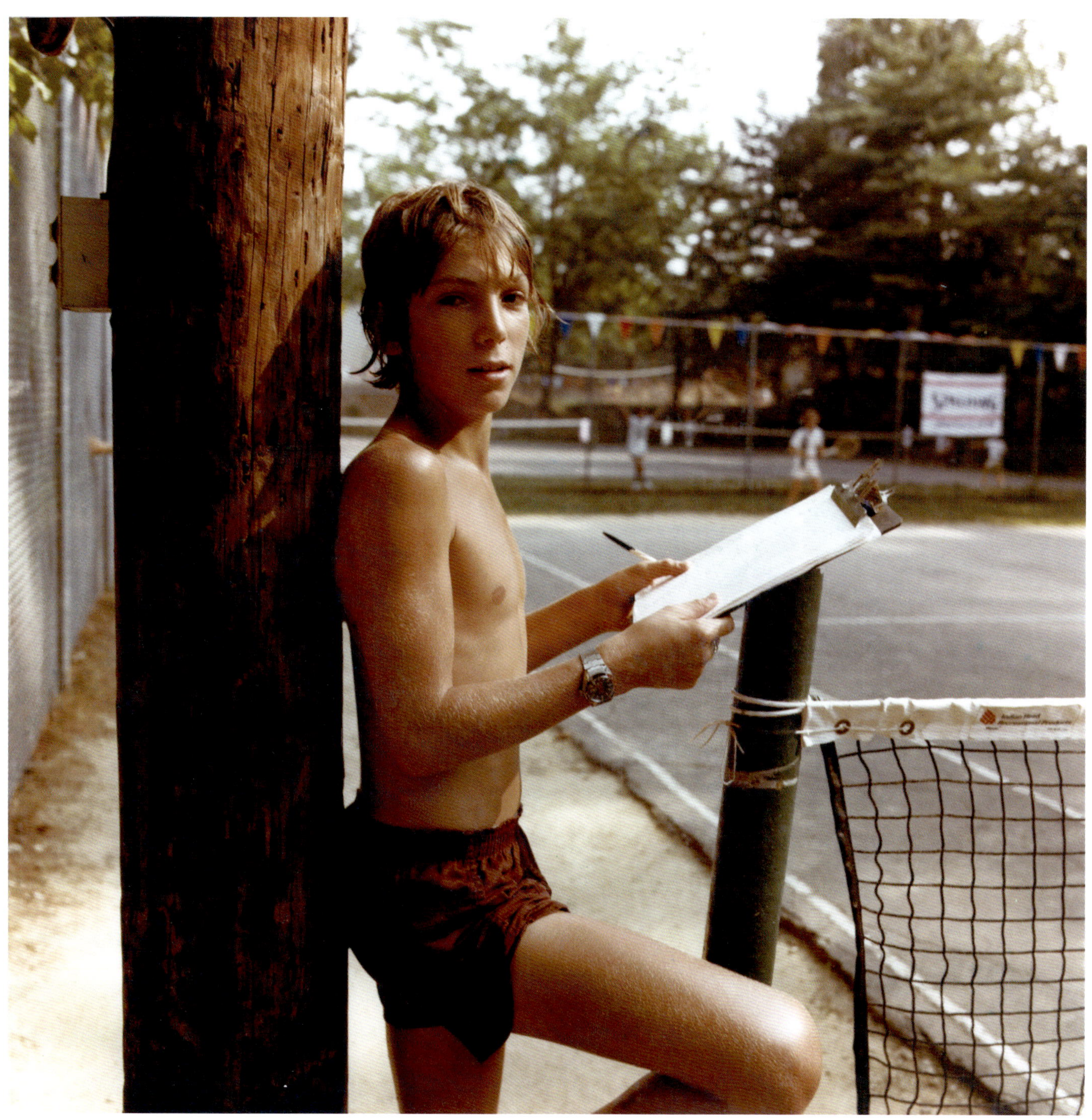

Letter16 Press, Inc.
www.letter16press.com

Book design: Francesco Casale
Editing: Brett Sokol

ISBN: 978-0-9893811-9-2
Library of Congress Control Number: 2019955399

First Edition

Printed in China.

K= **Knight Foundation**

This publication was made possible with the assistance of the John S. and James L.
Knight Foundation, through the Knight Arts Challenge.

Hello Muddah, Hello Faddah

Andy Sweet's Summer Camp 1977

Foreword by Brett Sokol
Introduction by Naomi Fry

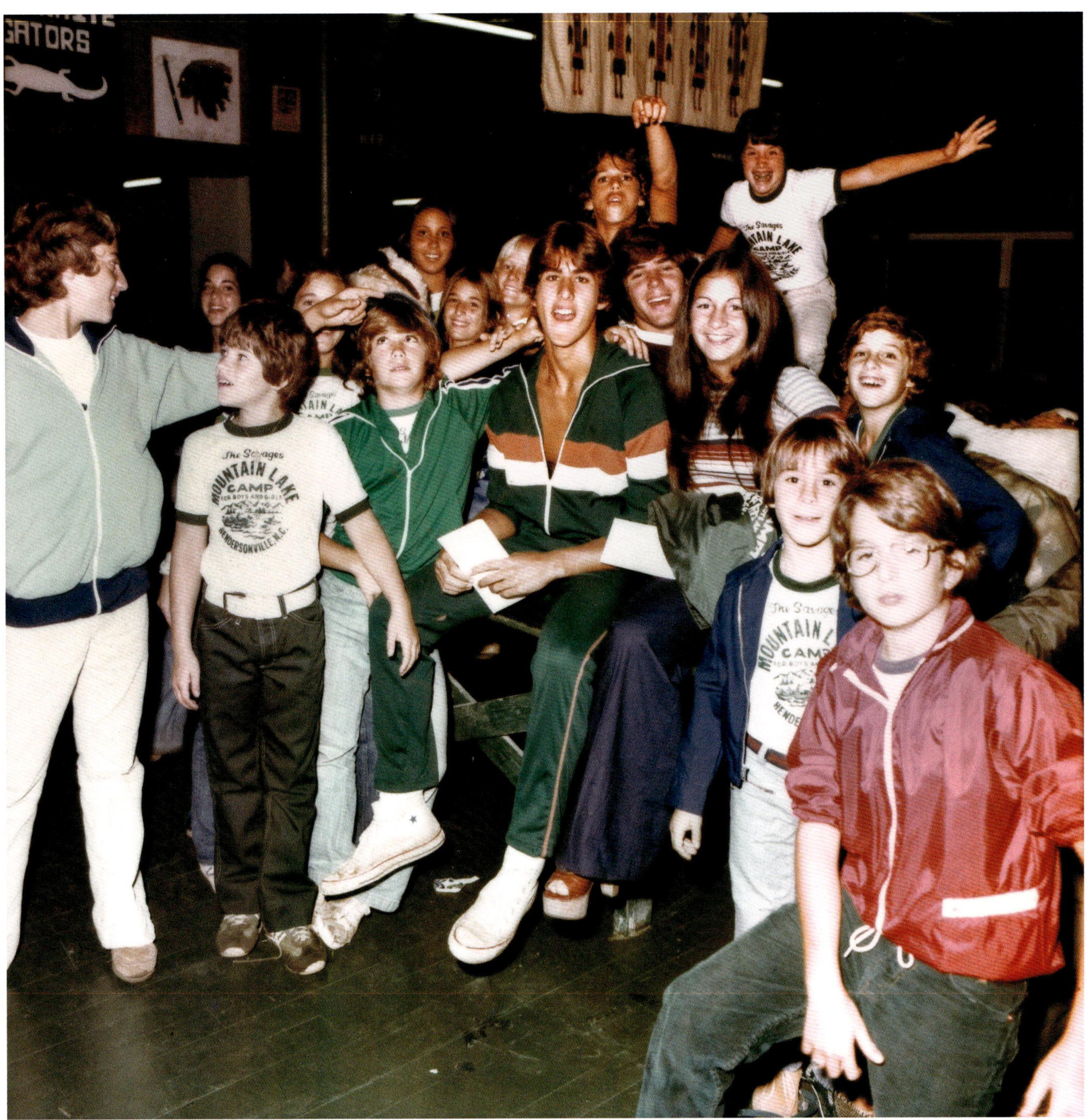

Foreward By Brett Sokol

In the fall of 1977, Andy Sweet was a man on a mission, set on, as he wrote at the time, "telling my own story about the truth of something." Unlike many of his fellow art students in the University of Colorado at Boulder's MFA program, then-twenty-four-year-old Sweet knew exactly what he wanted to do—and how he would do it—upon graduating that December.

A self-described "documentary photographer" who shot exclusively in color after having switched over from black-and-white only the previous year, Sweet carried himself with a remarkable air of self-assurance. Eschewing the dense theory and obfuscating artspeak so common to many of today's MFA students, he used a statement accompanying his master's thesis to place himself on an aesthetic path laid out by several of the mid-'70s brightest emerging photographic figures.

"Robert Adams did not move to the eastern front of the Rockies to photograph the land and its changes," Sweet wrote. "Emmet Gowin did not have a family so he could have subject matter for his pictures and Bill Owens did not move to suburbia for the purpose of making photos; he lived there first. These three photographers all have something in common with the way I work. Their photographs are not the reason of their subject matter. The subject matter is the reason of their work. Belonging, knowing, and understanding, before picking up the camera, is the most determining factor."

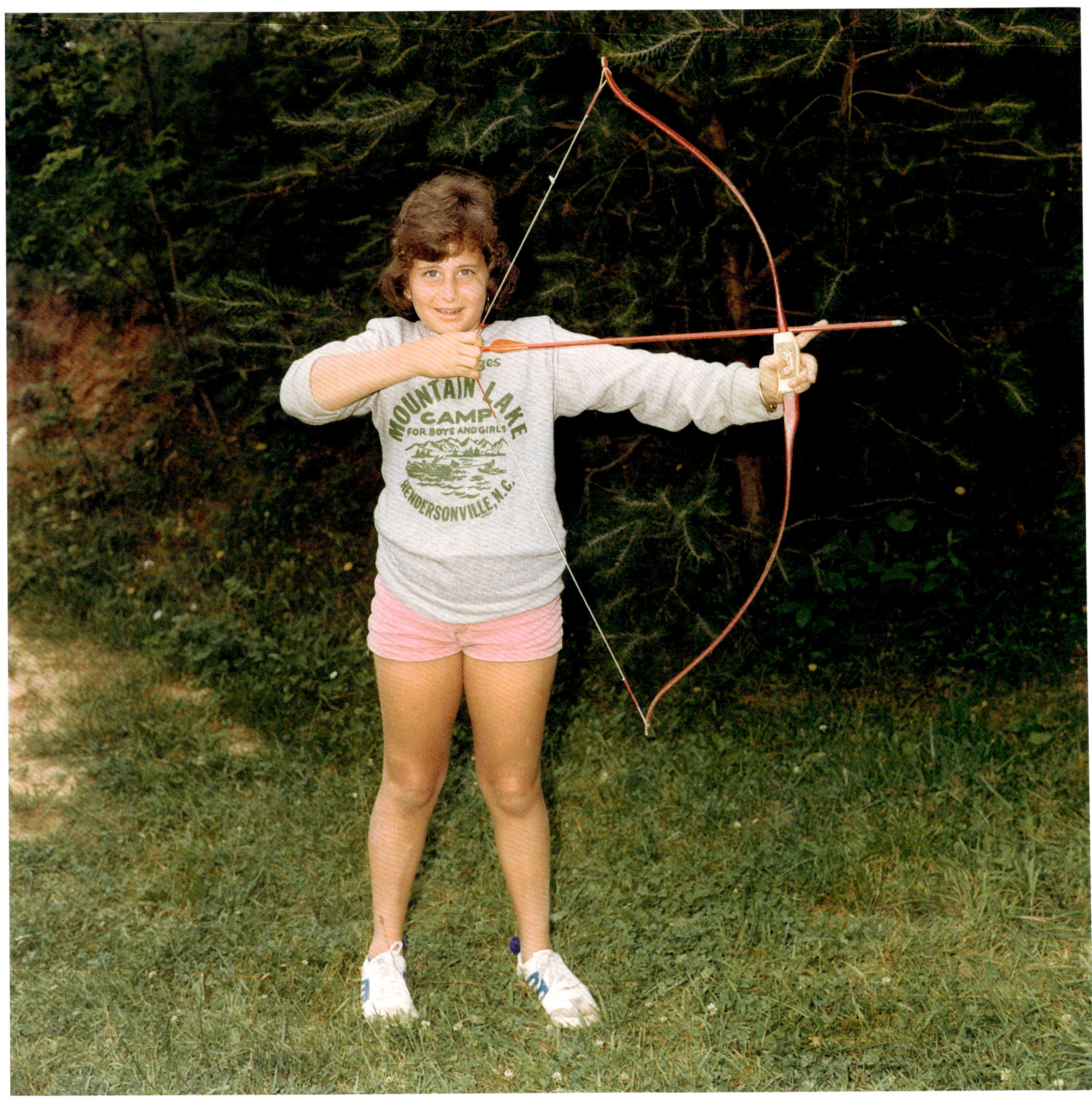

MOUNTAIN LAKE
CAMP
FOR BOYS AND GIRLS
HENDERSONVILLE, N.C.

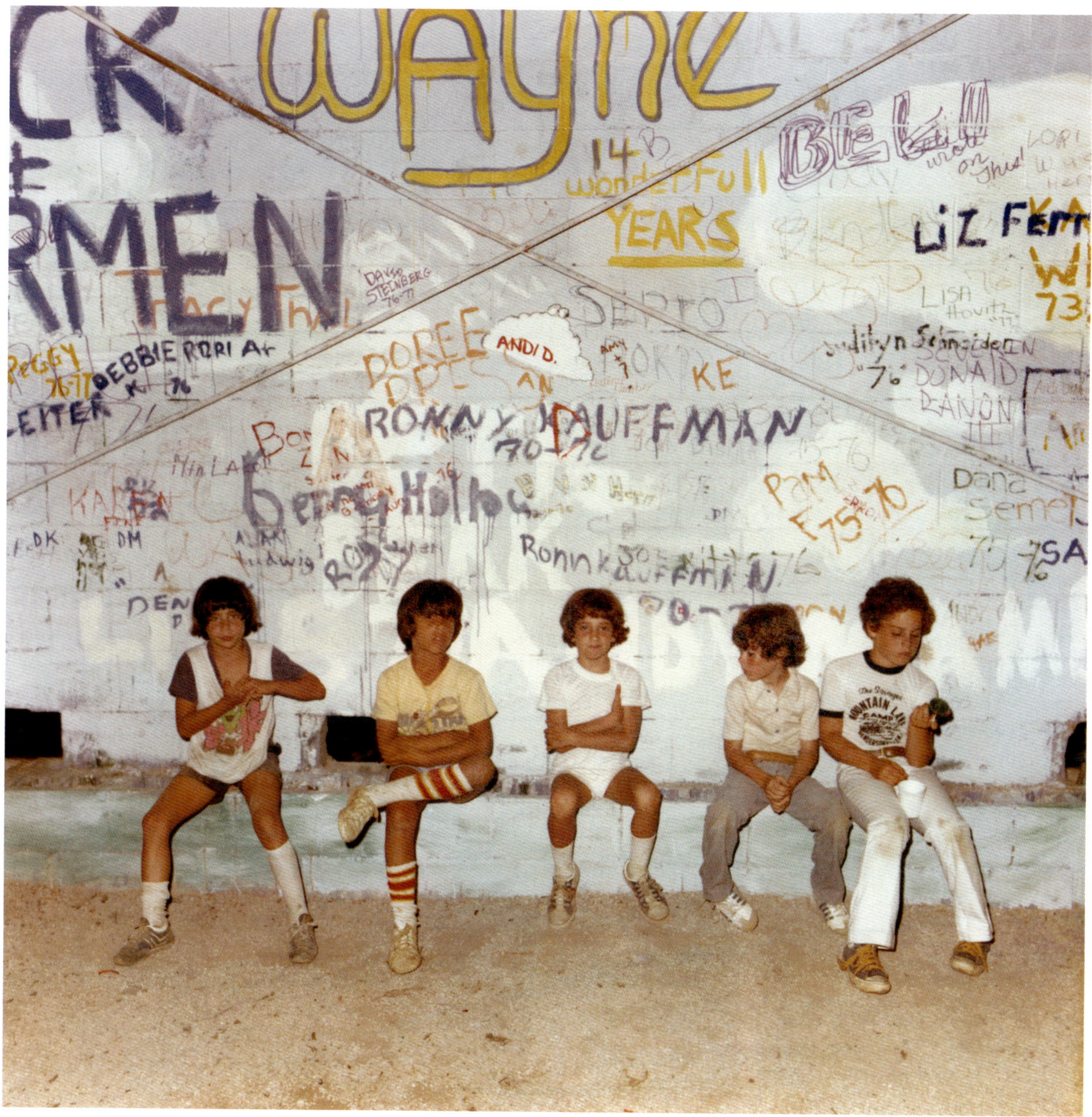

CK WAYNE
MEN
14 B
wonderFull
YEARS
BE
LiZ Fenn
LISA
73
Judilyn Schneider
'76
DONALD
DAVON
DEBBIE RORI A
POREE
AND/ D.
KE
RONNY KAUFFMAN
PAM
F 75 76
Dana
Semel
75 76 SA
RonnKauFFMAN

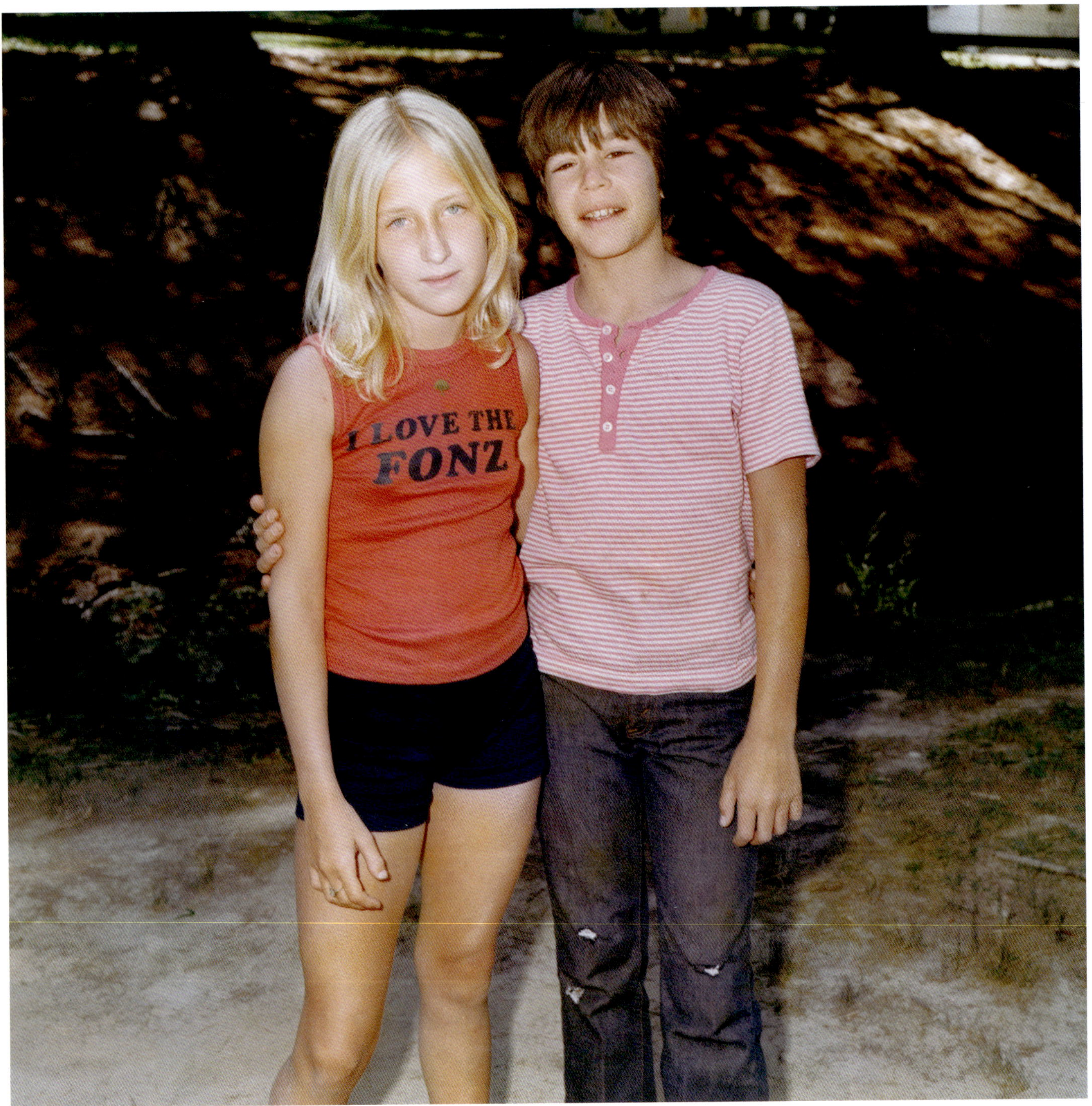
I LOVE THE
FONZ

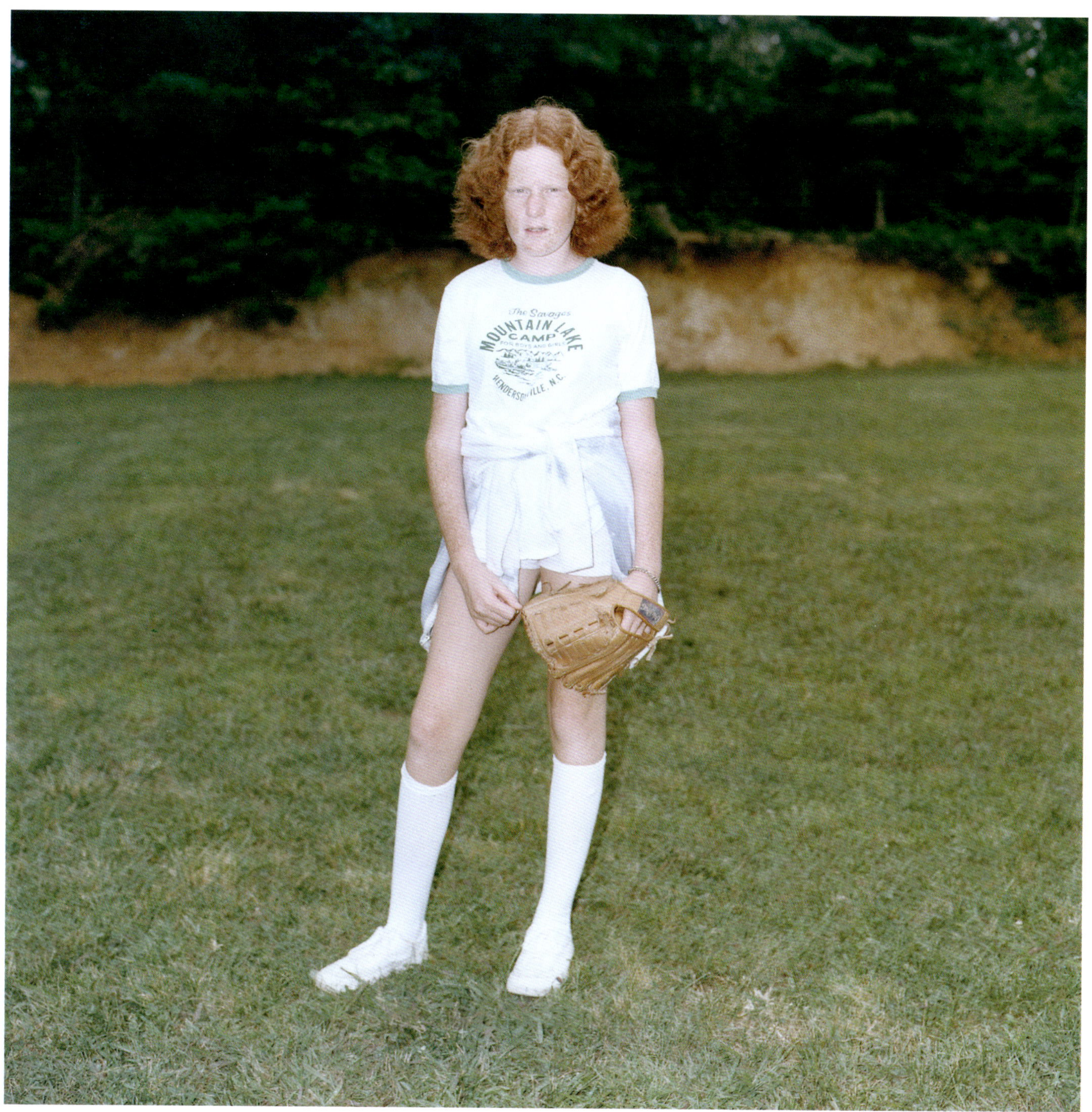
The Savages
MOUNTAIN LAKE
CAMP
FOR BOYS AND GIRLS
HENDERSONVILLE, N.C.

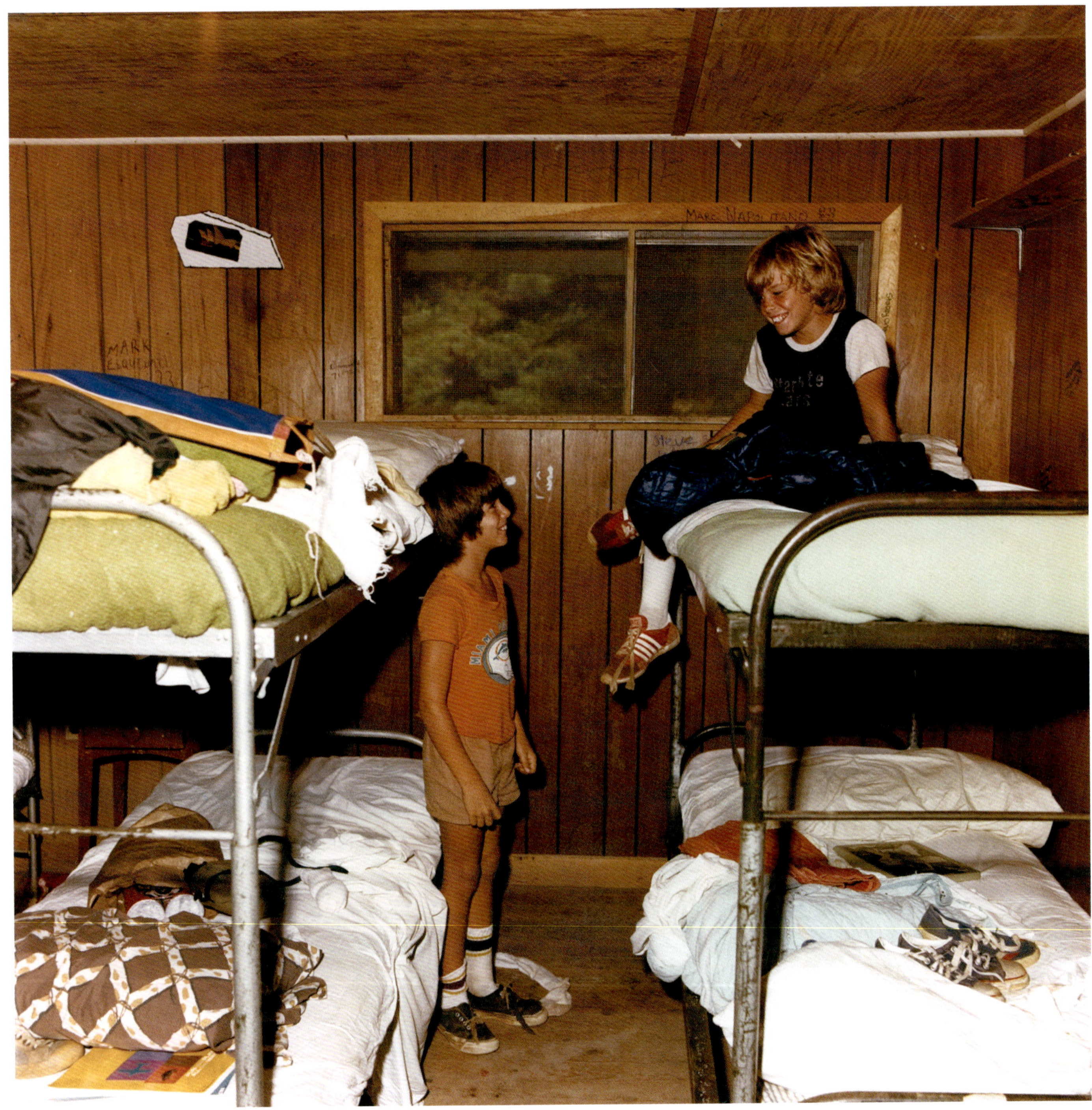

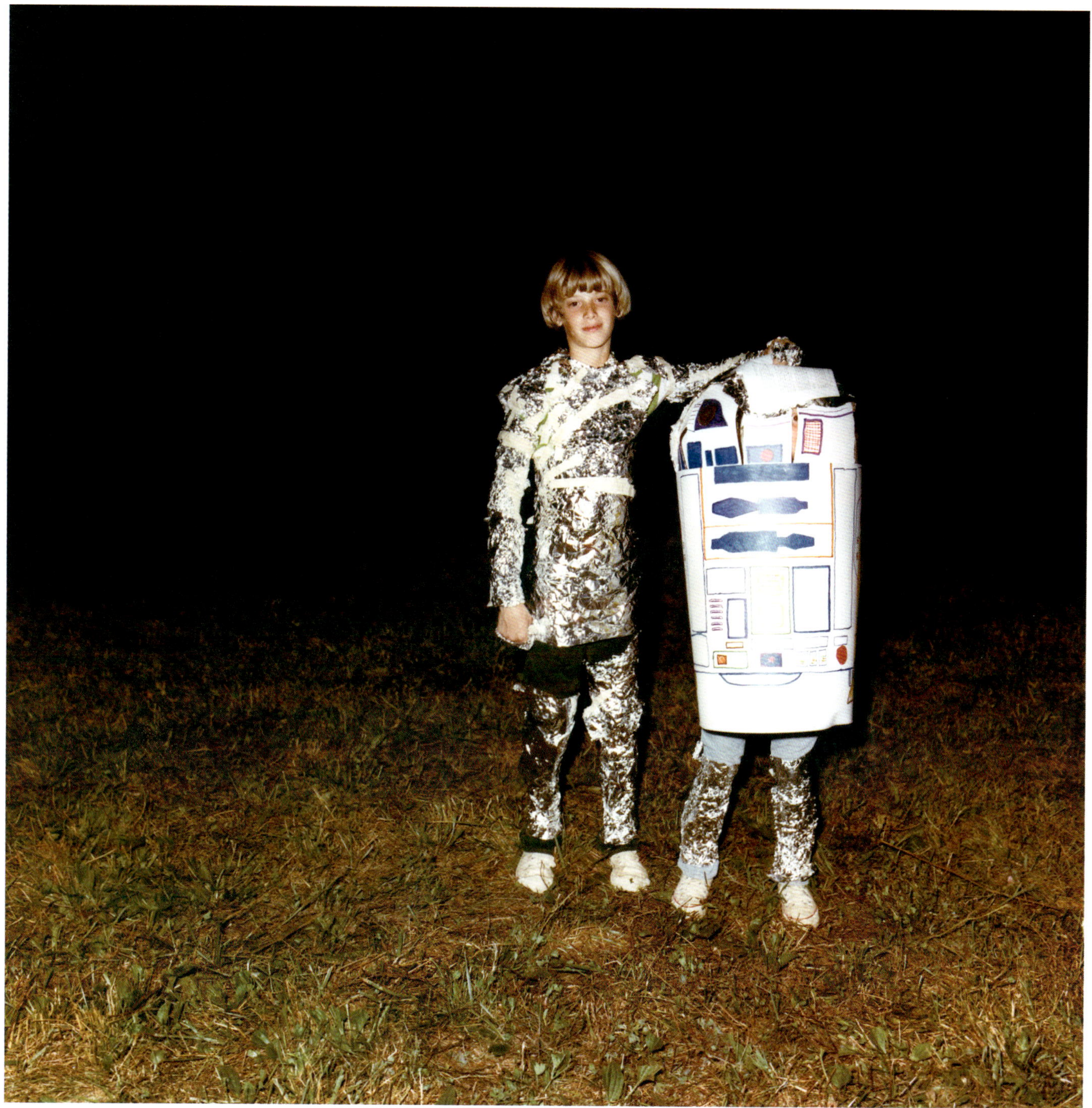

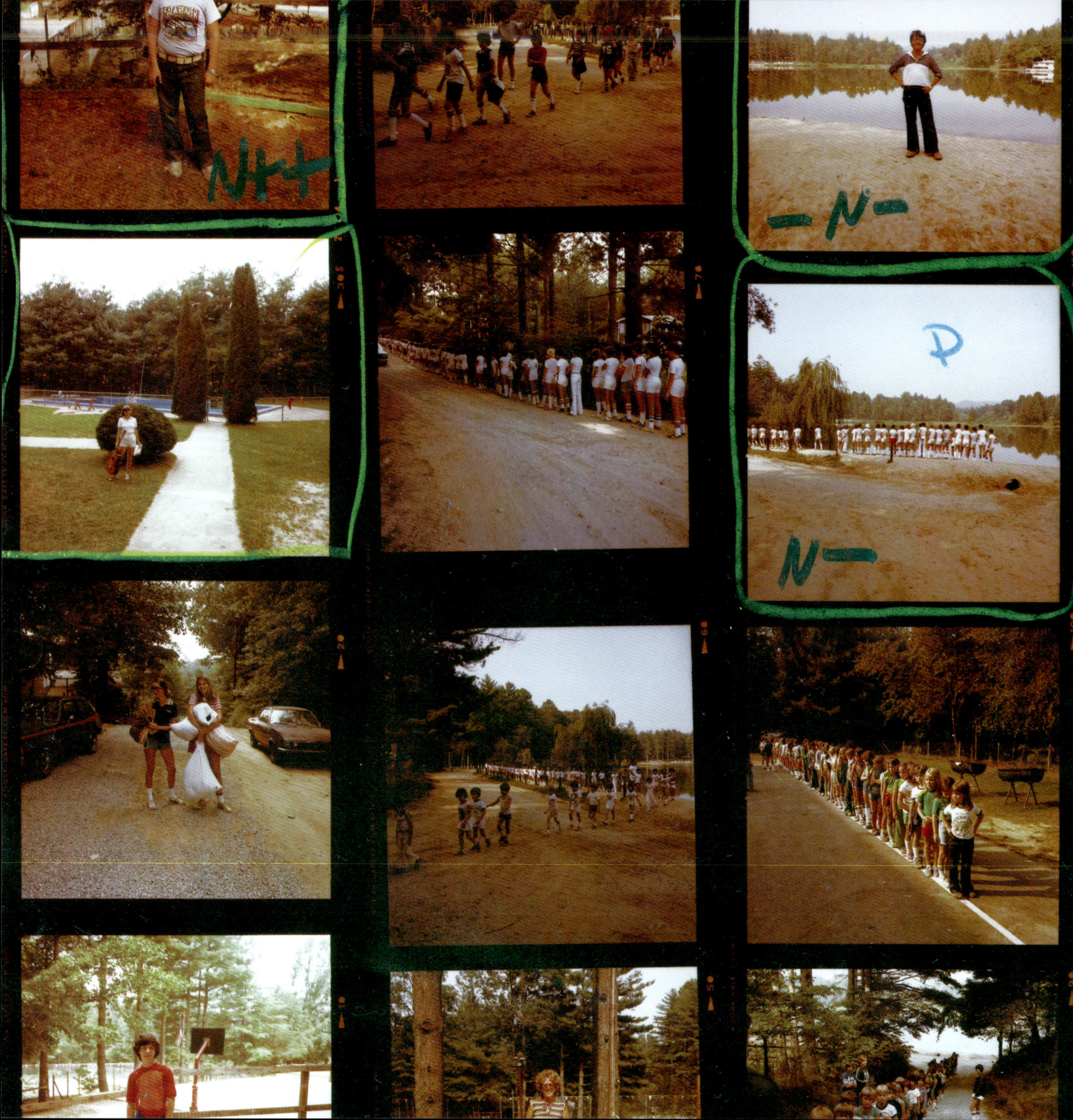

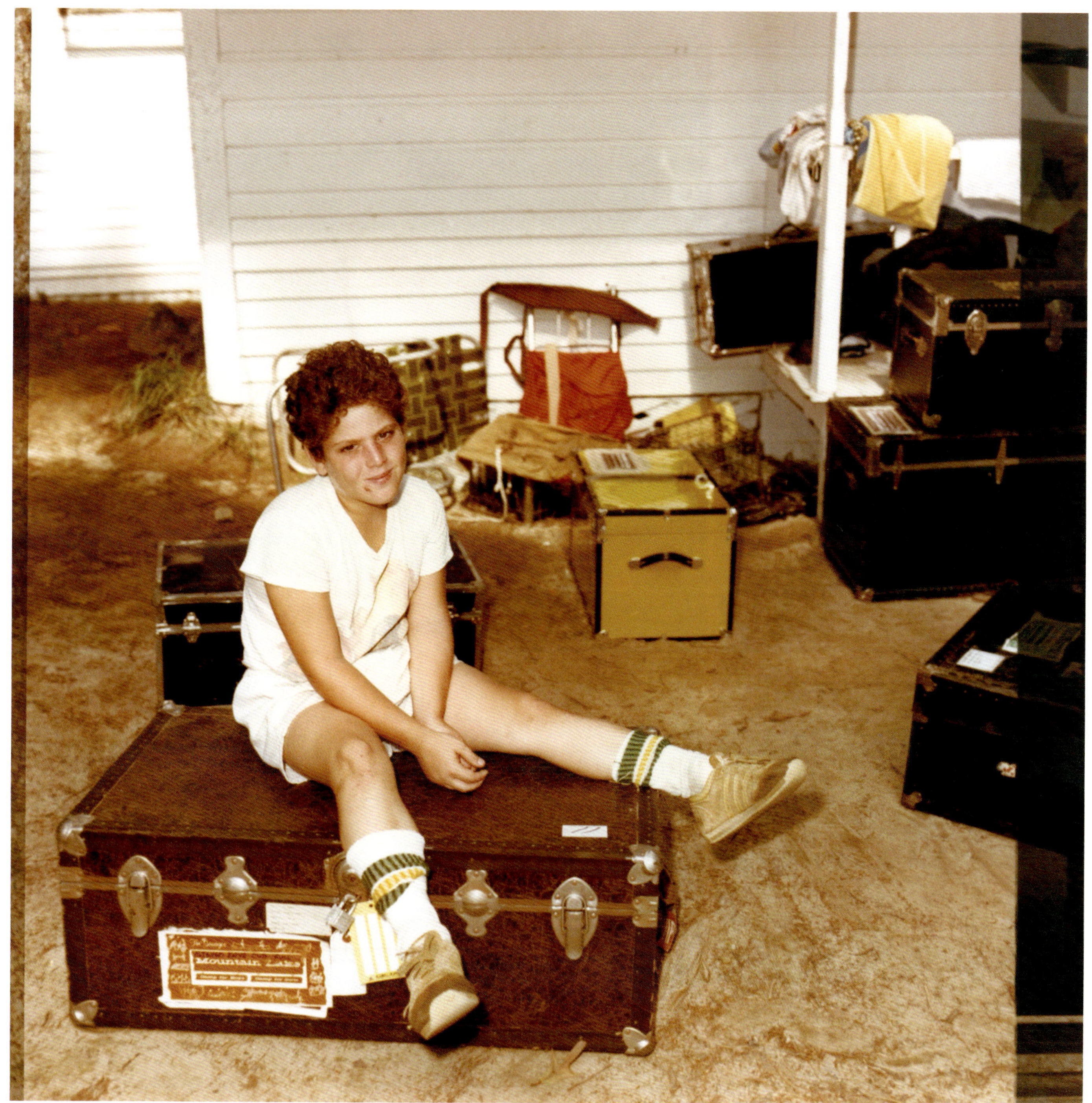
Mountain Lake

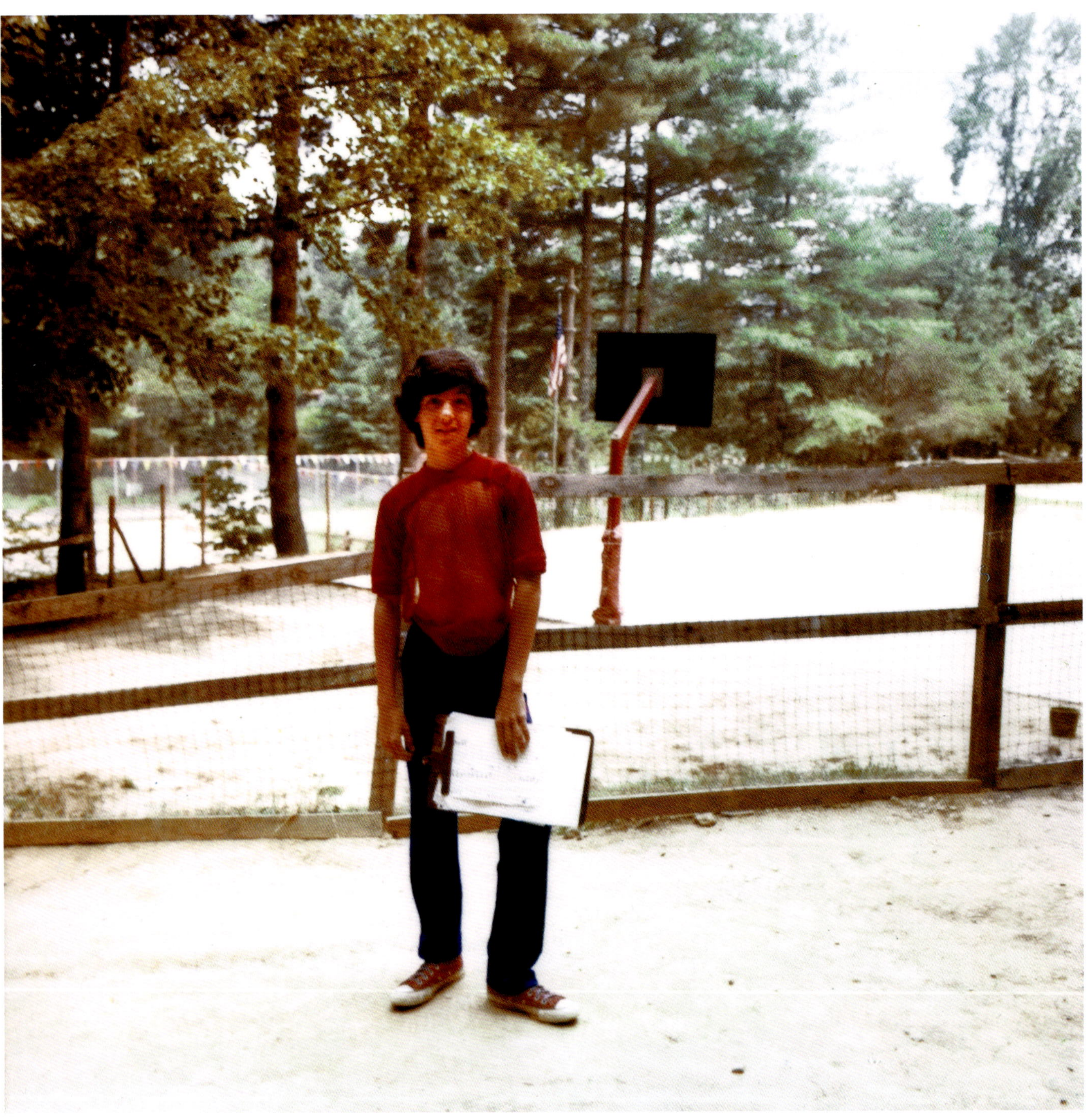

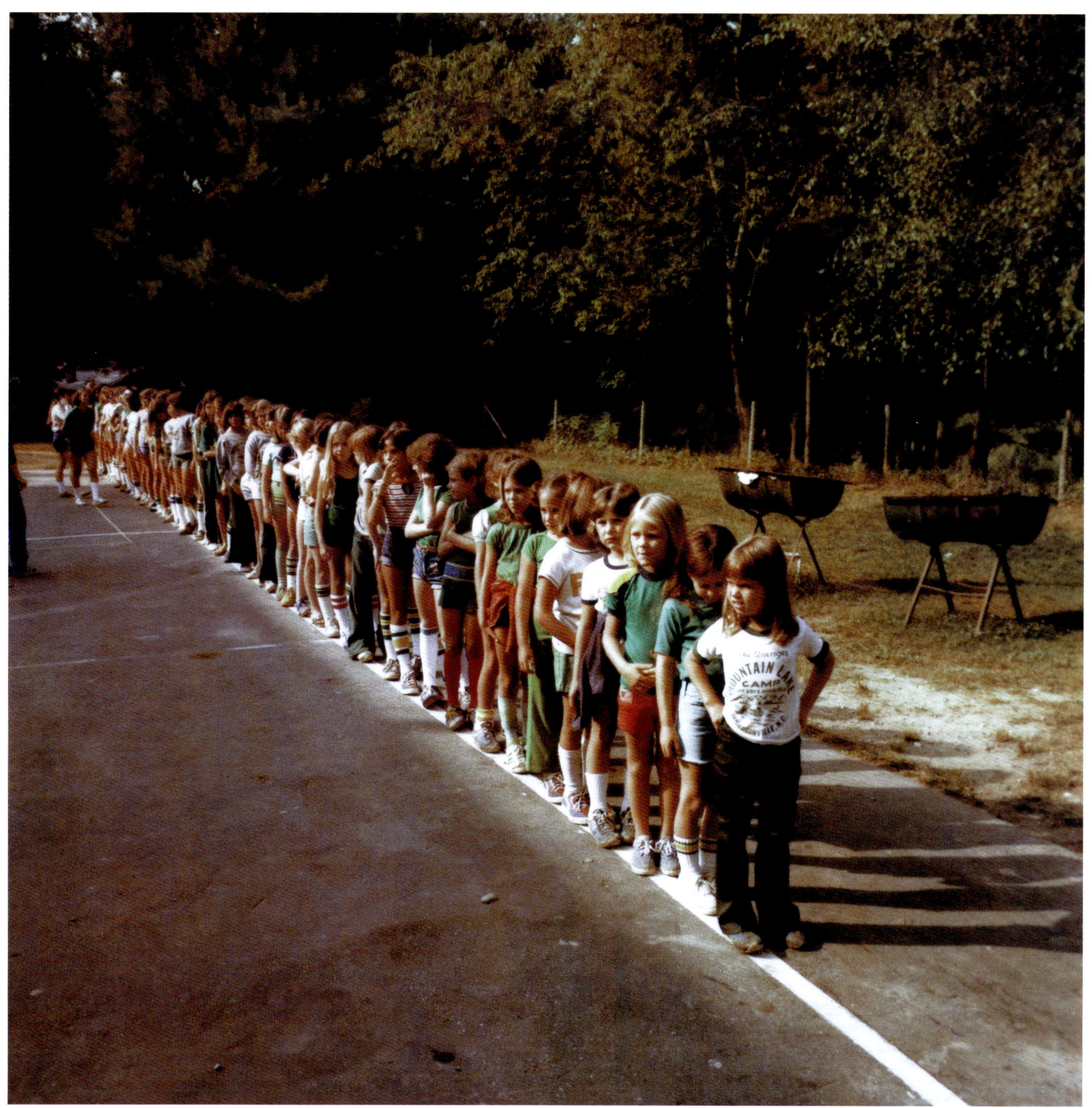

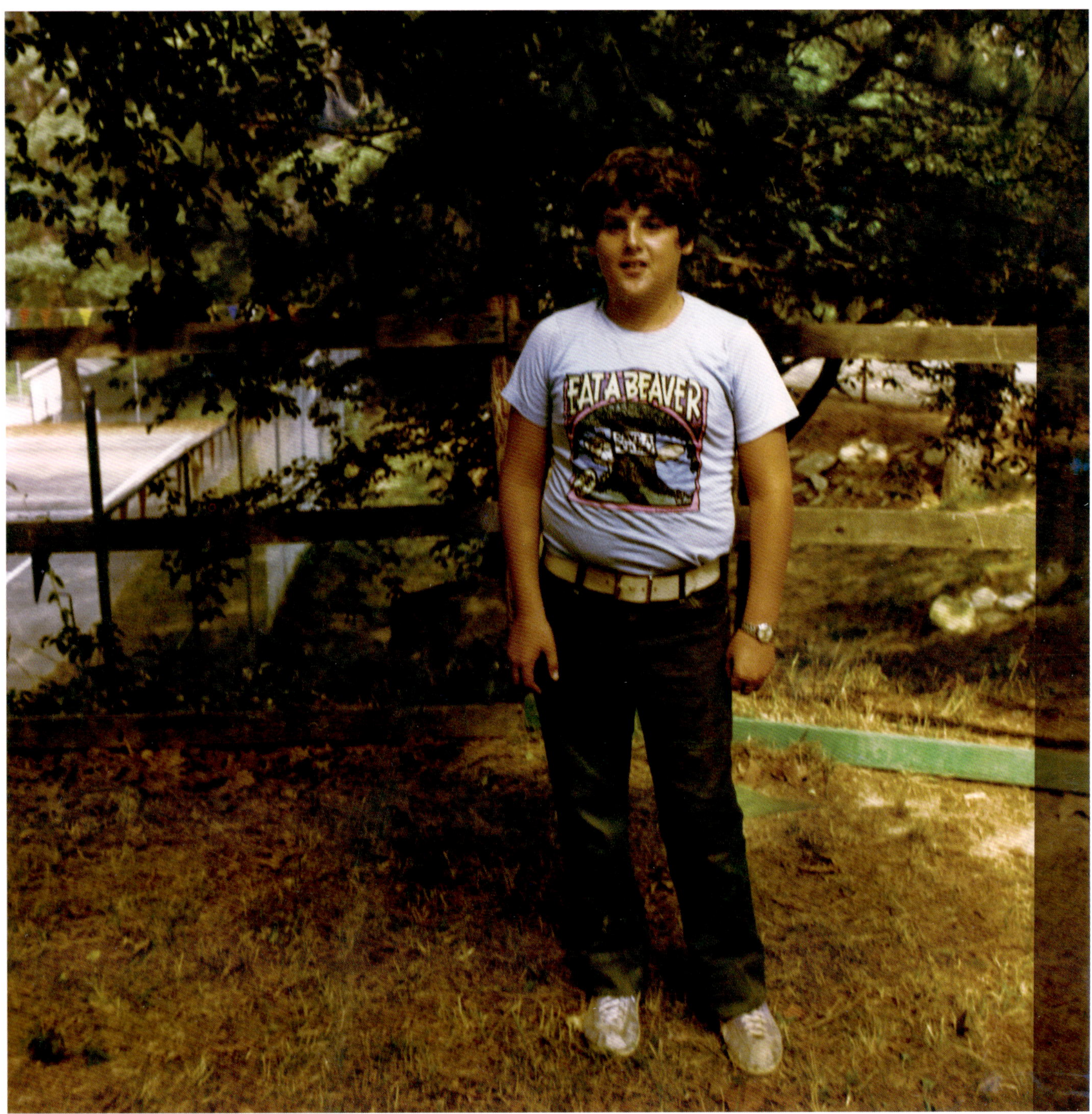

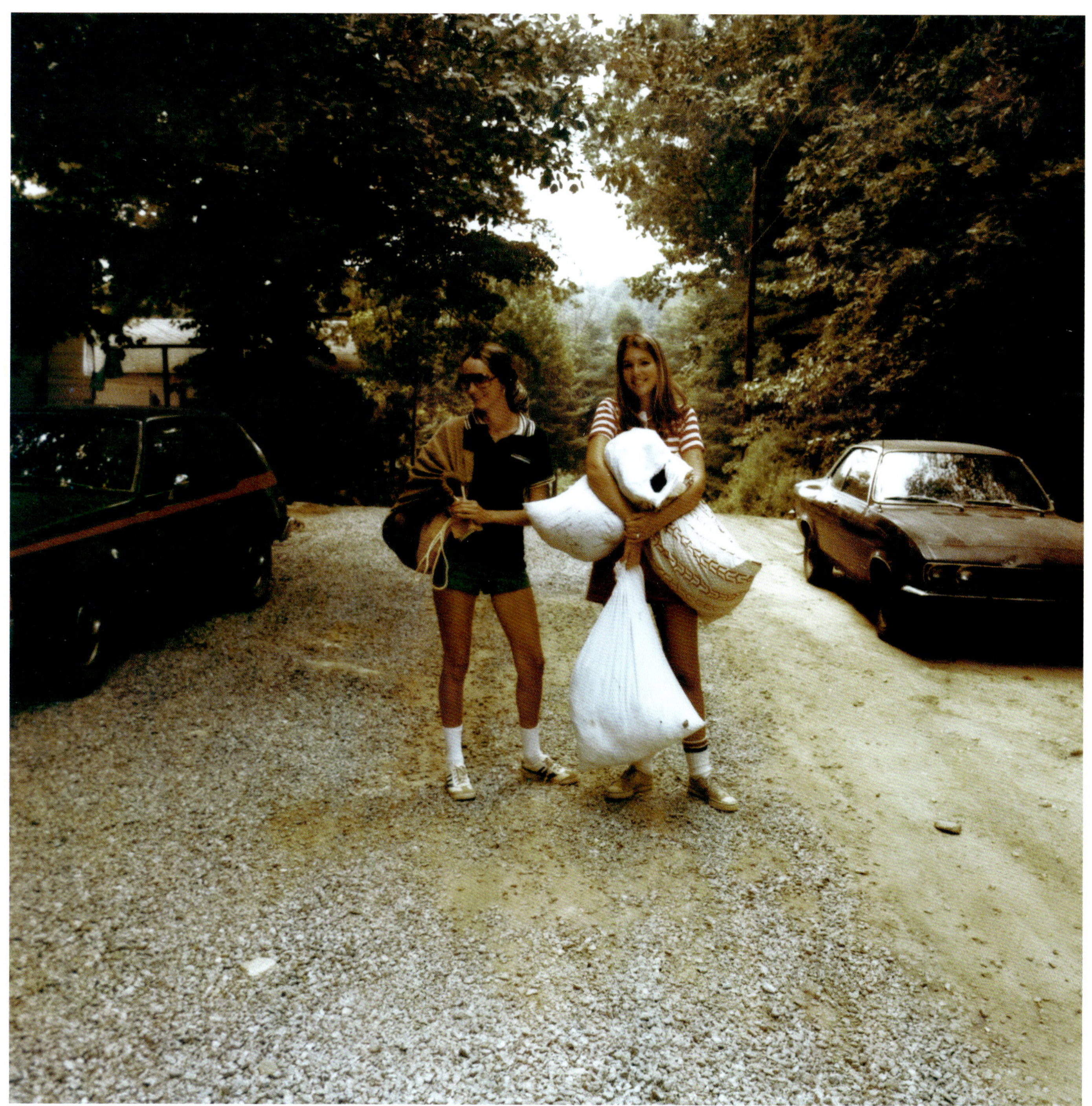

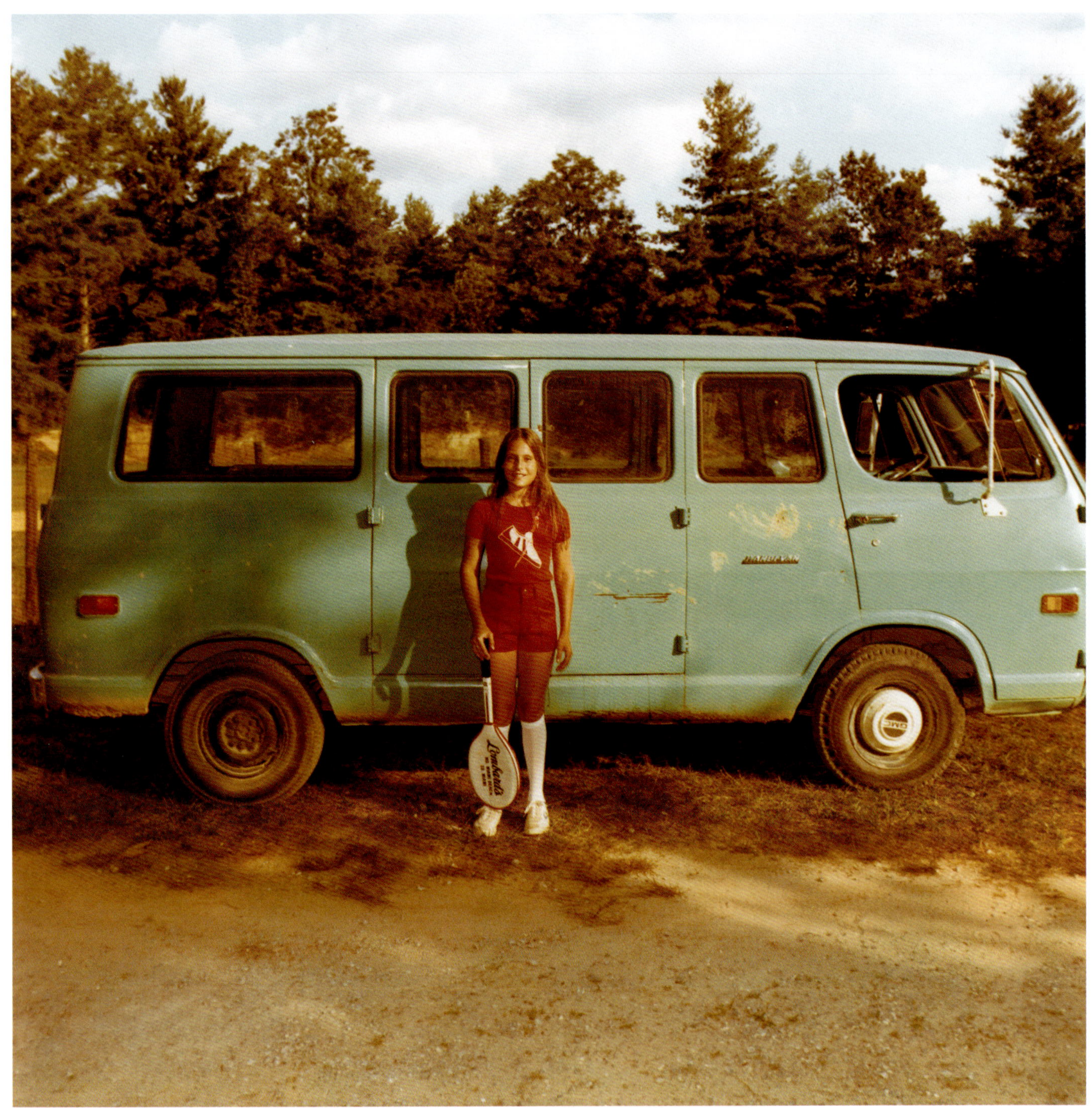

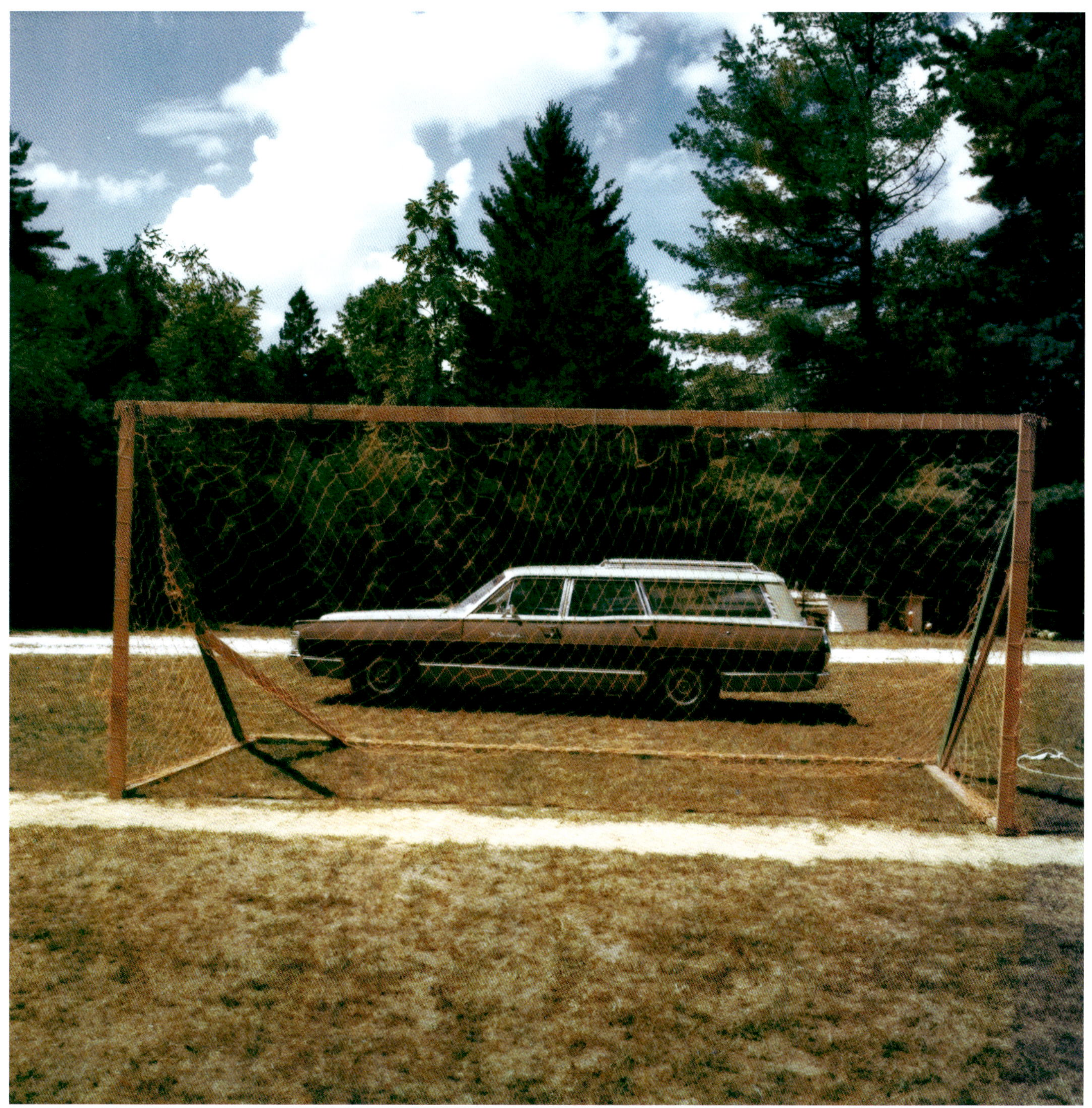

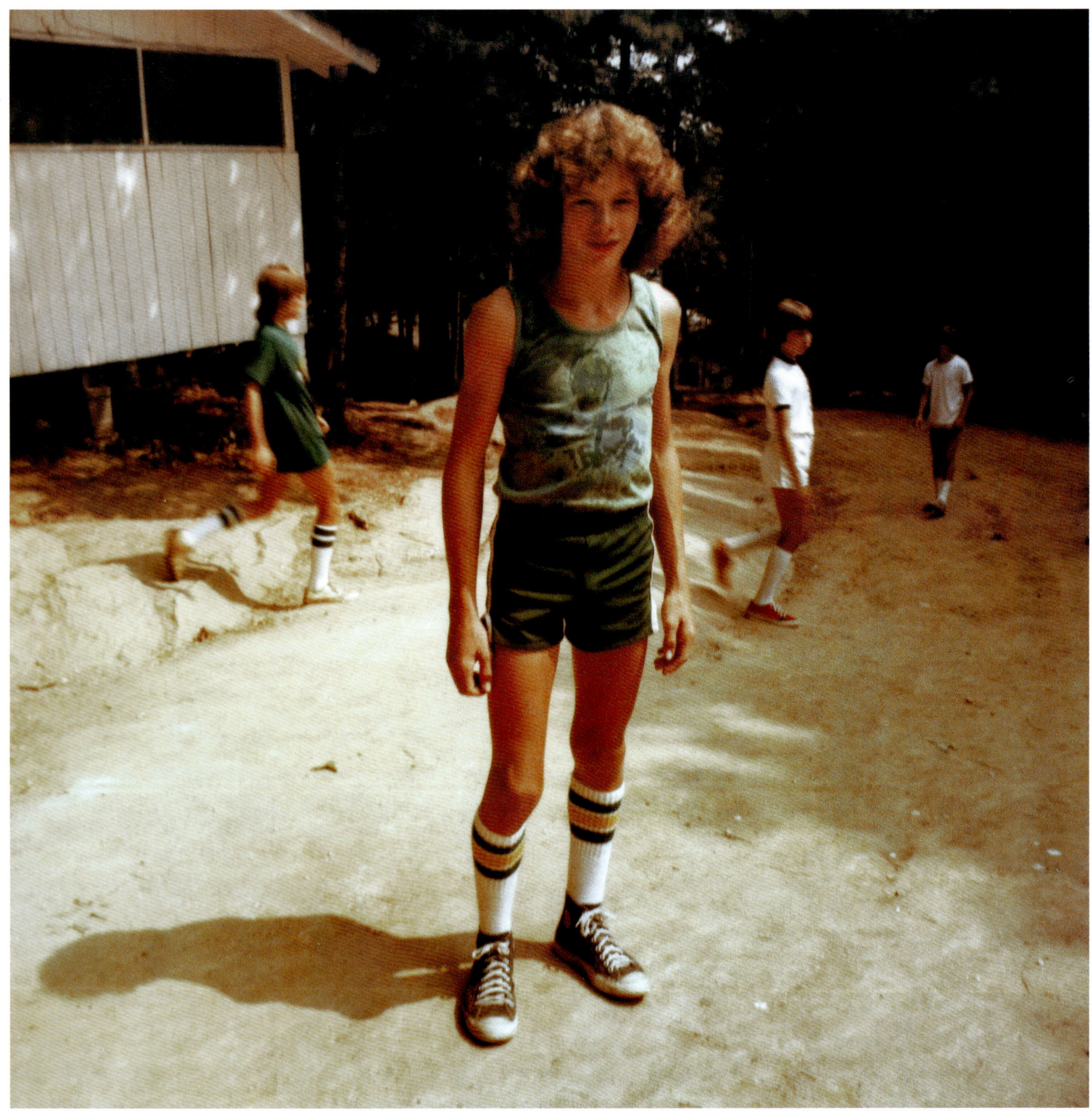

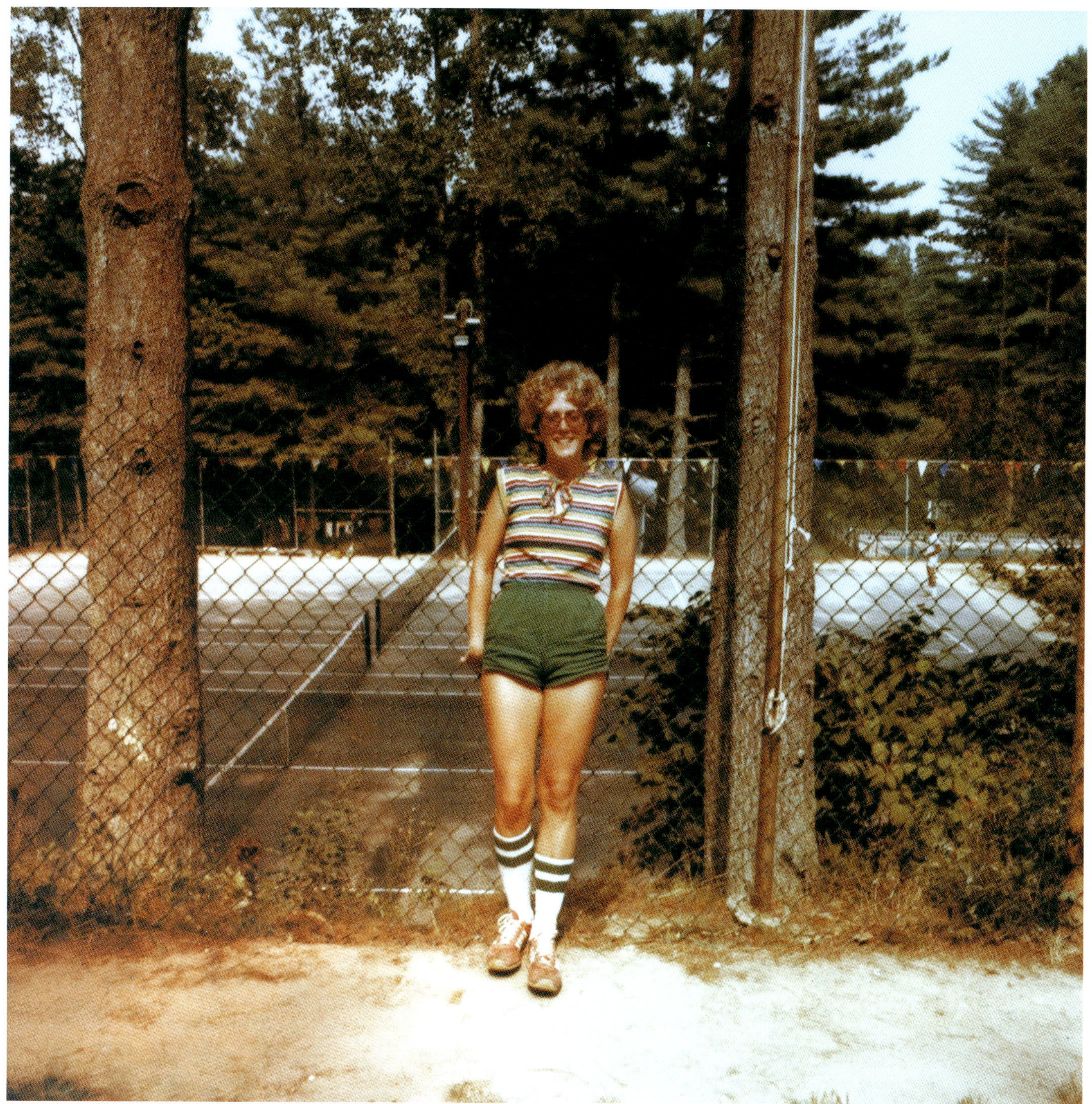

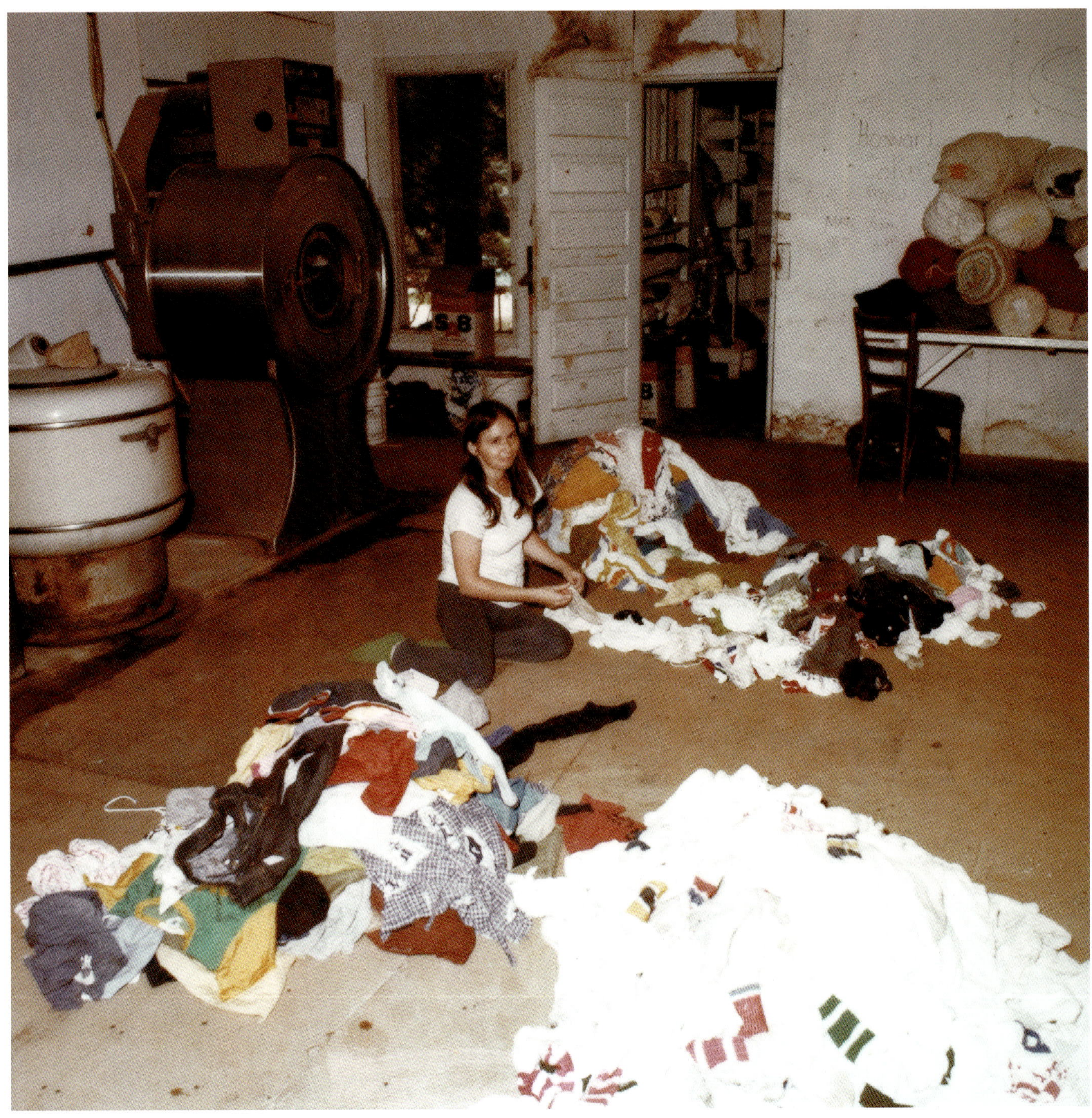

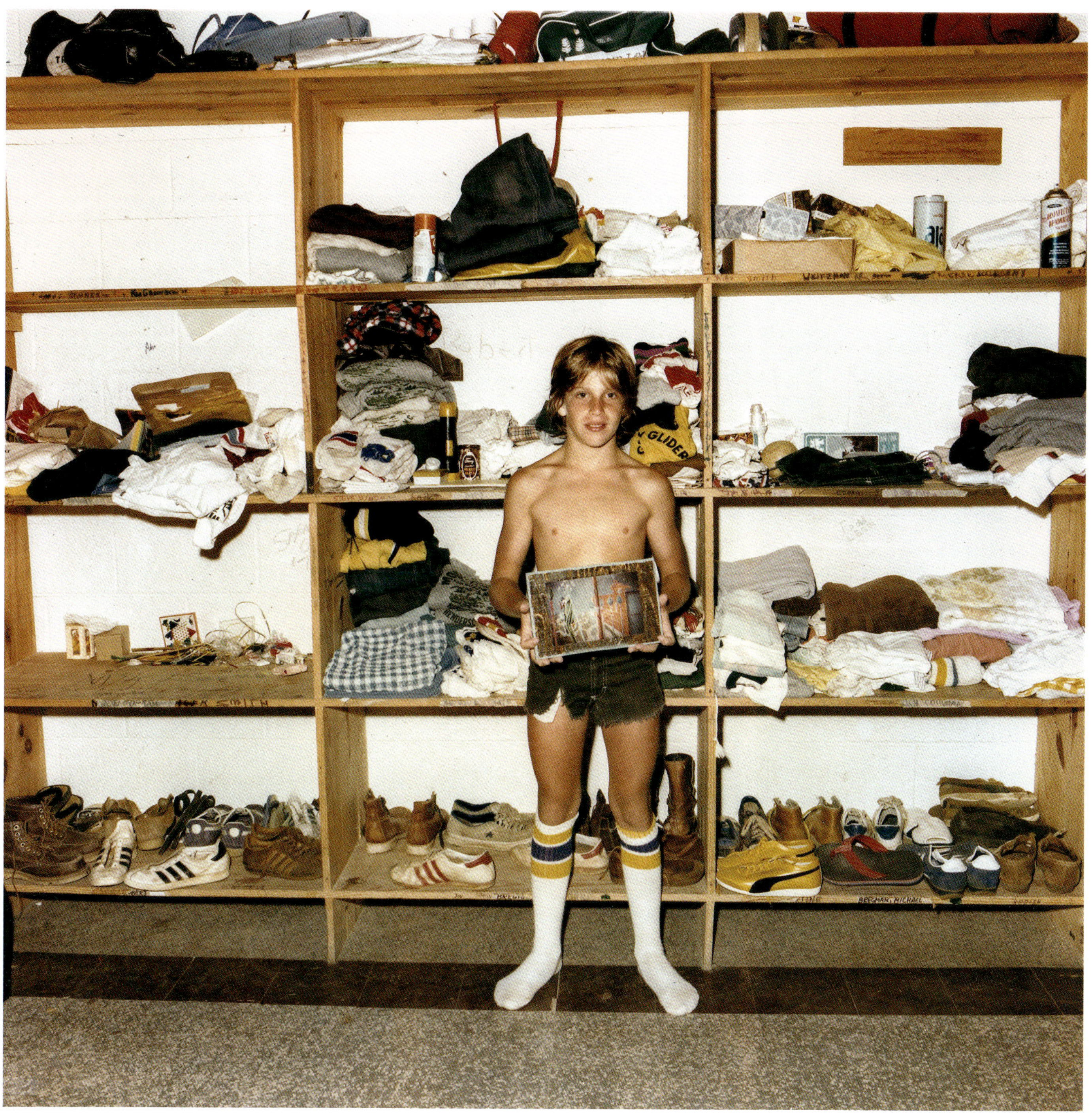

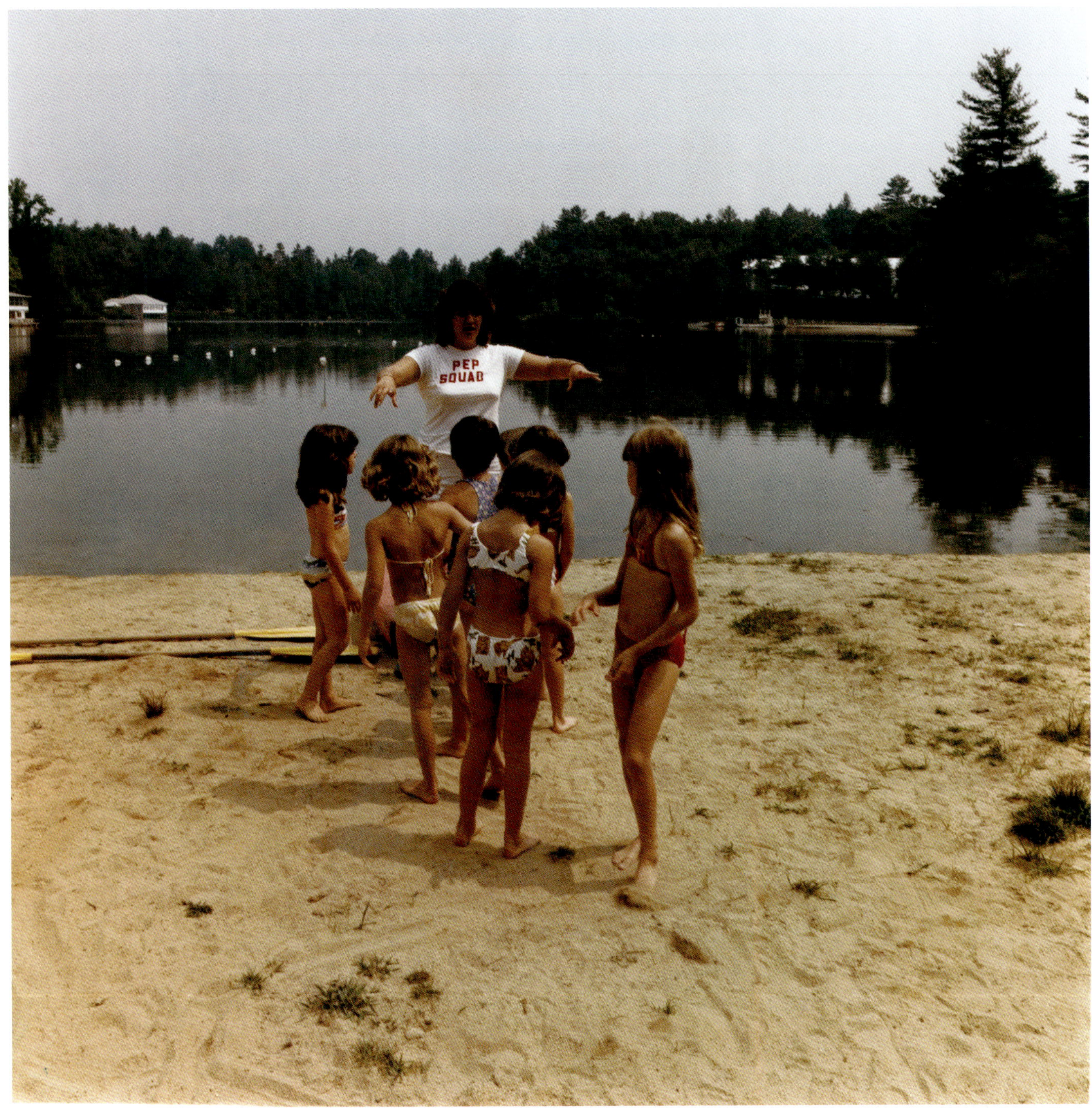
PEP
SQUAD

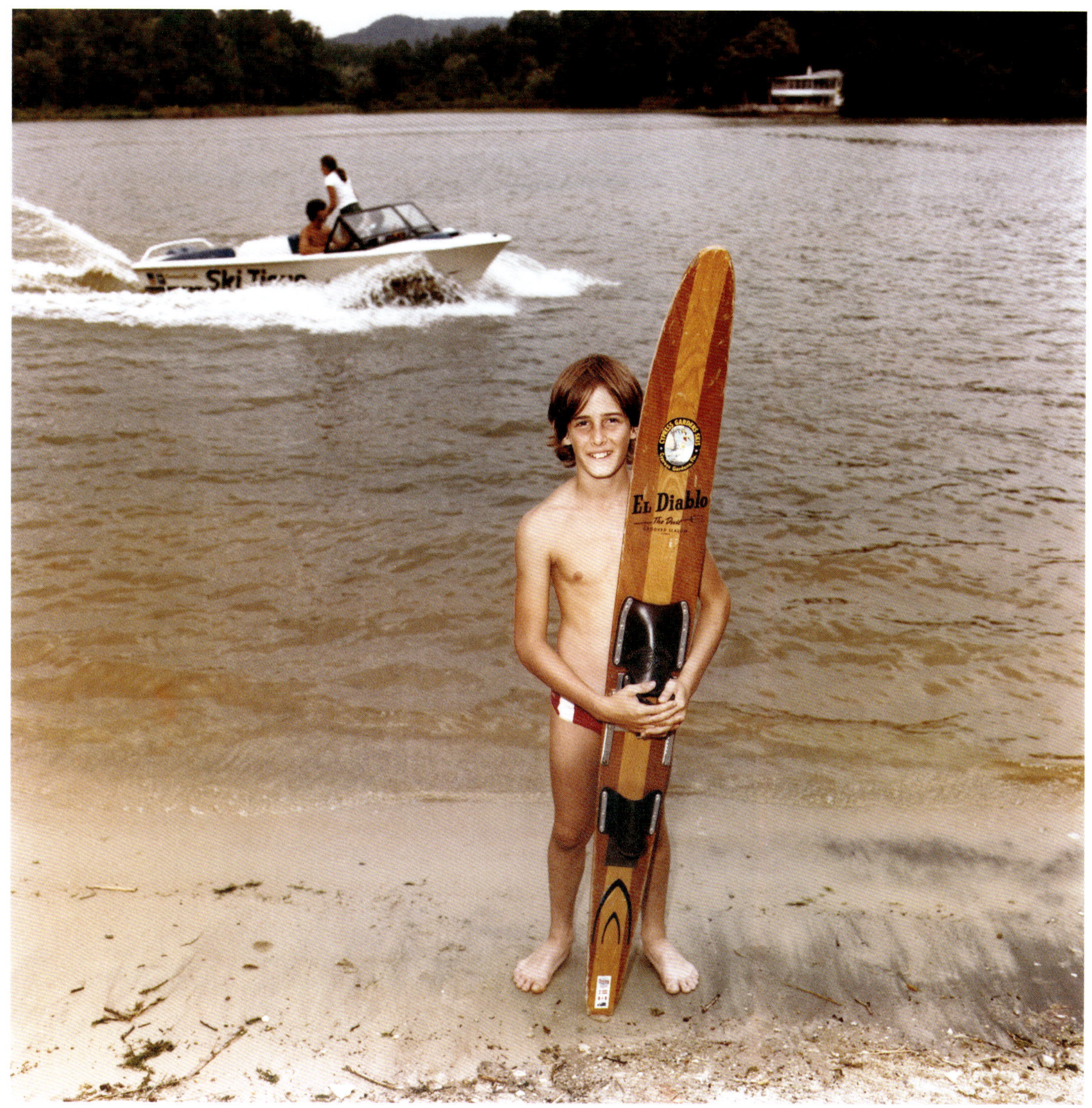
Ski Tique
El Diablo

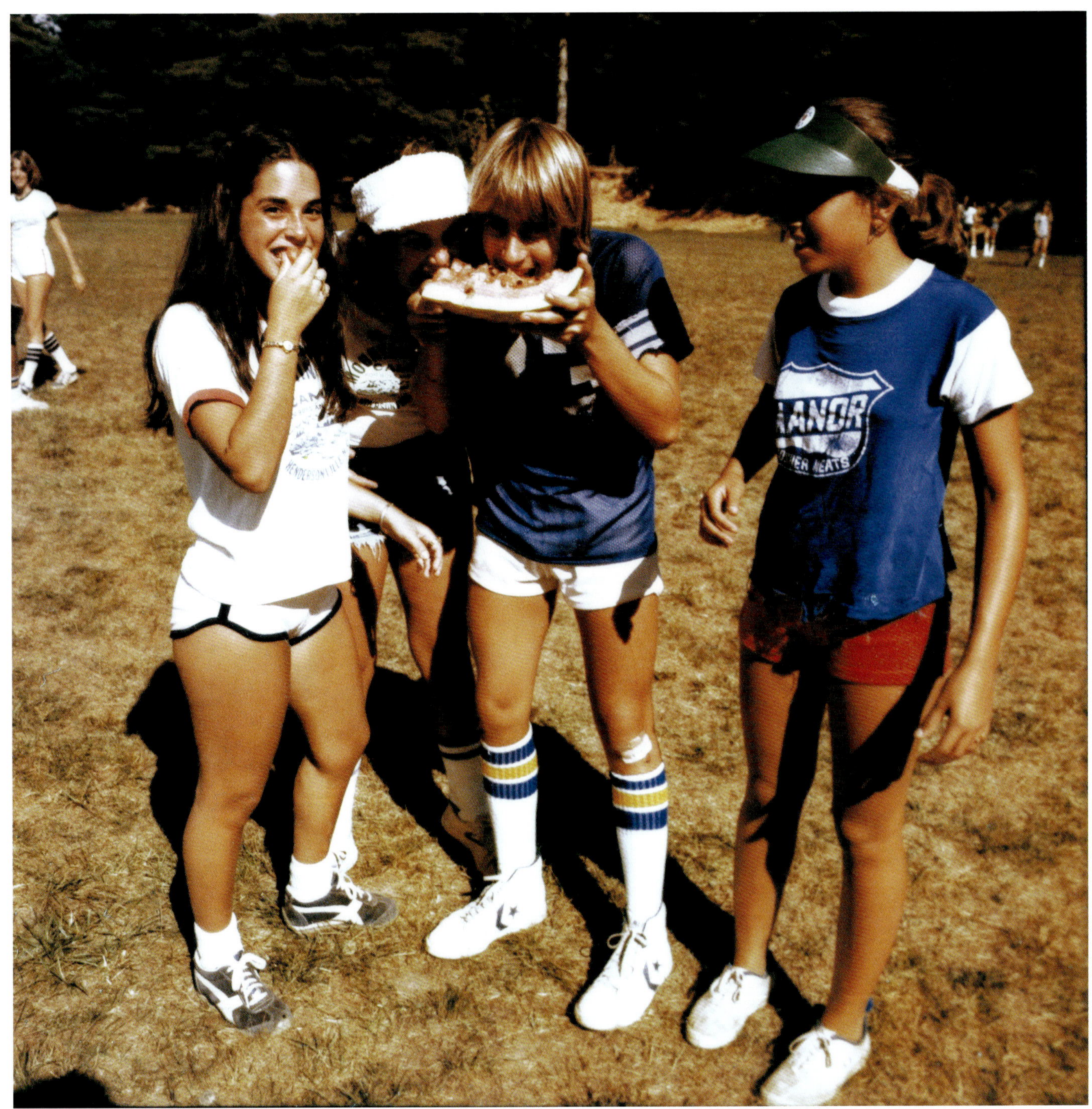

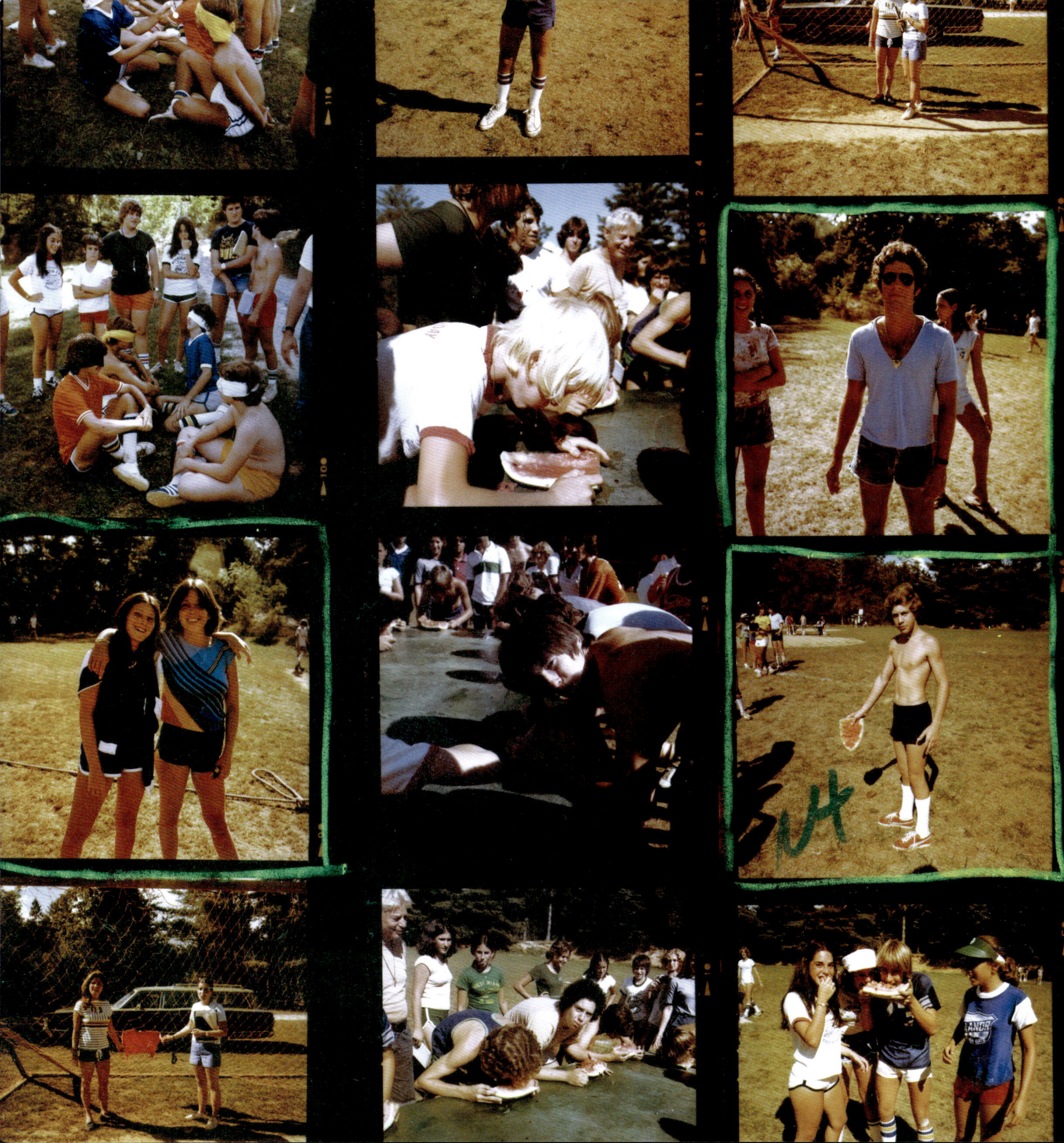

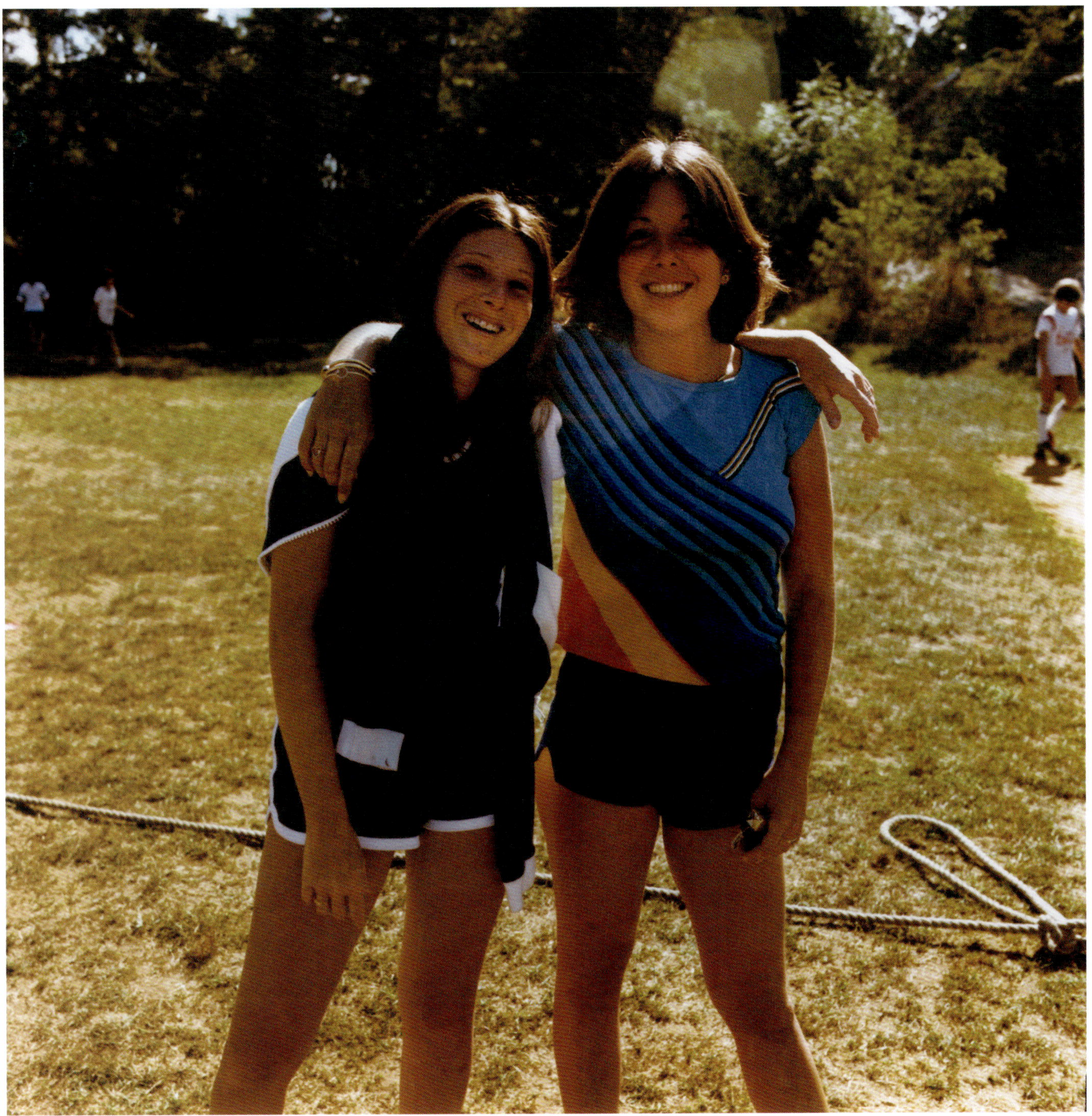

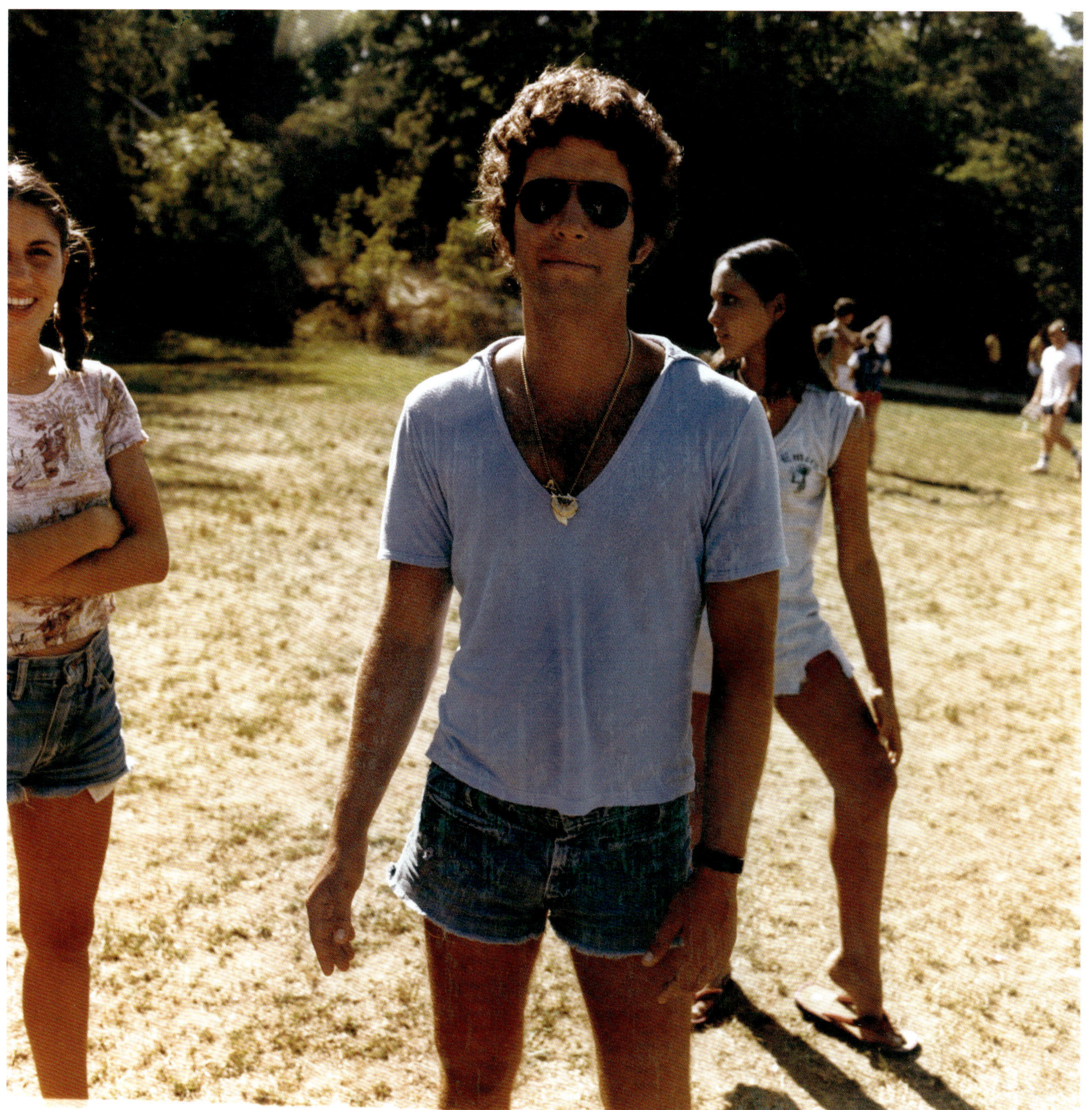

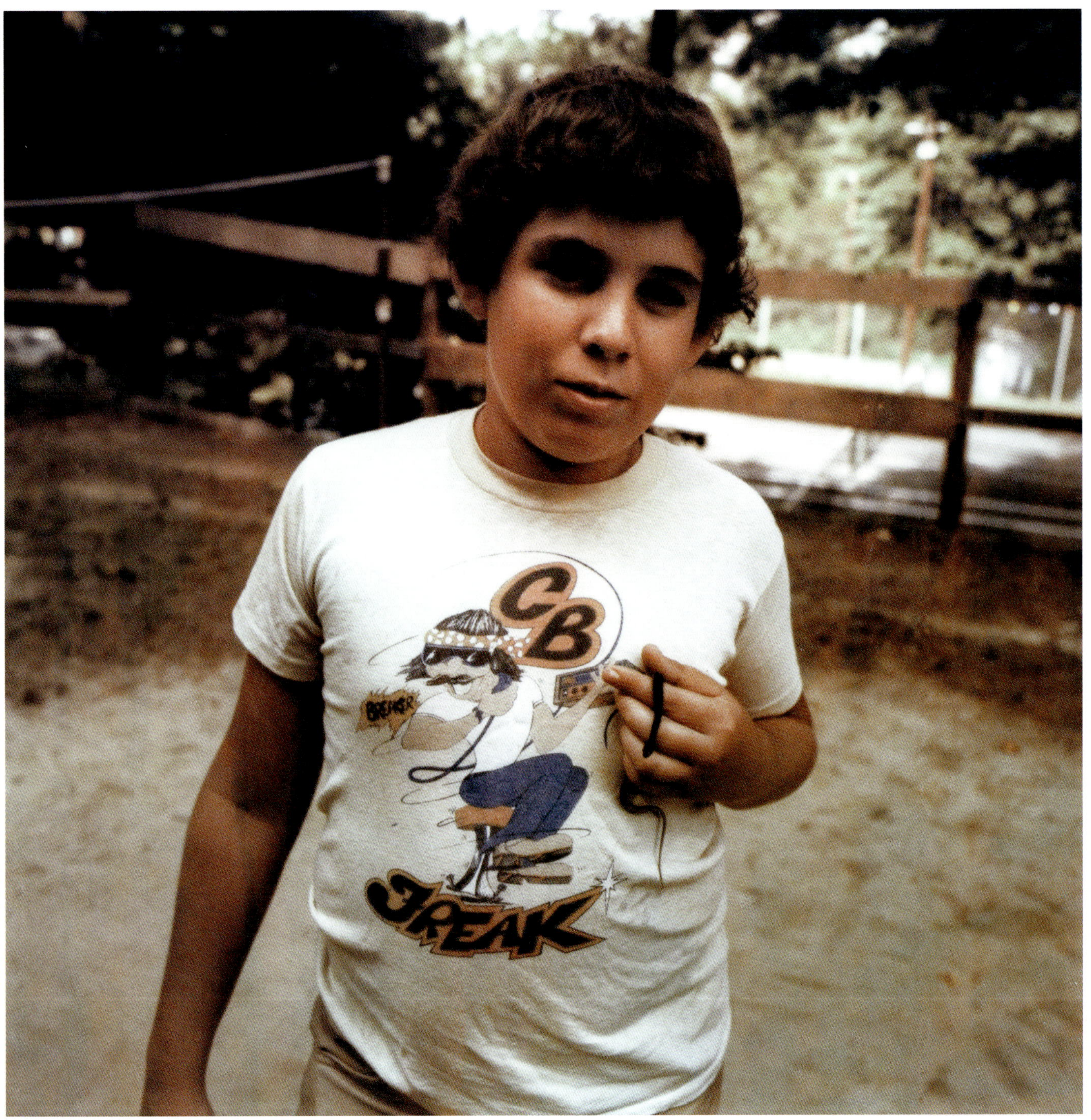
CB
BREAKER
FREAK

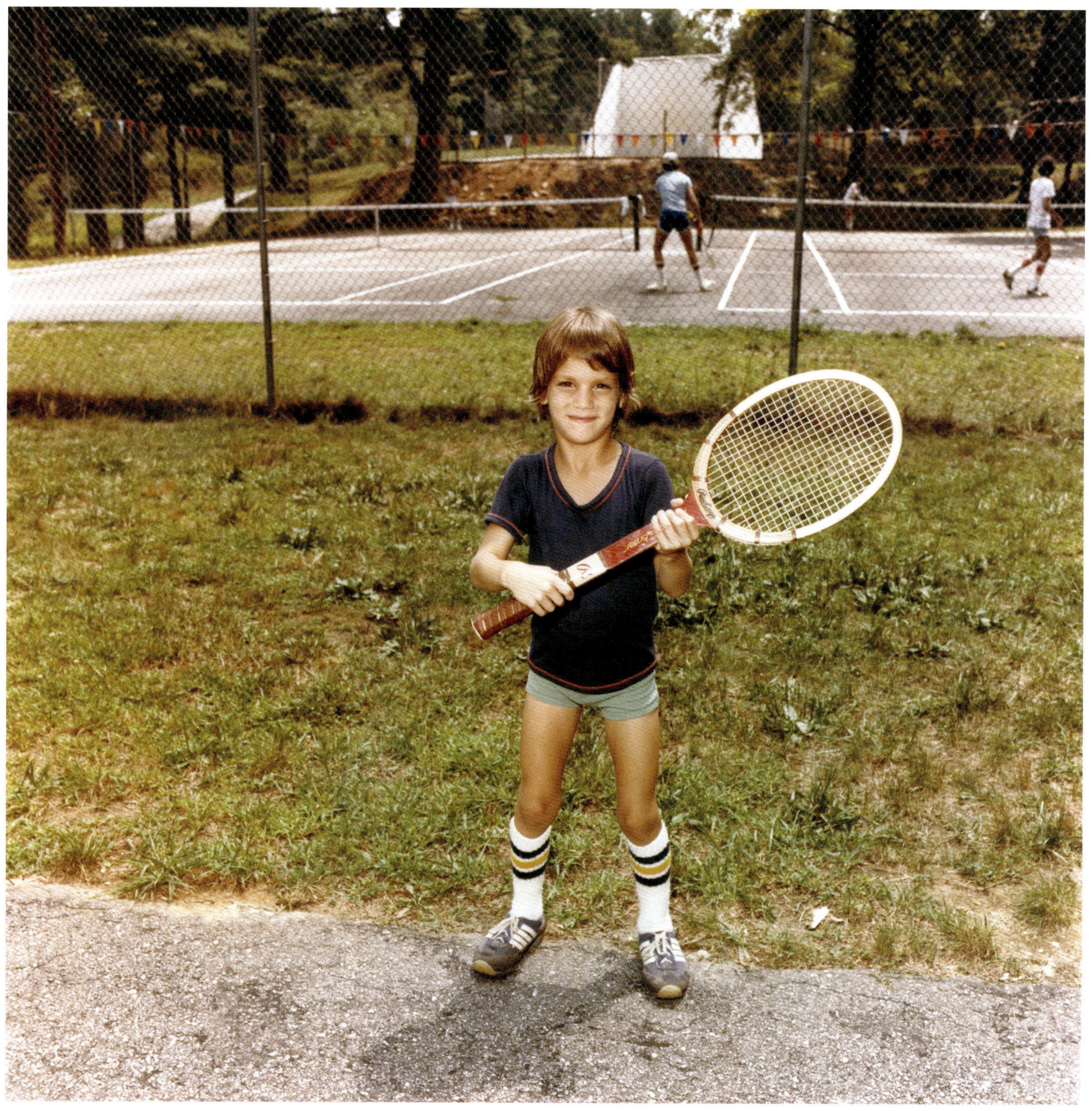

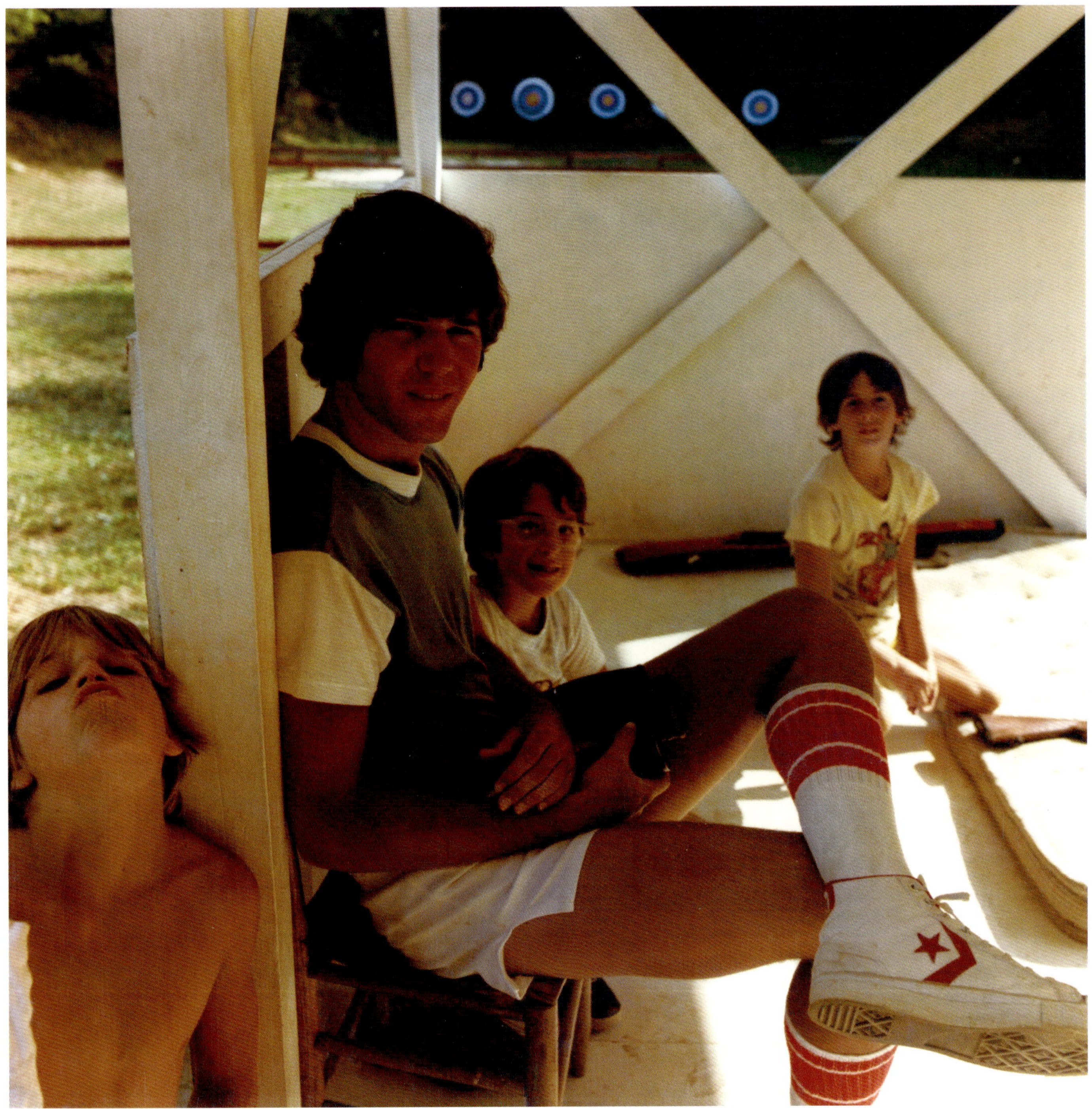

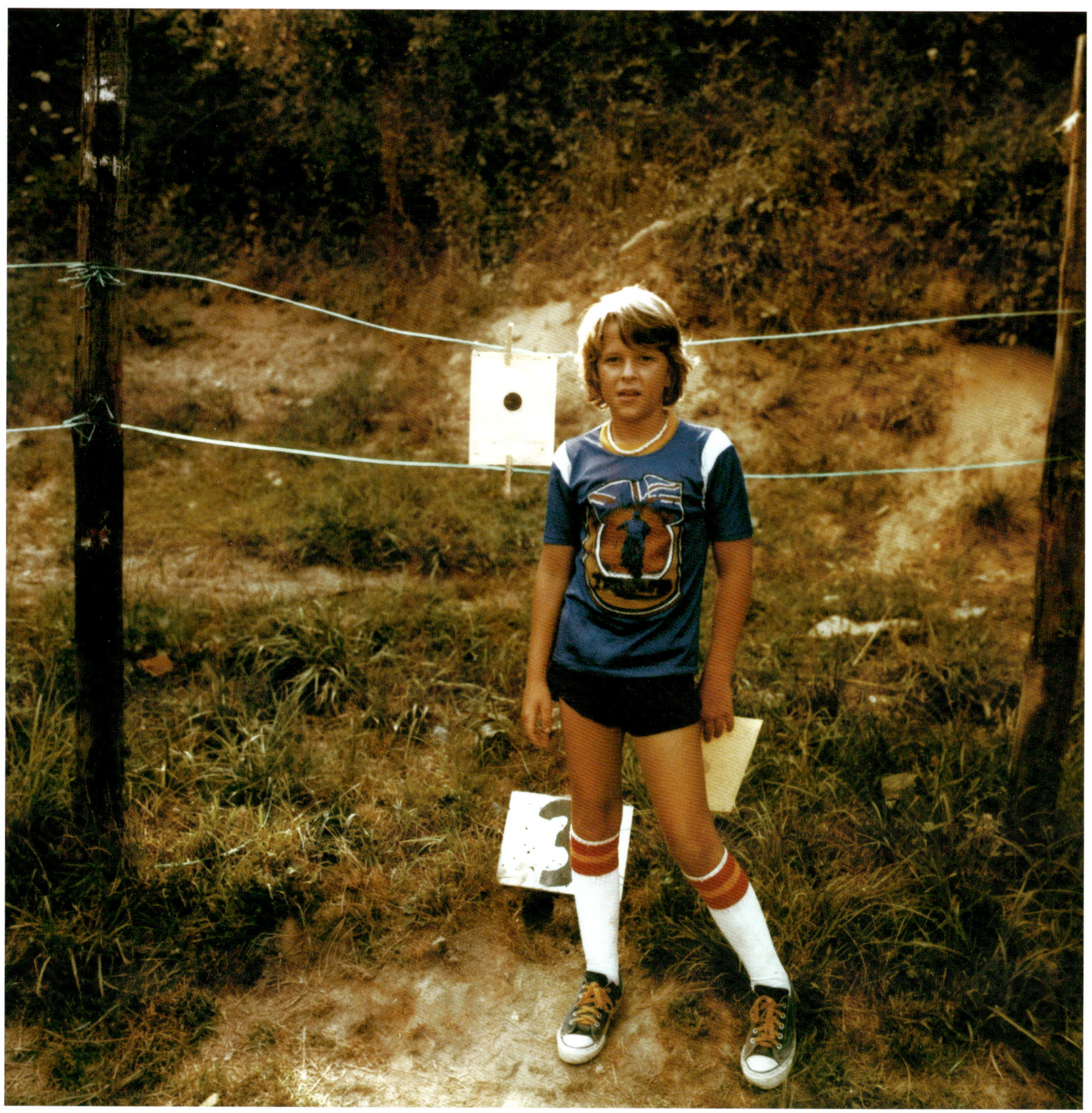

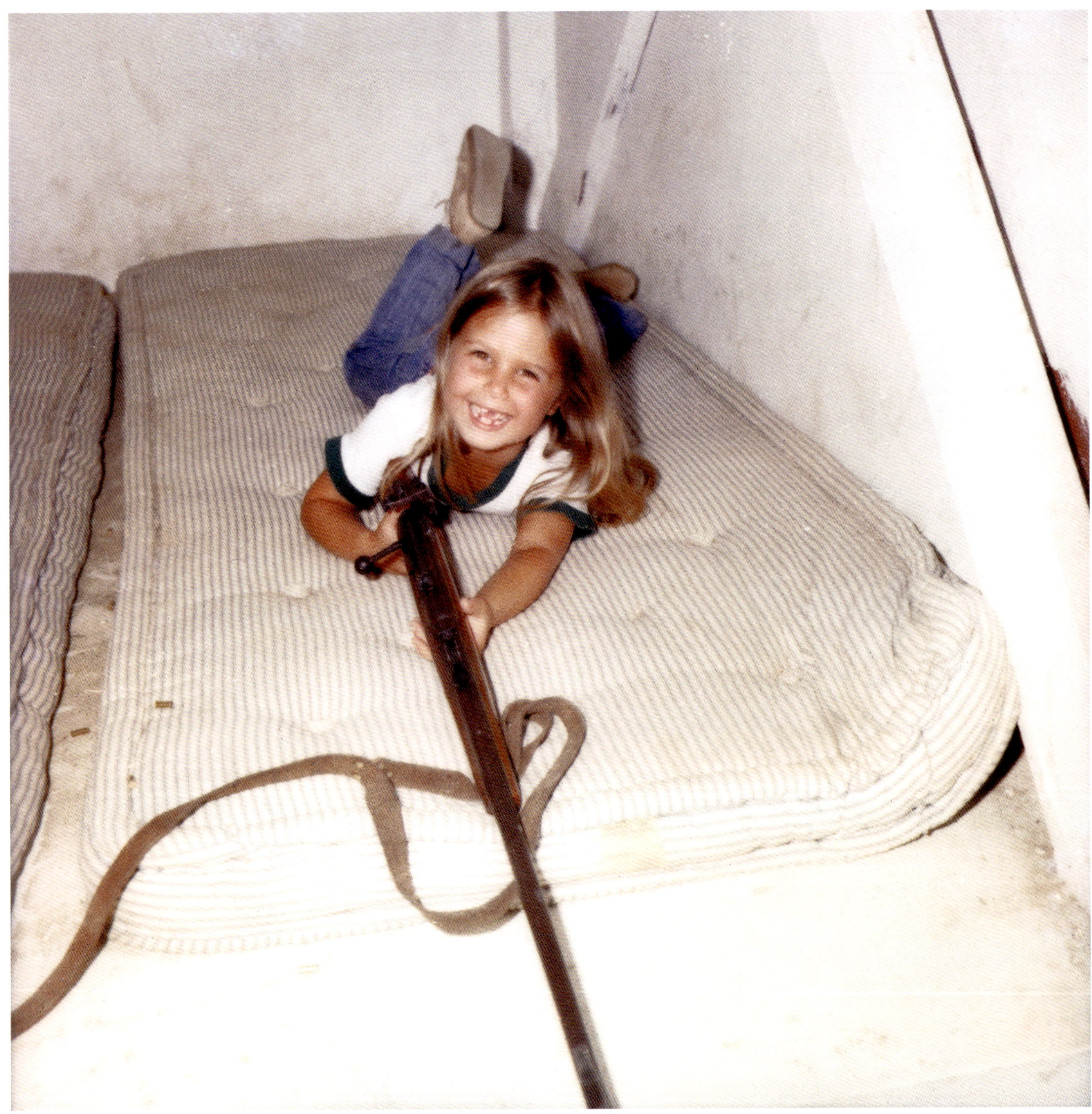

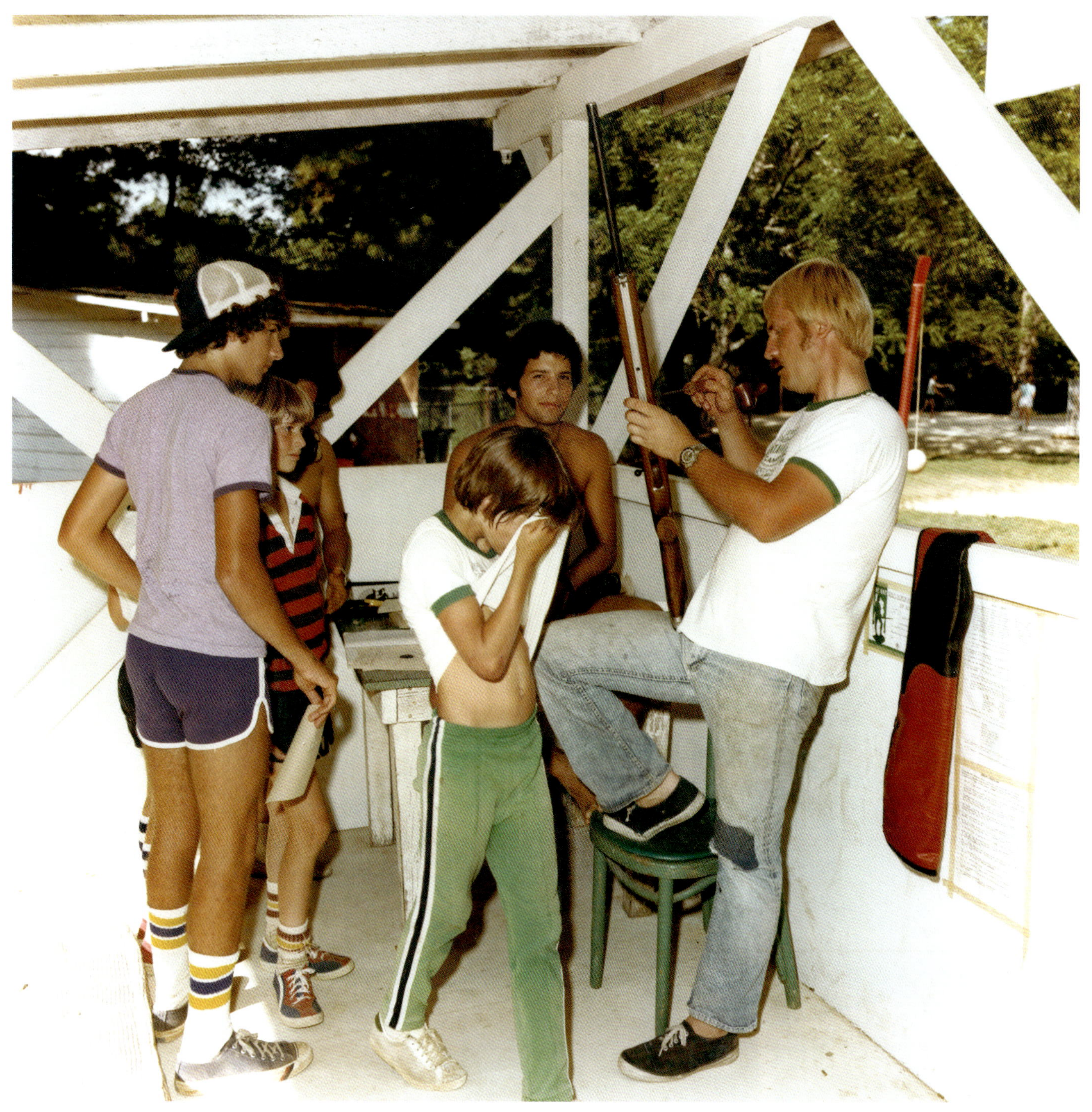

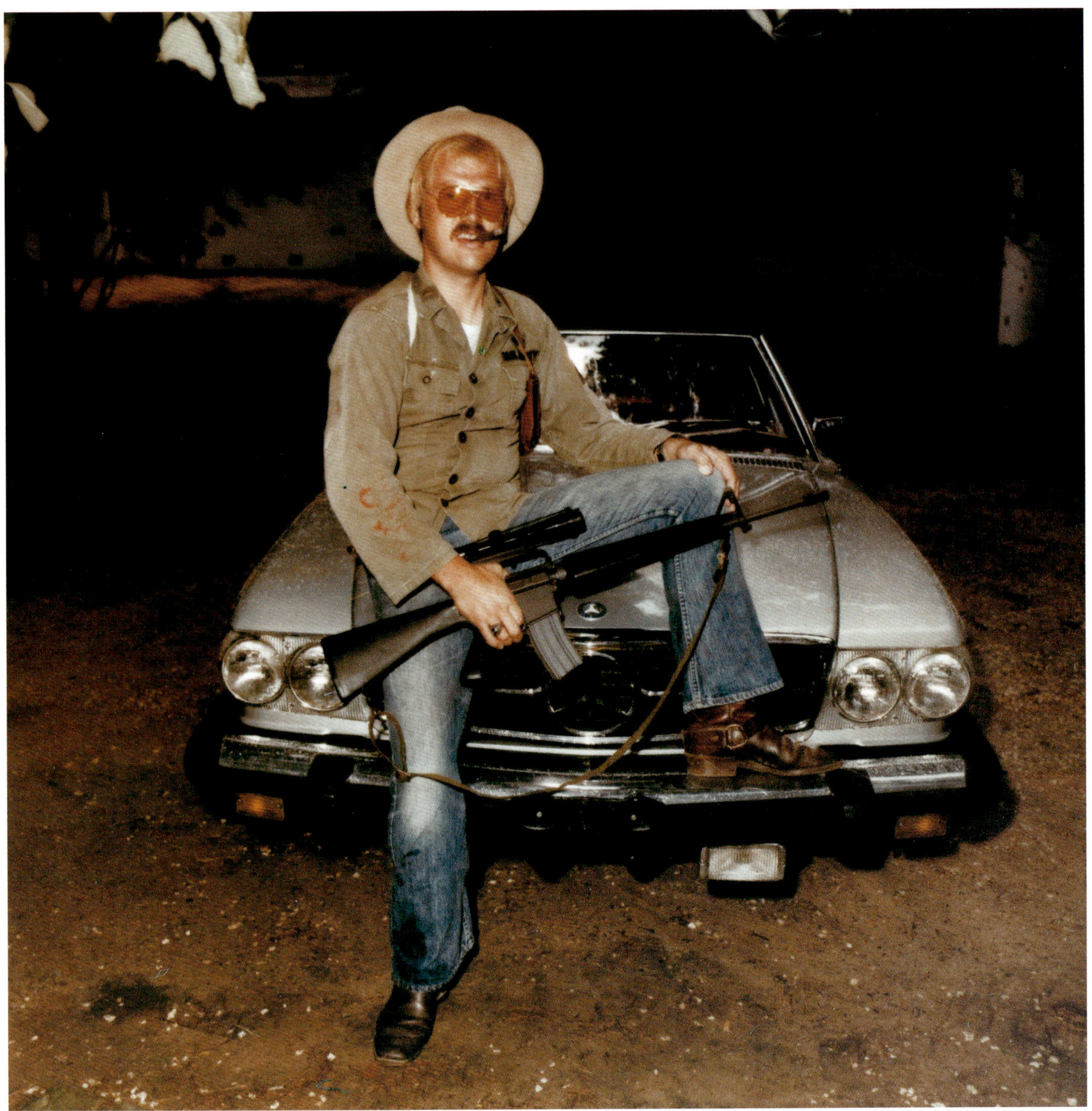

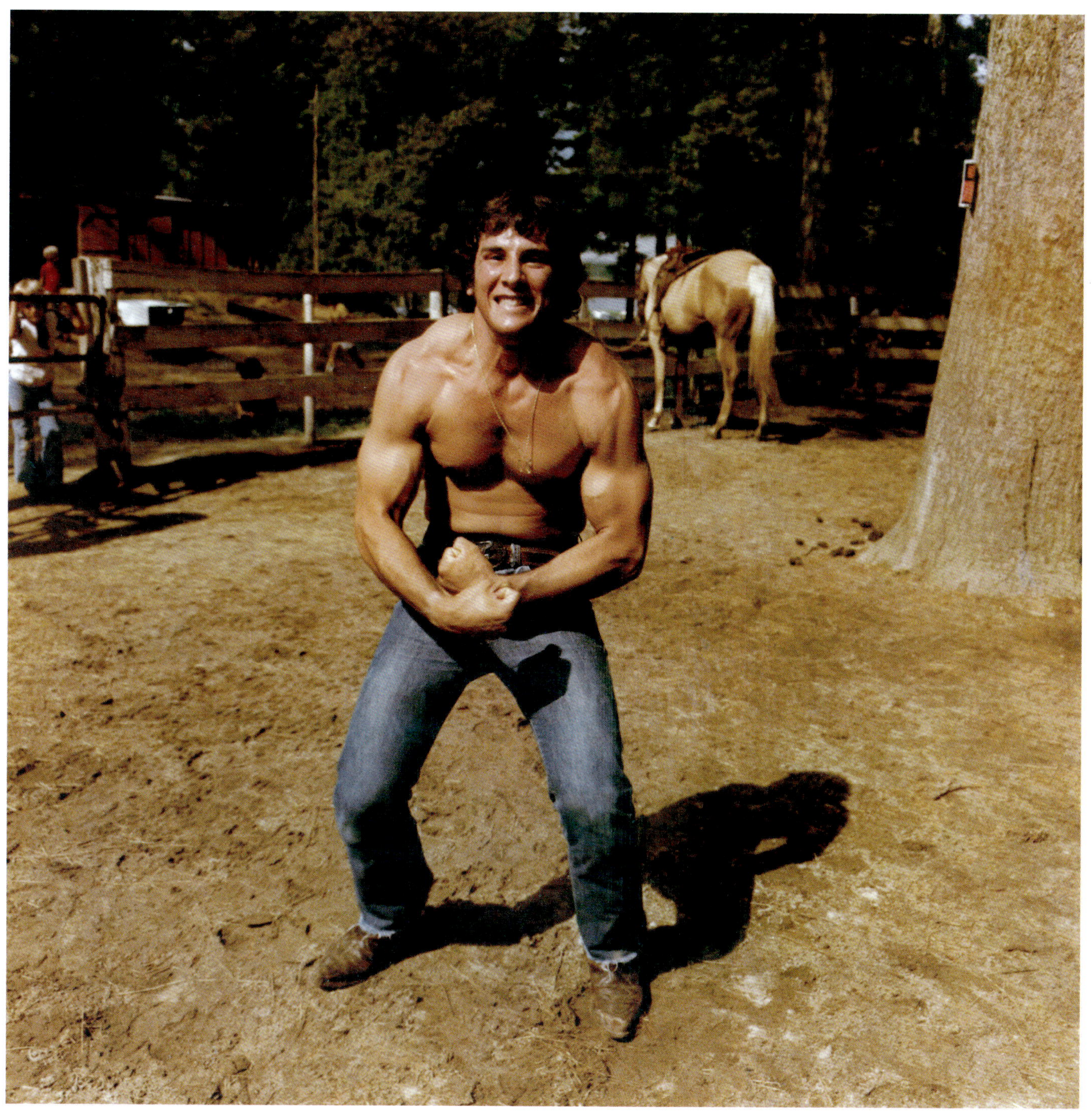

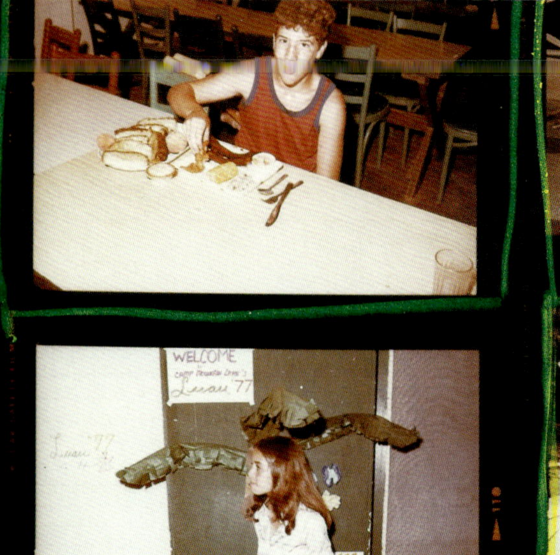
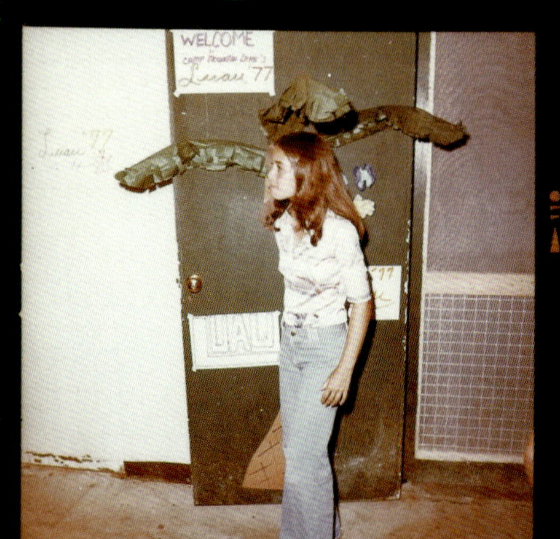
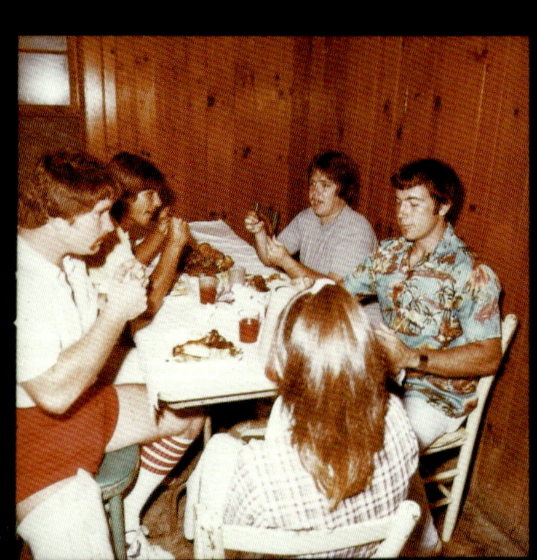
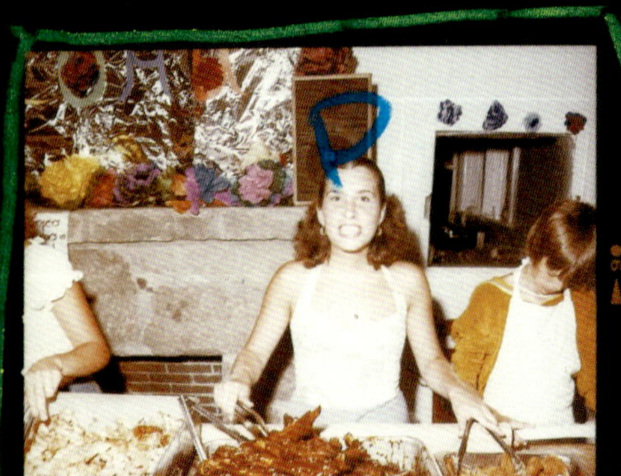
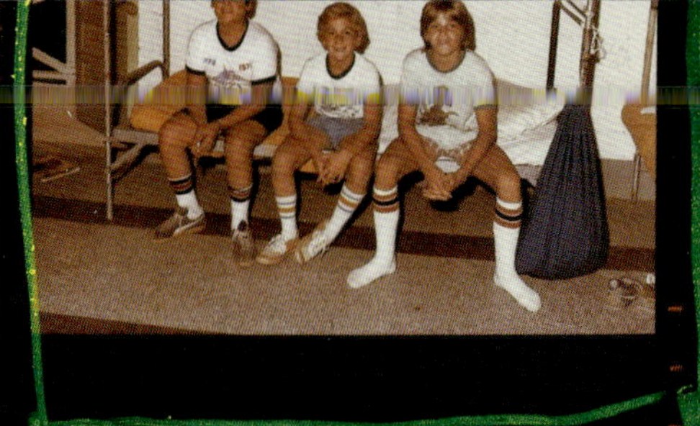
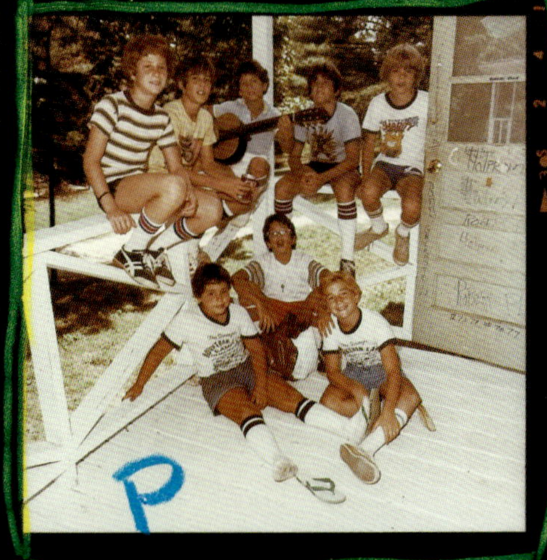
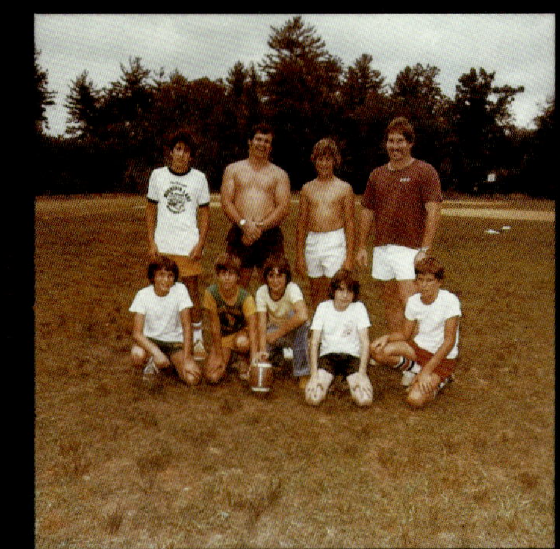
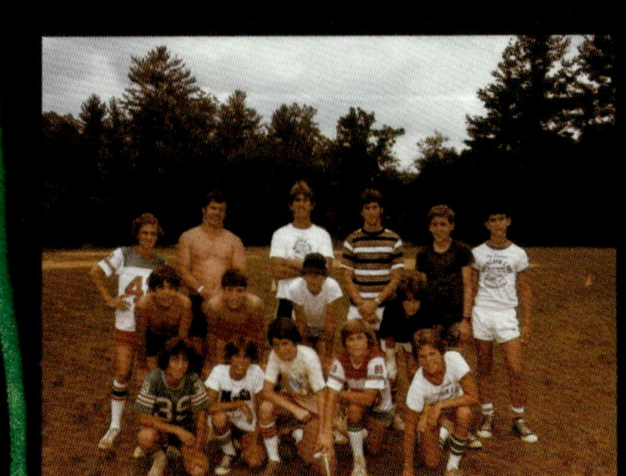
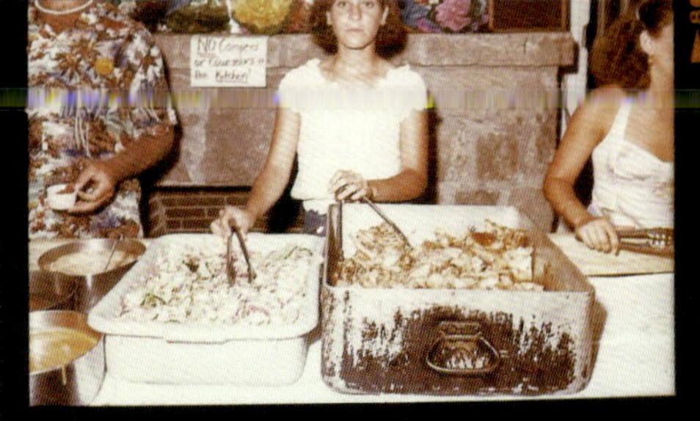
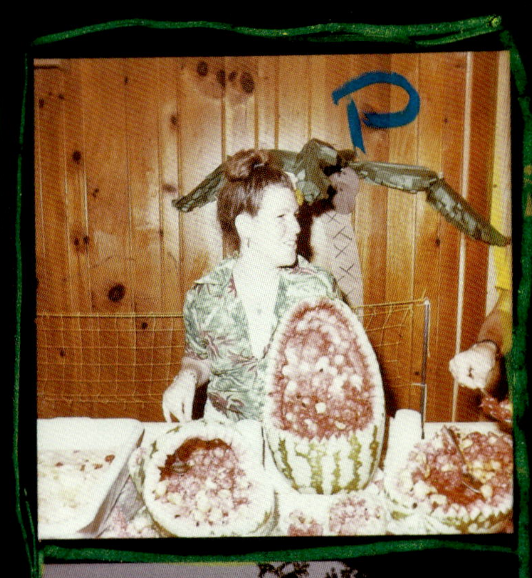
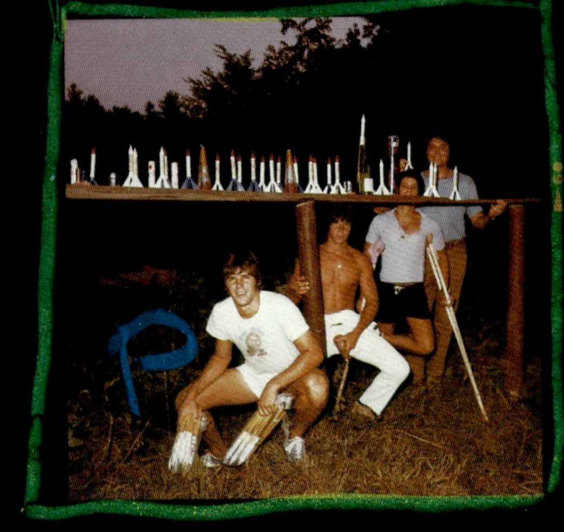
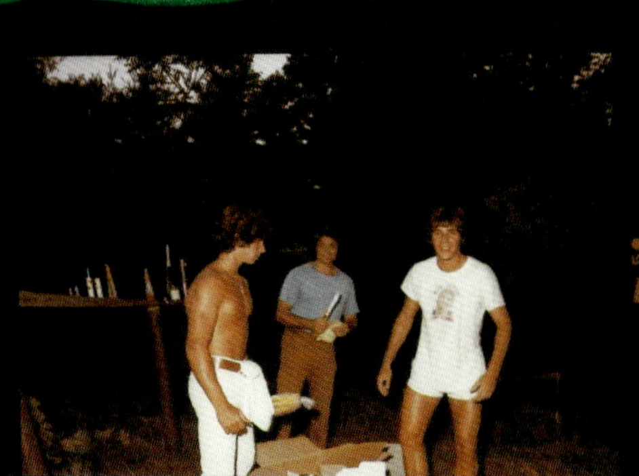

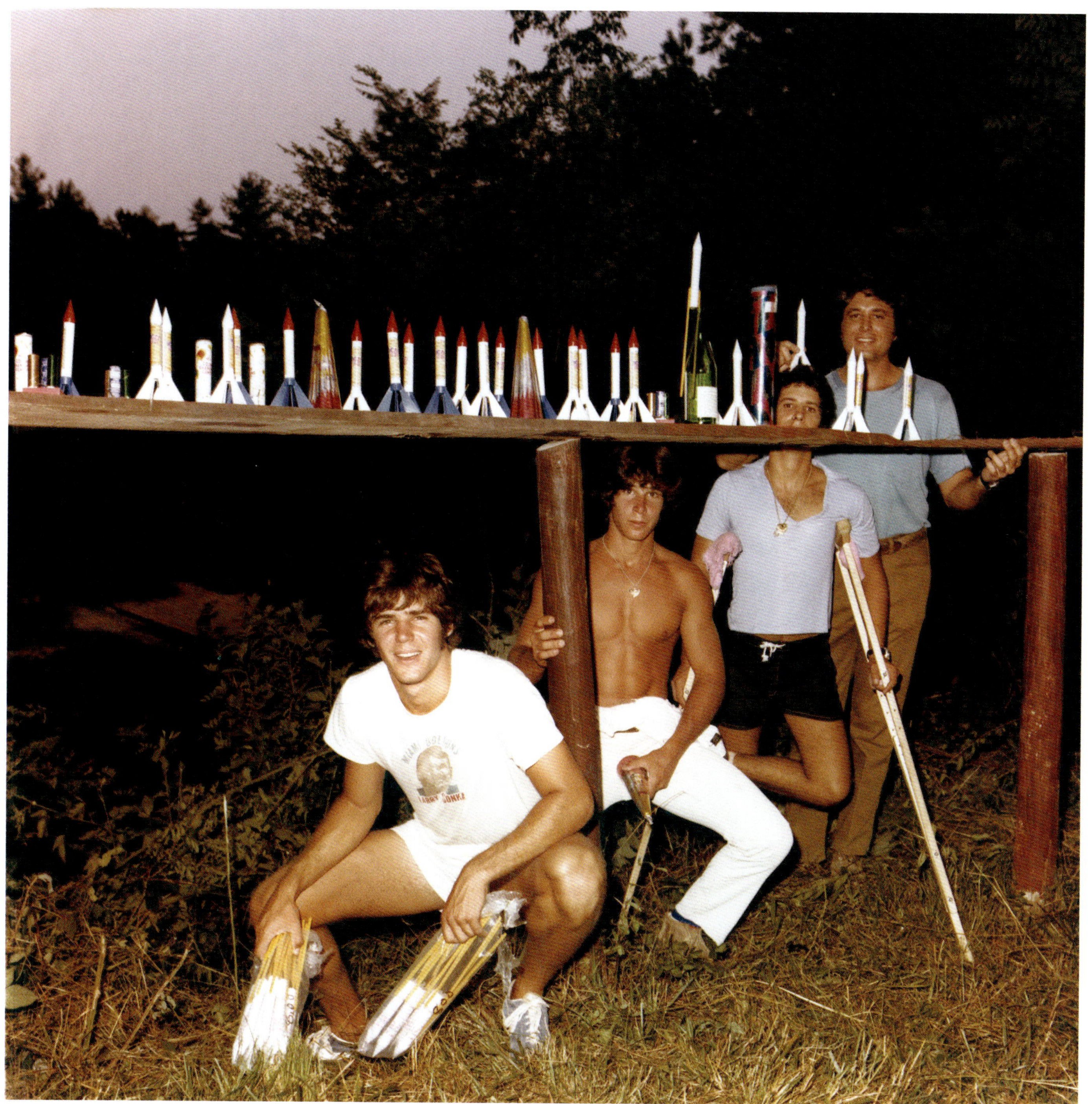

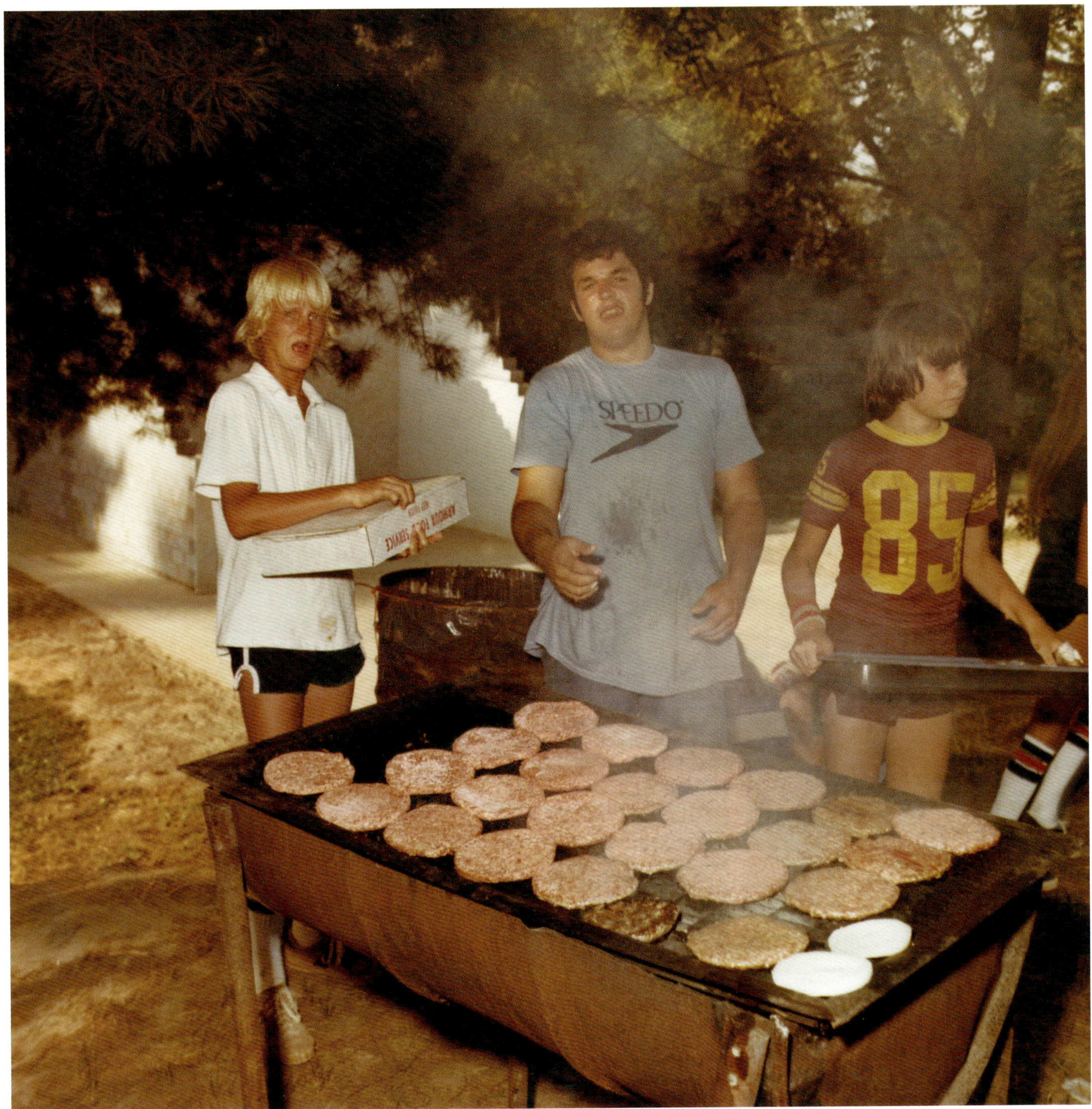

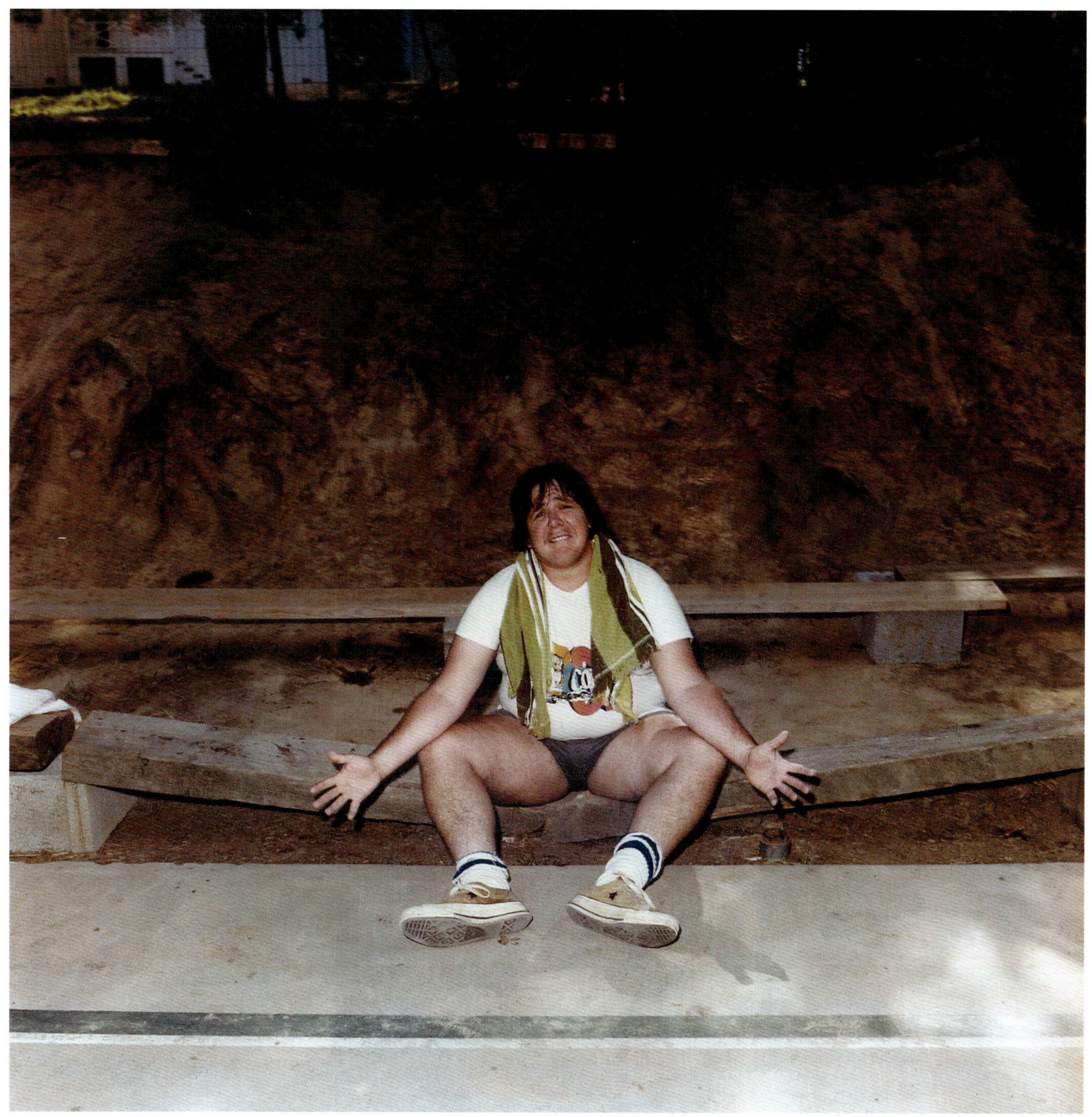

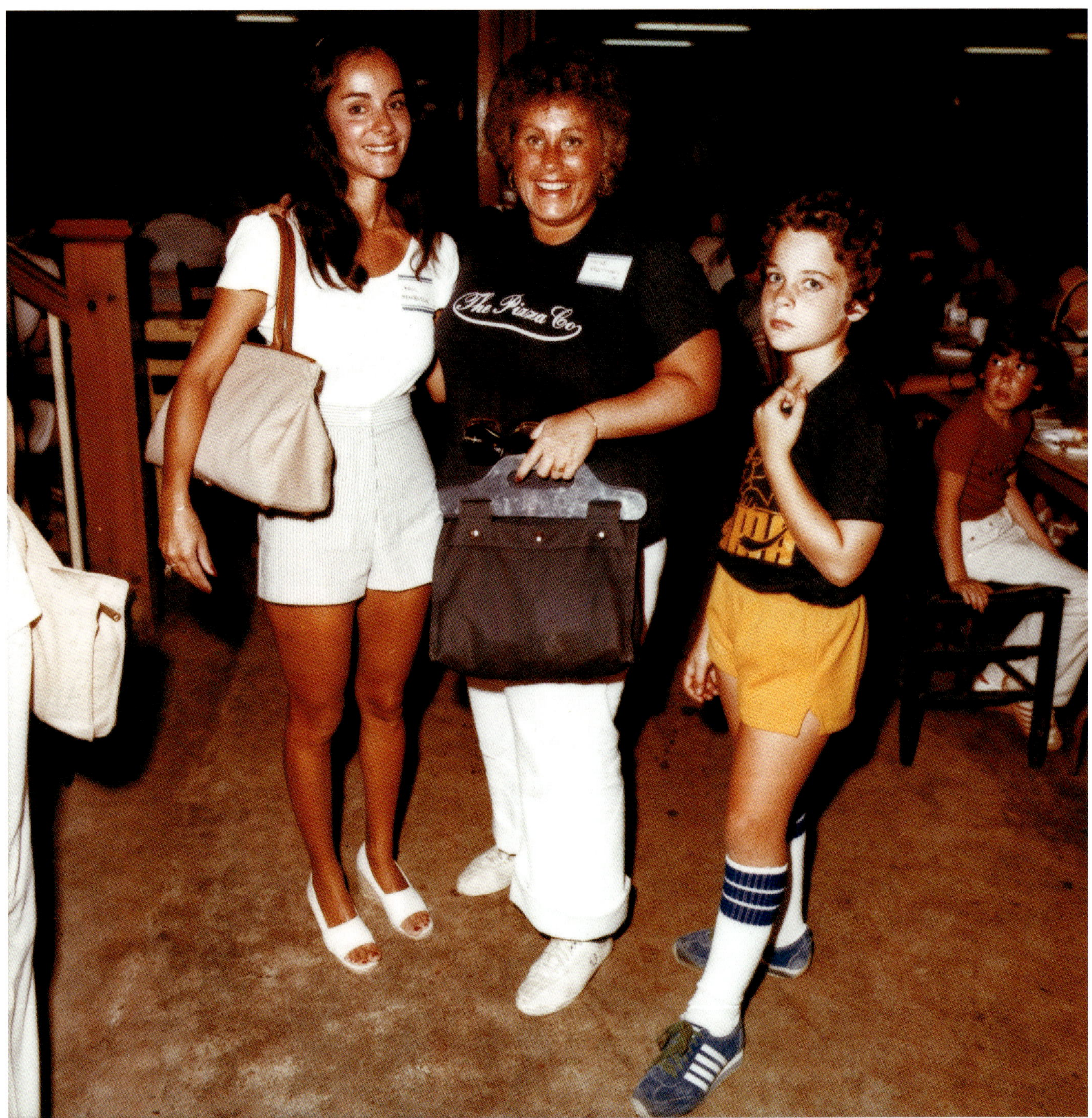

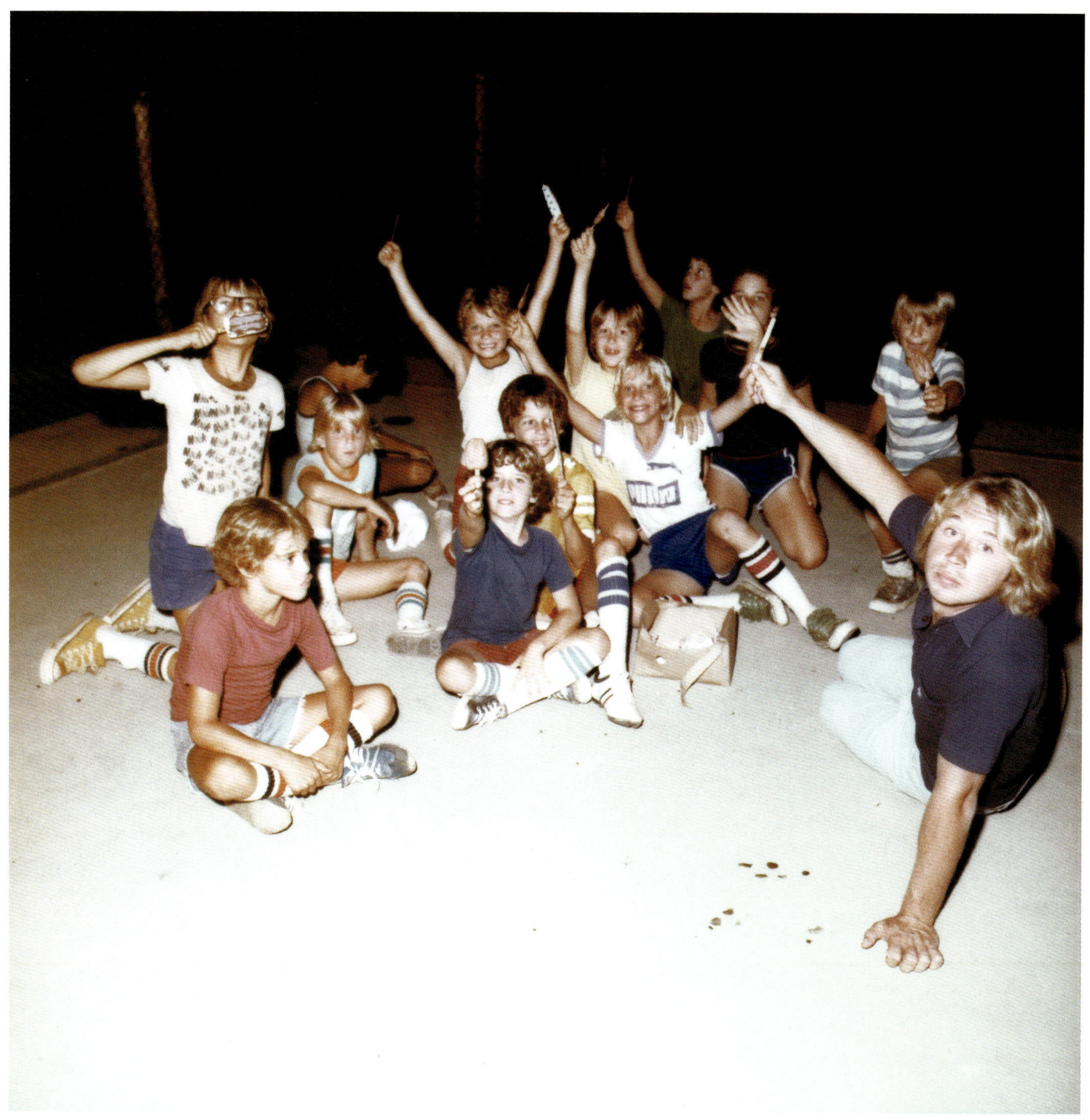

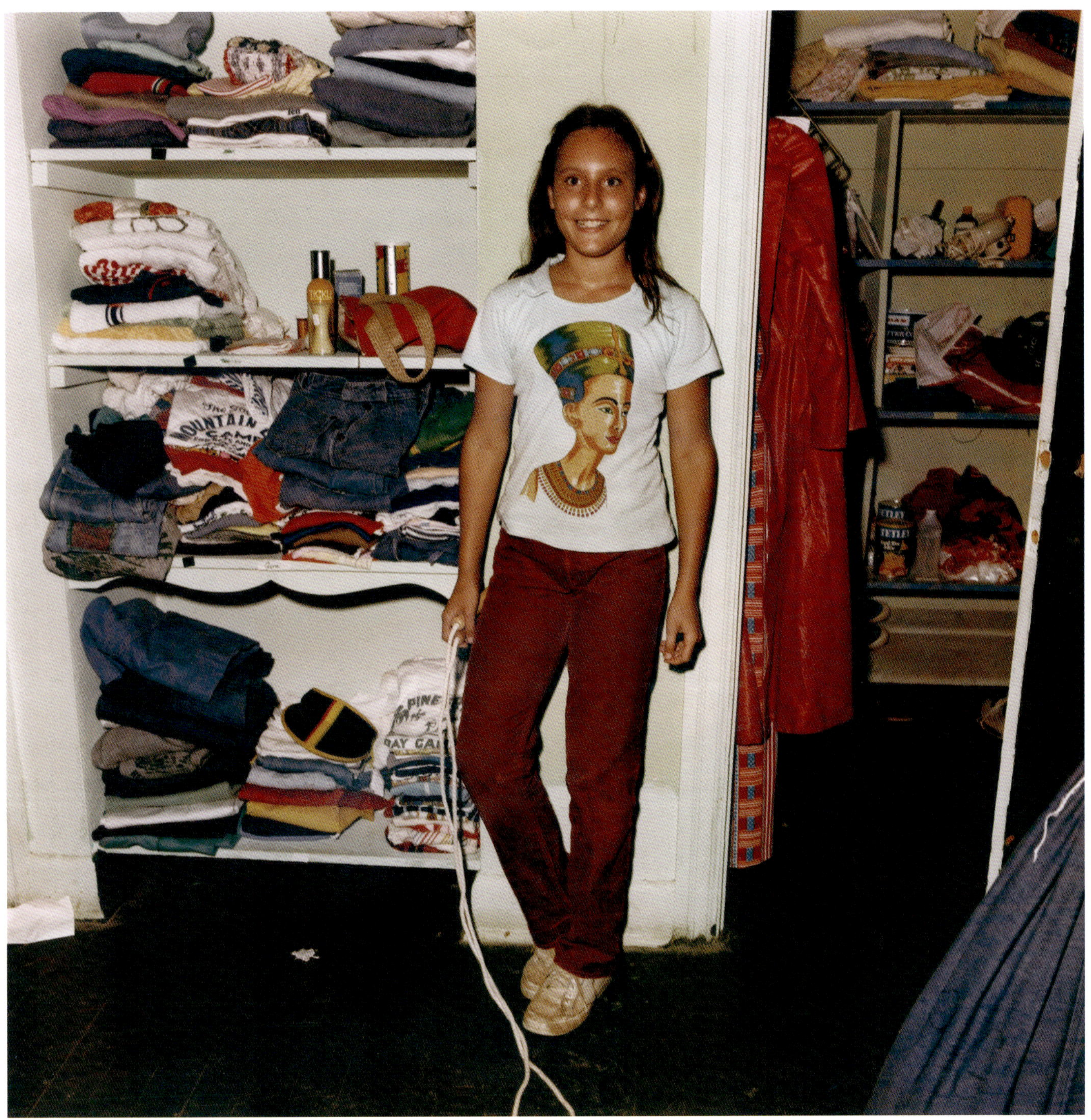

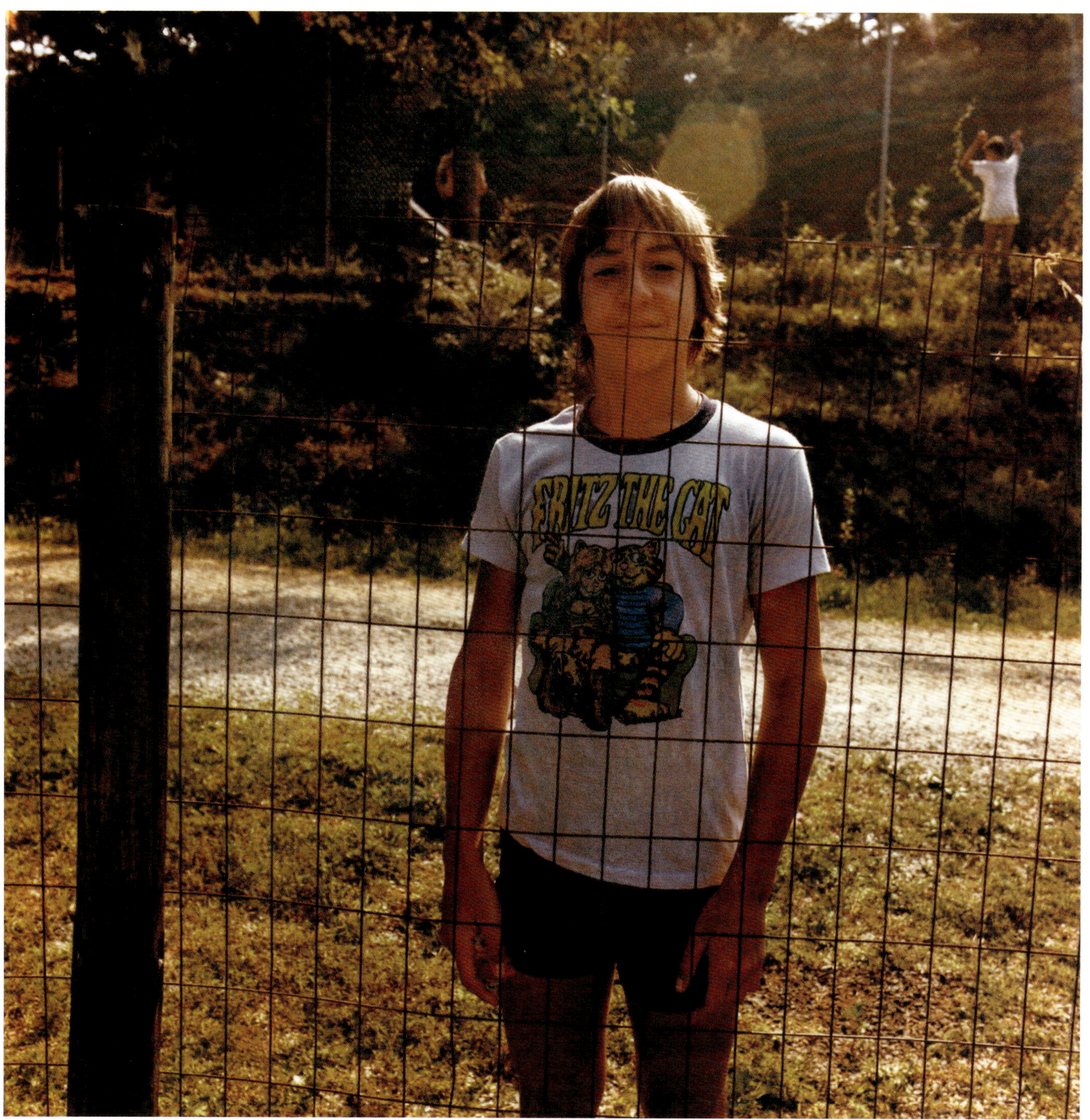

FRITZ THE CAT

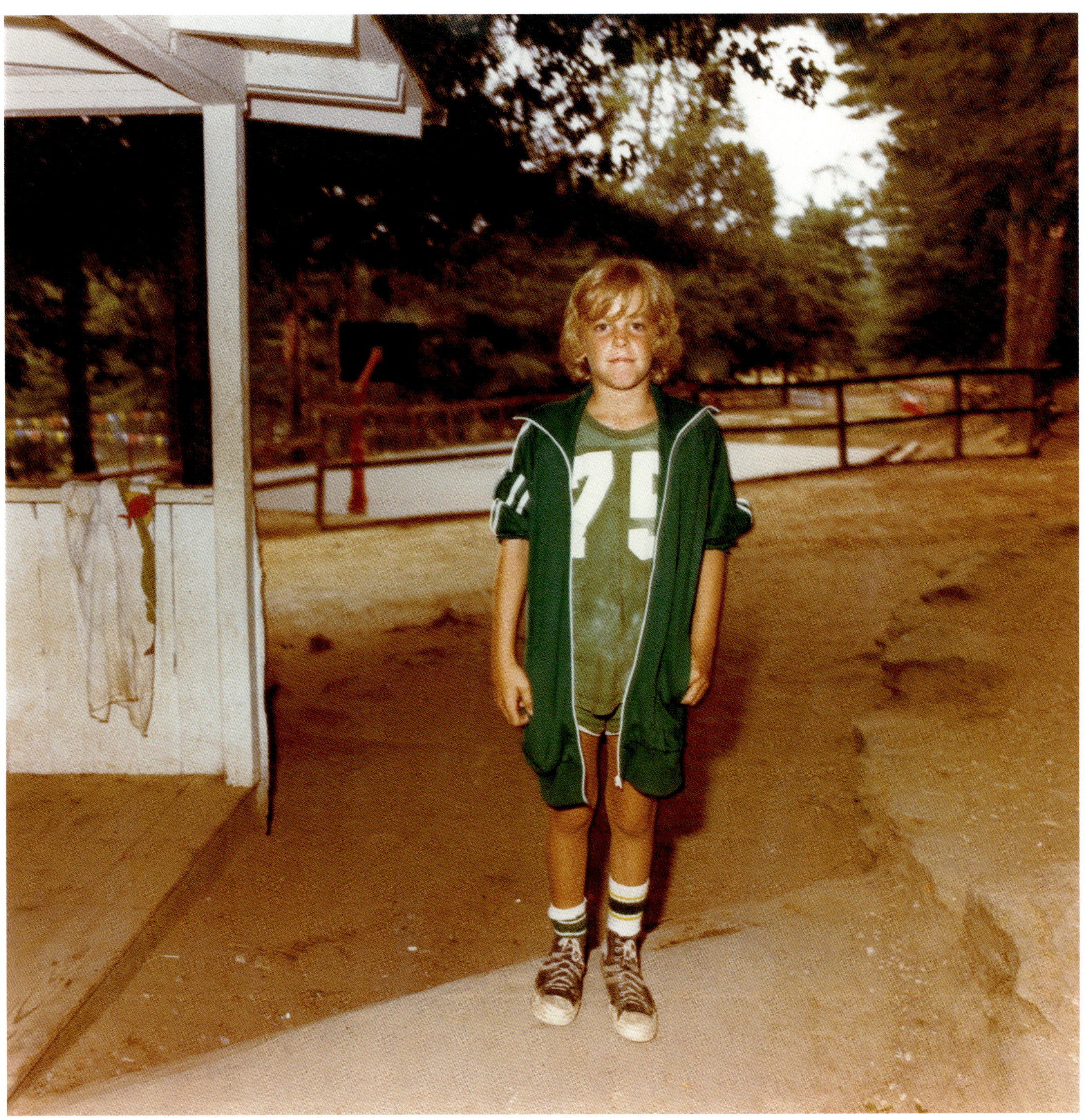

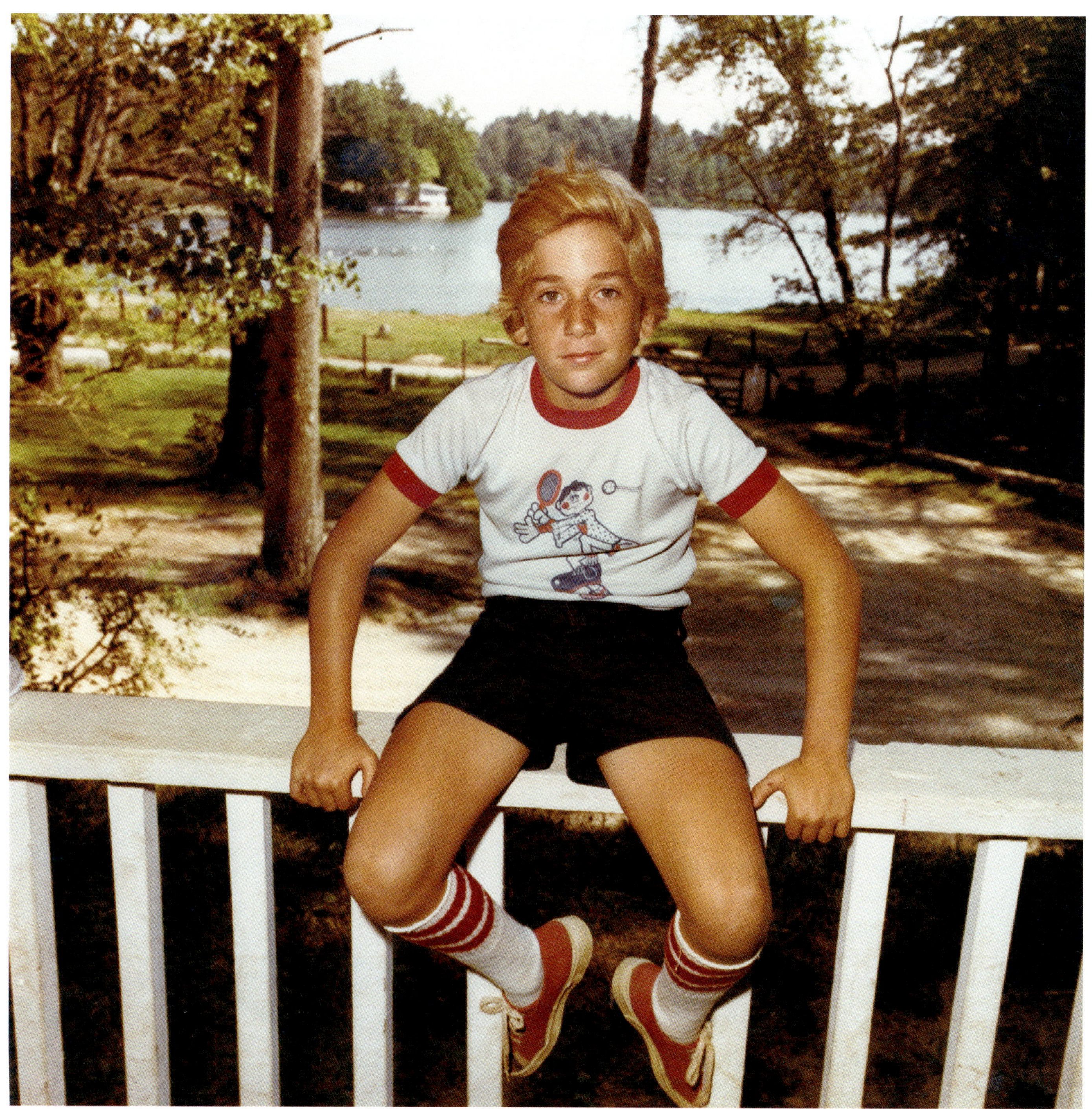

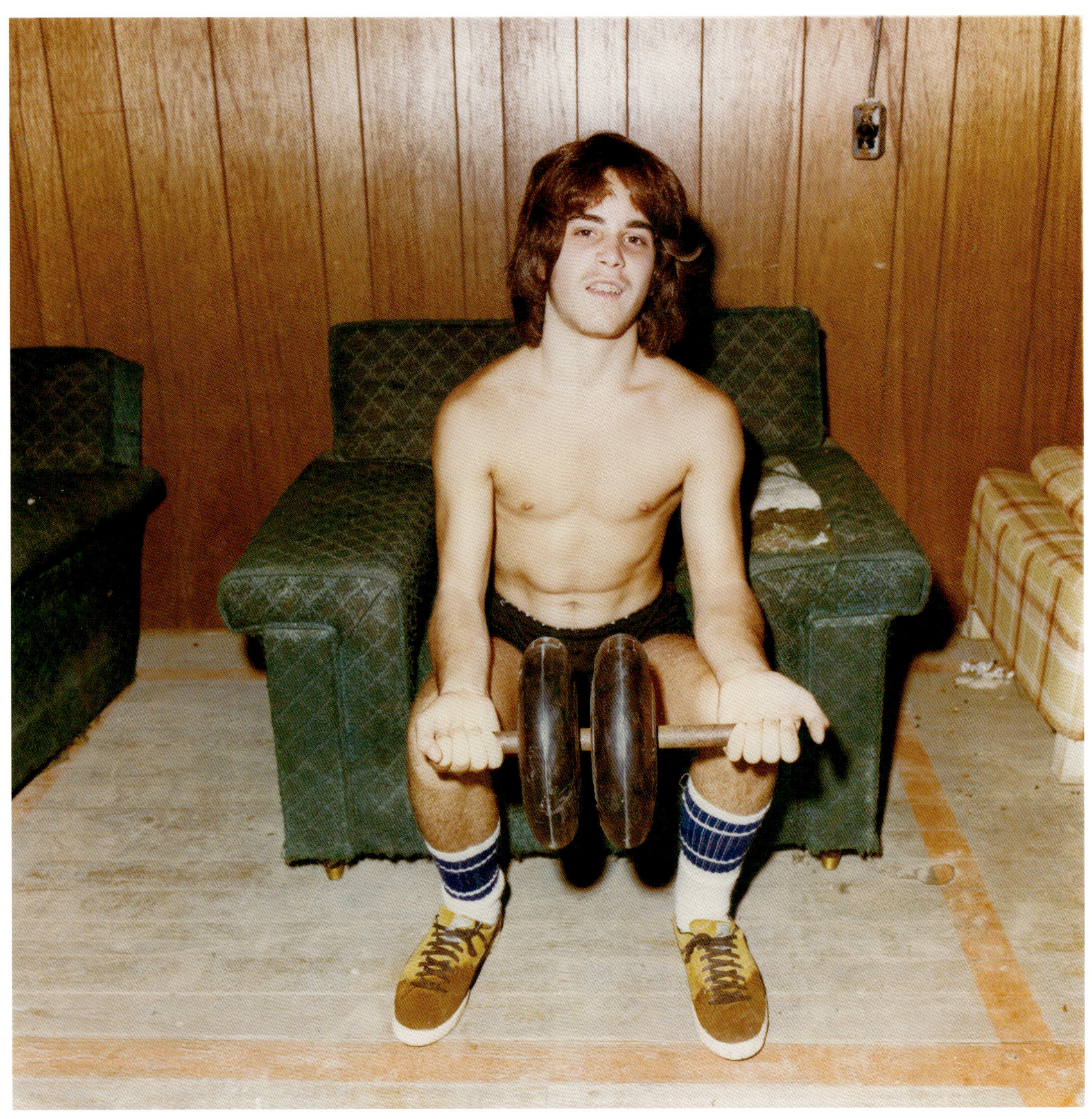

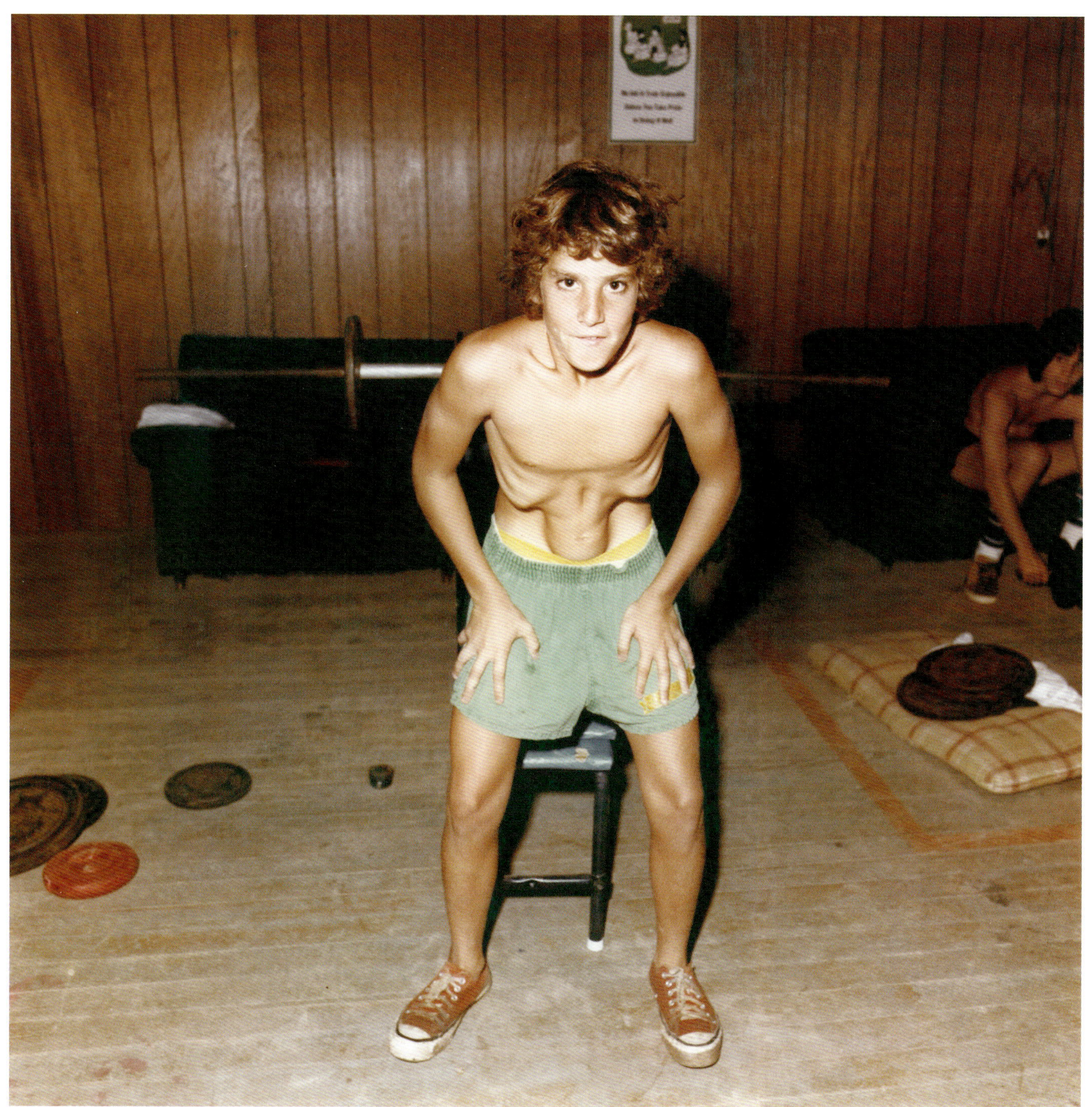

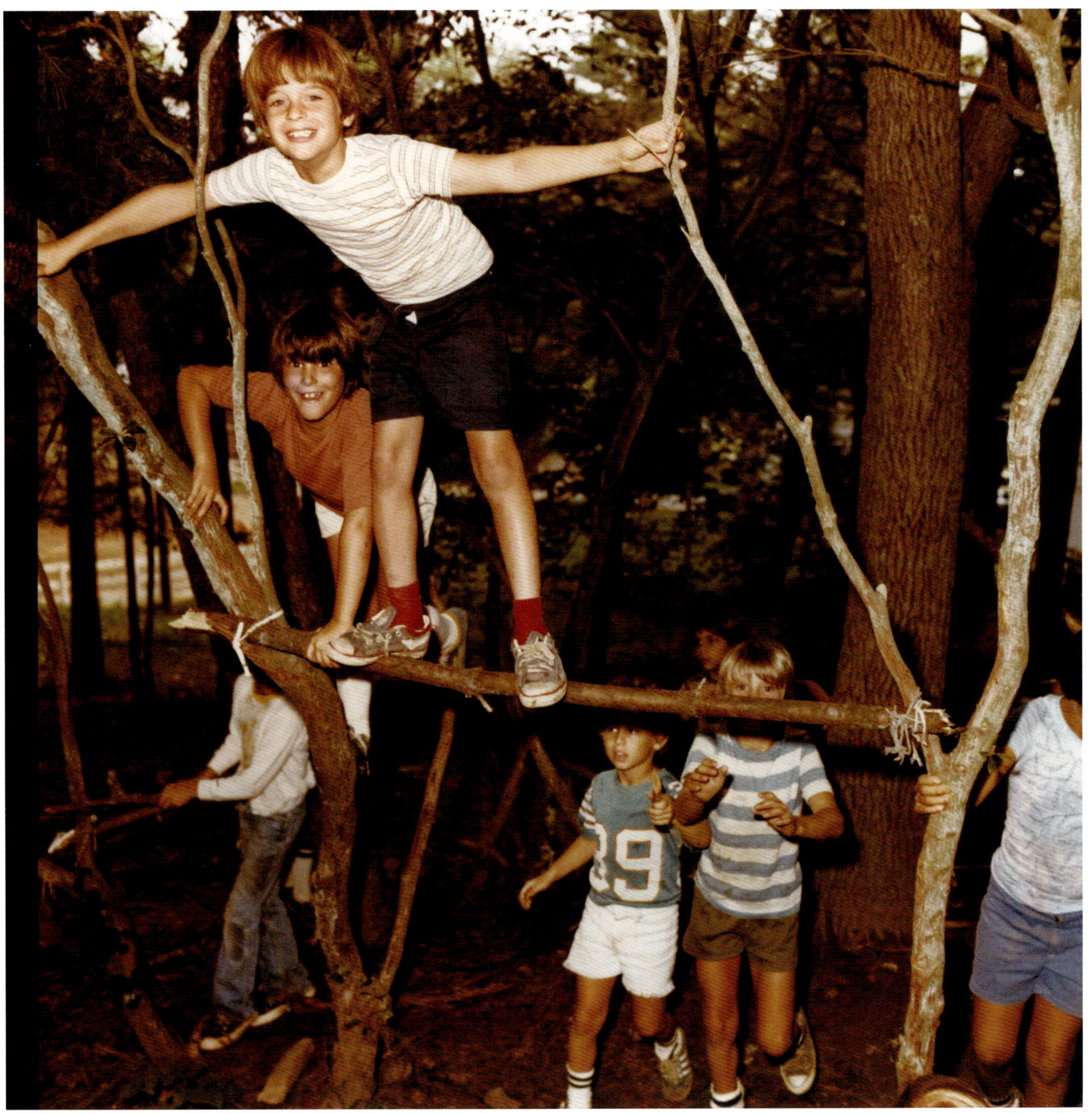

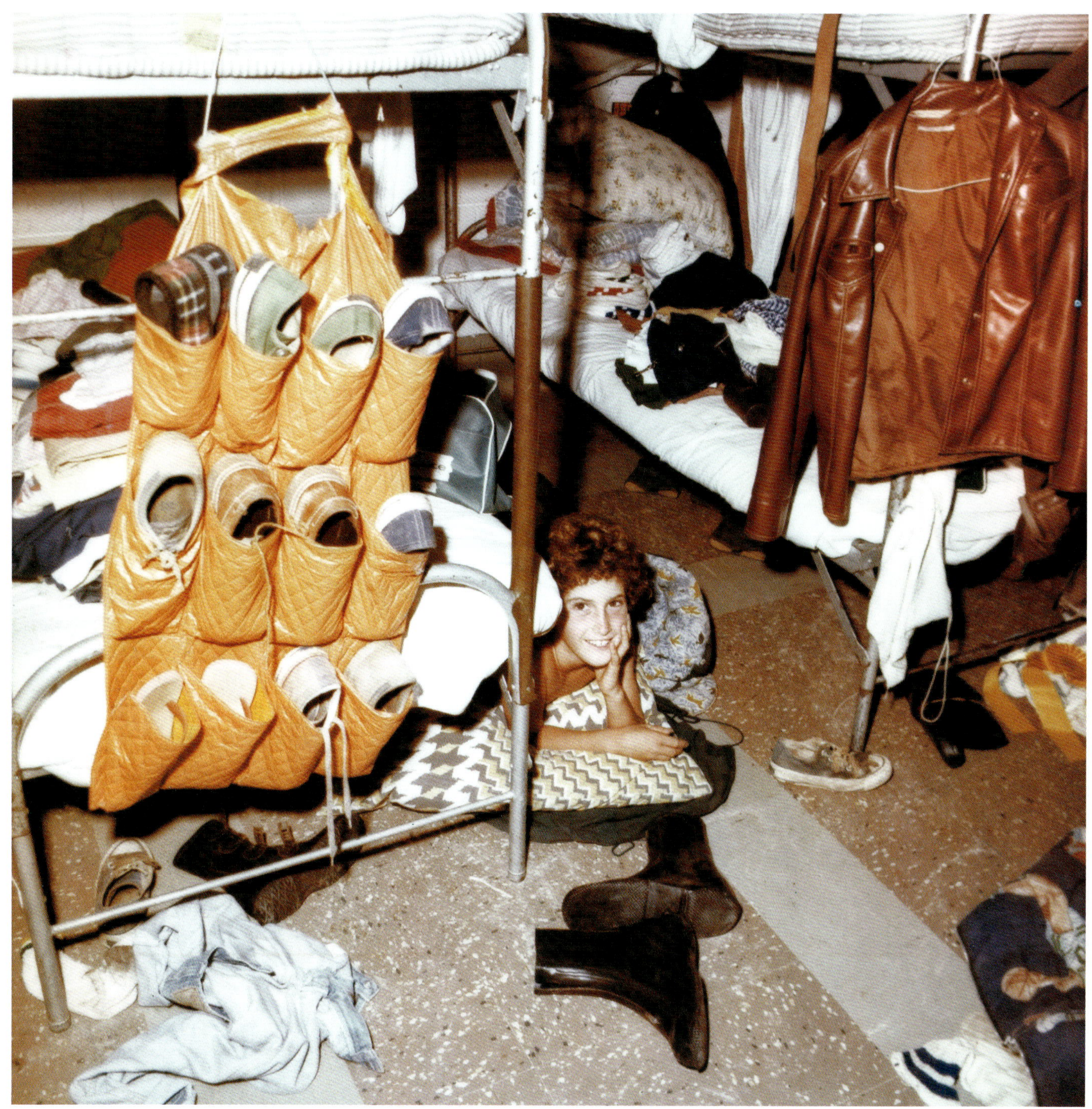

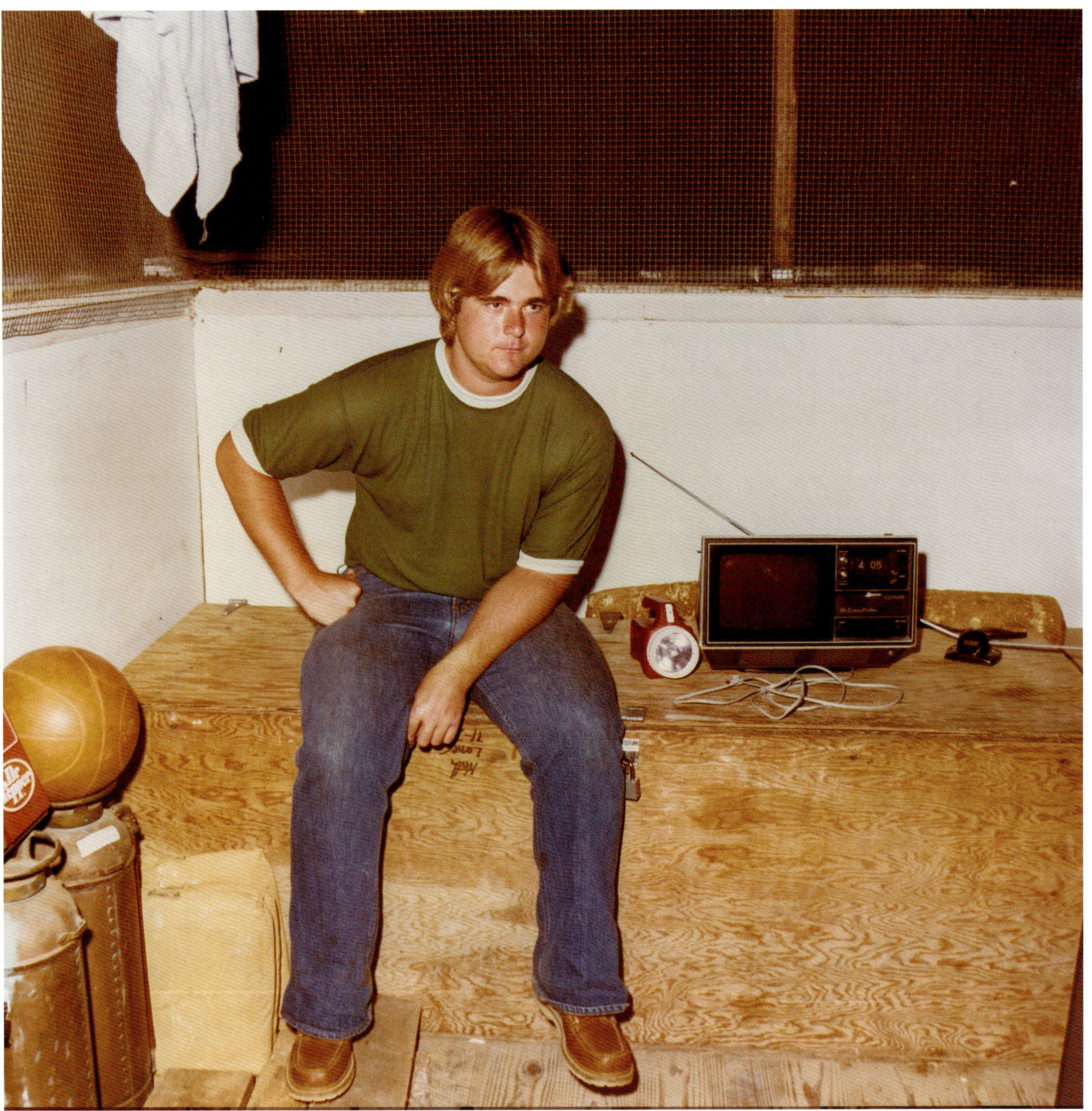

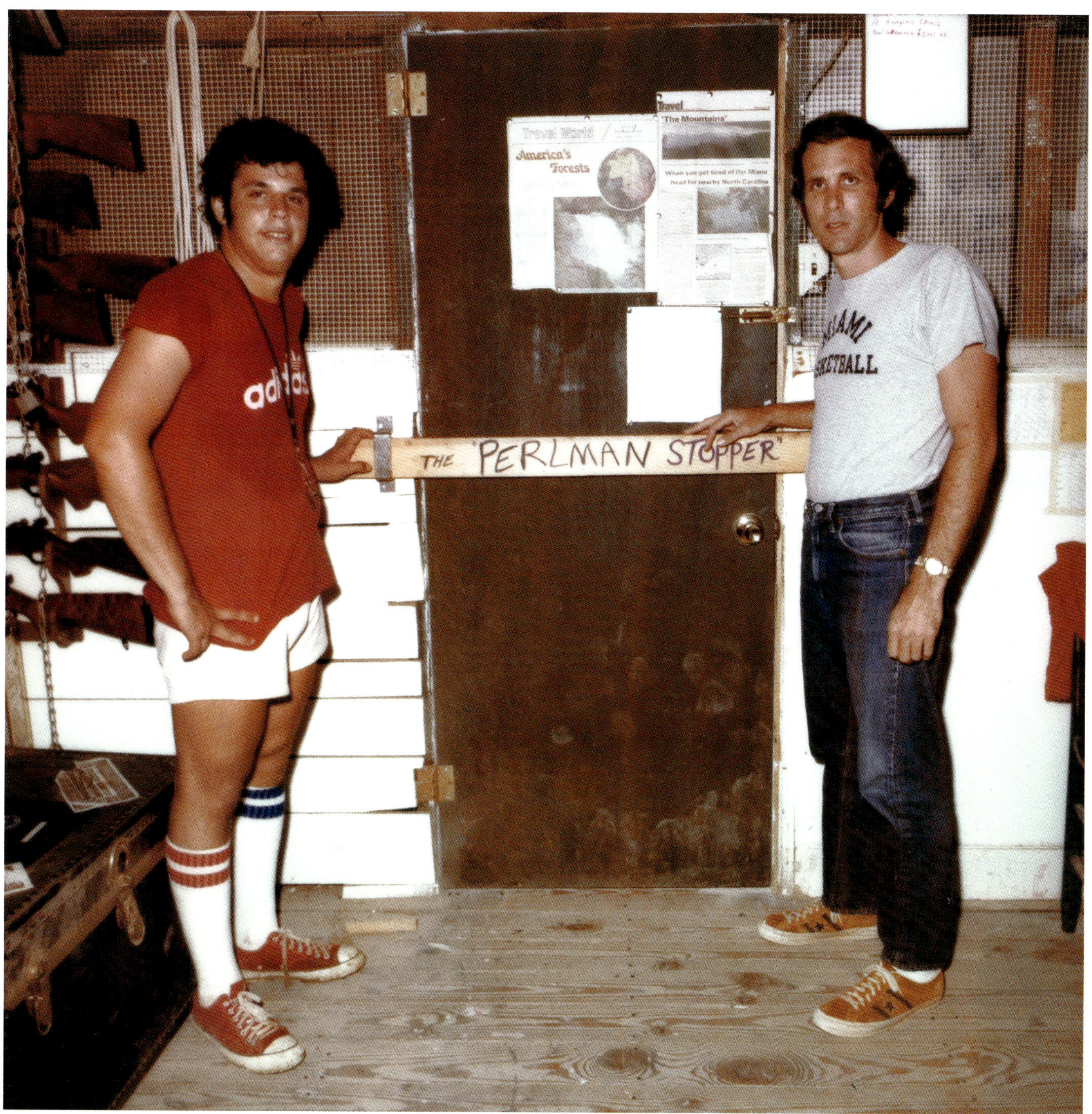
adidas
Travel World
America's Forests
Travel
'The Mountains'
When you get tired of flat Miami
head for nearby North Carolina
MIAMI
BASKETBALL
THE "PERLMAN STOPPER"

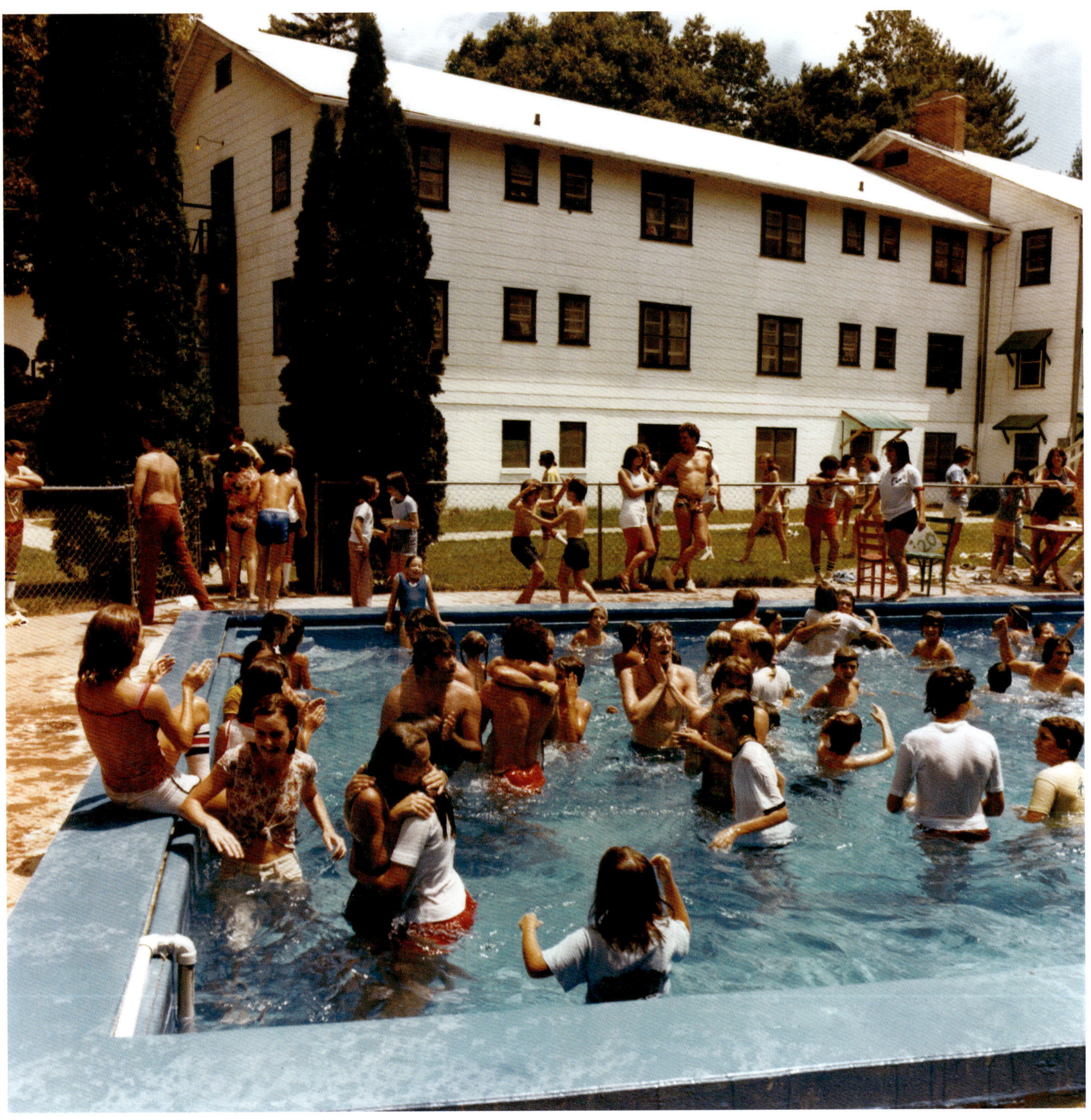

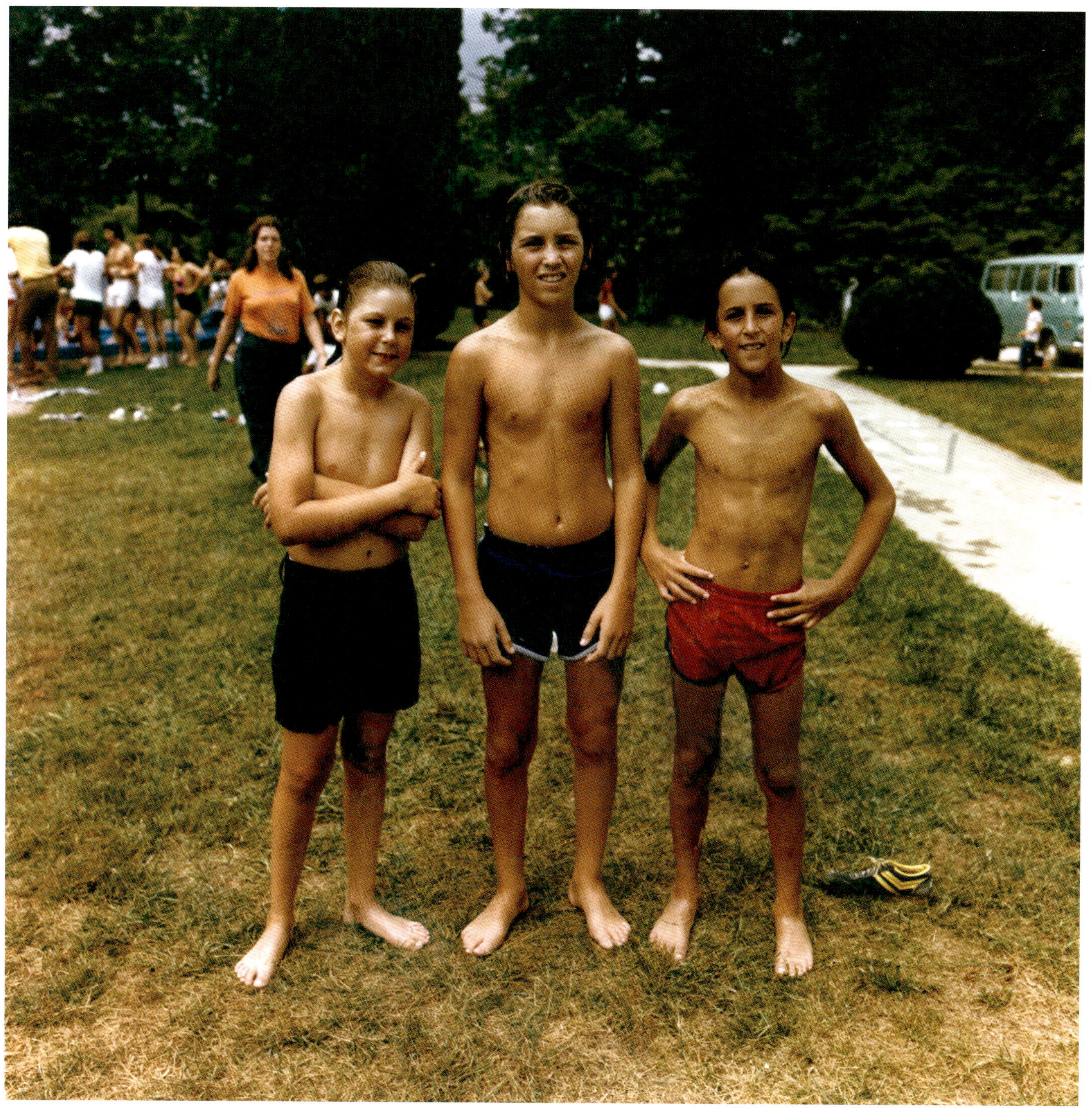

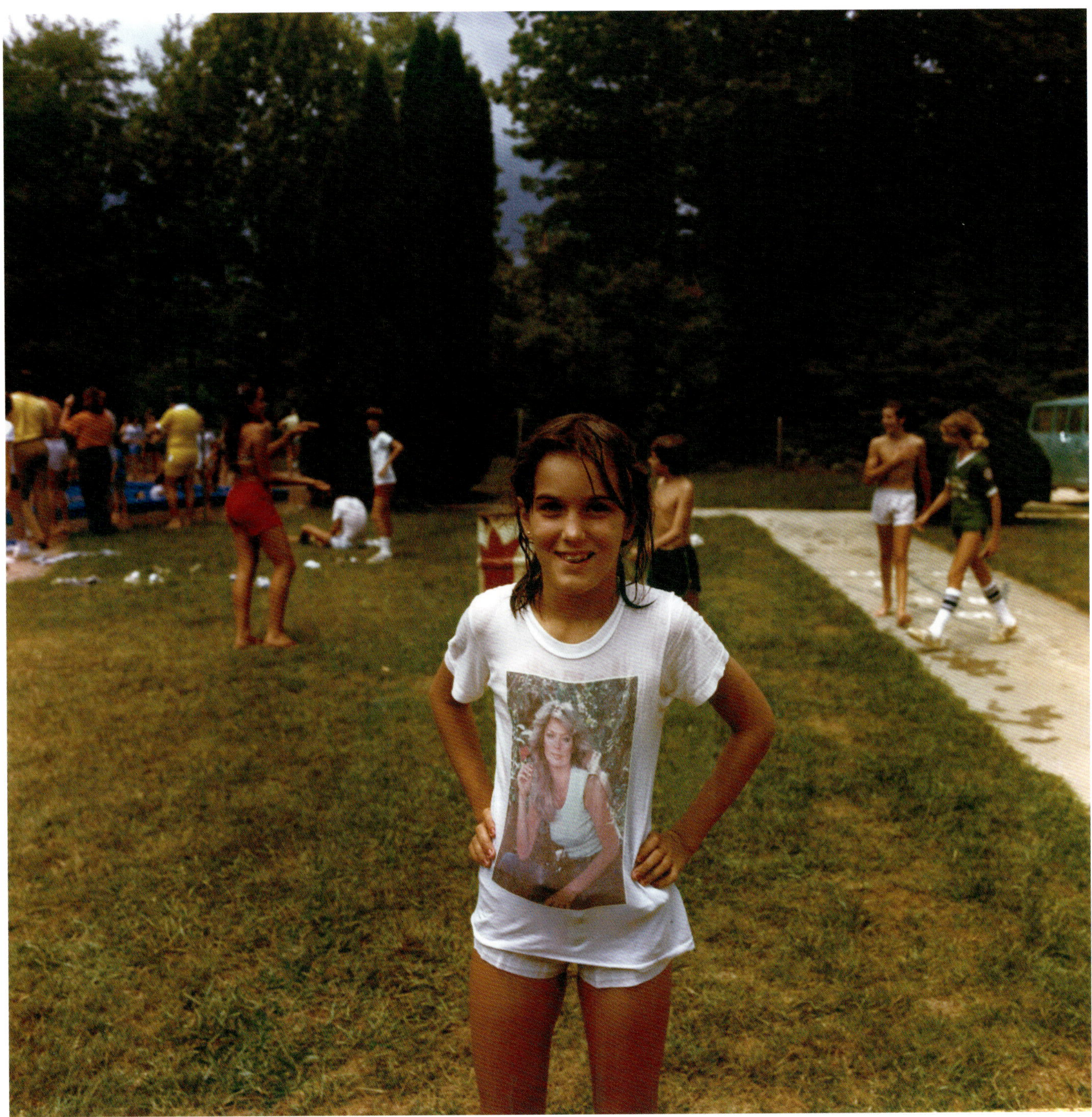

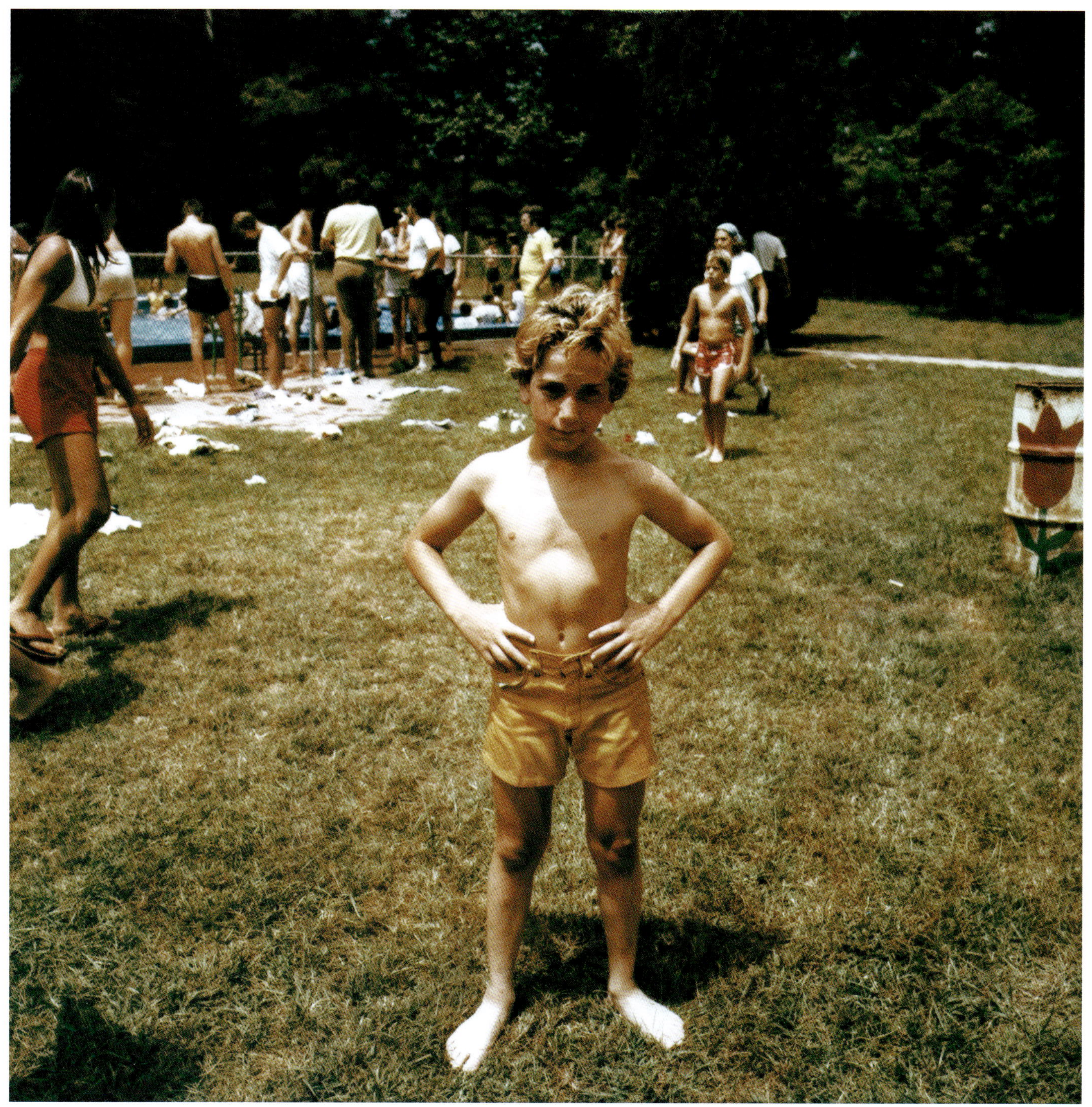

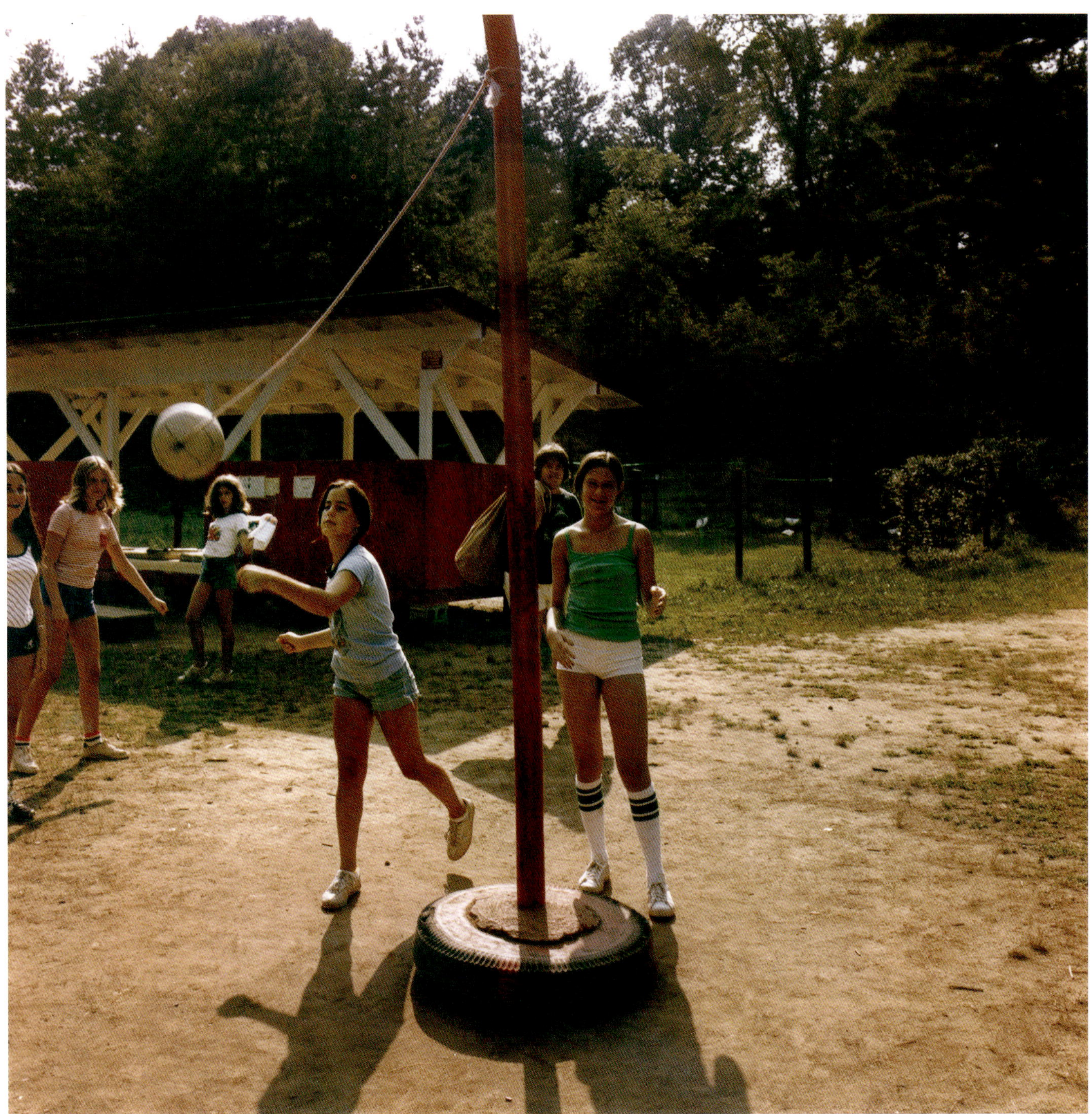

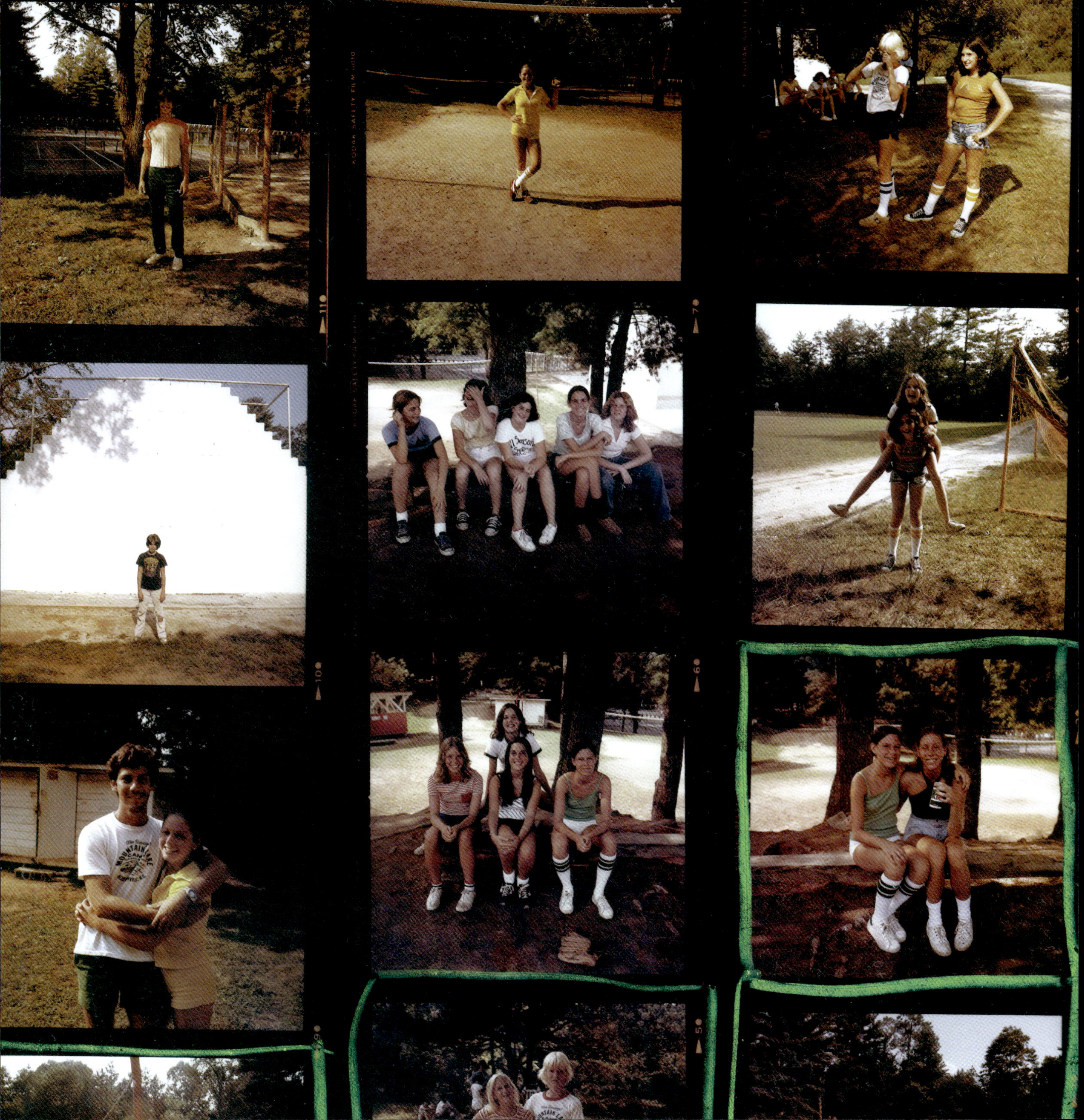

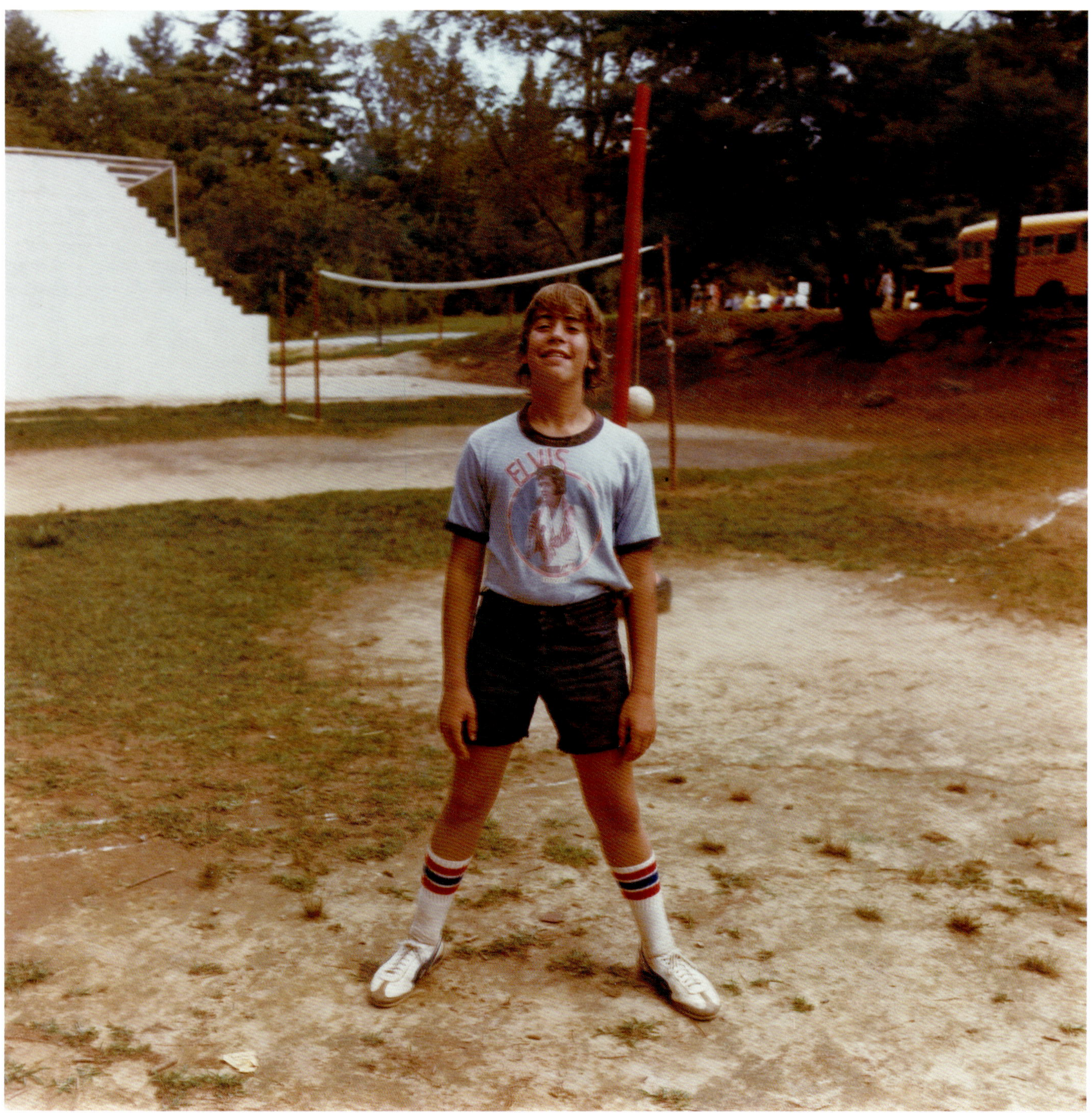

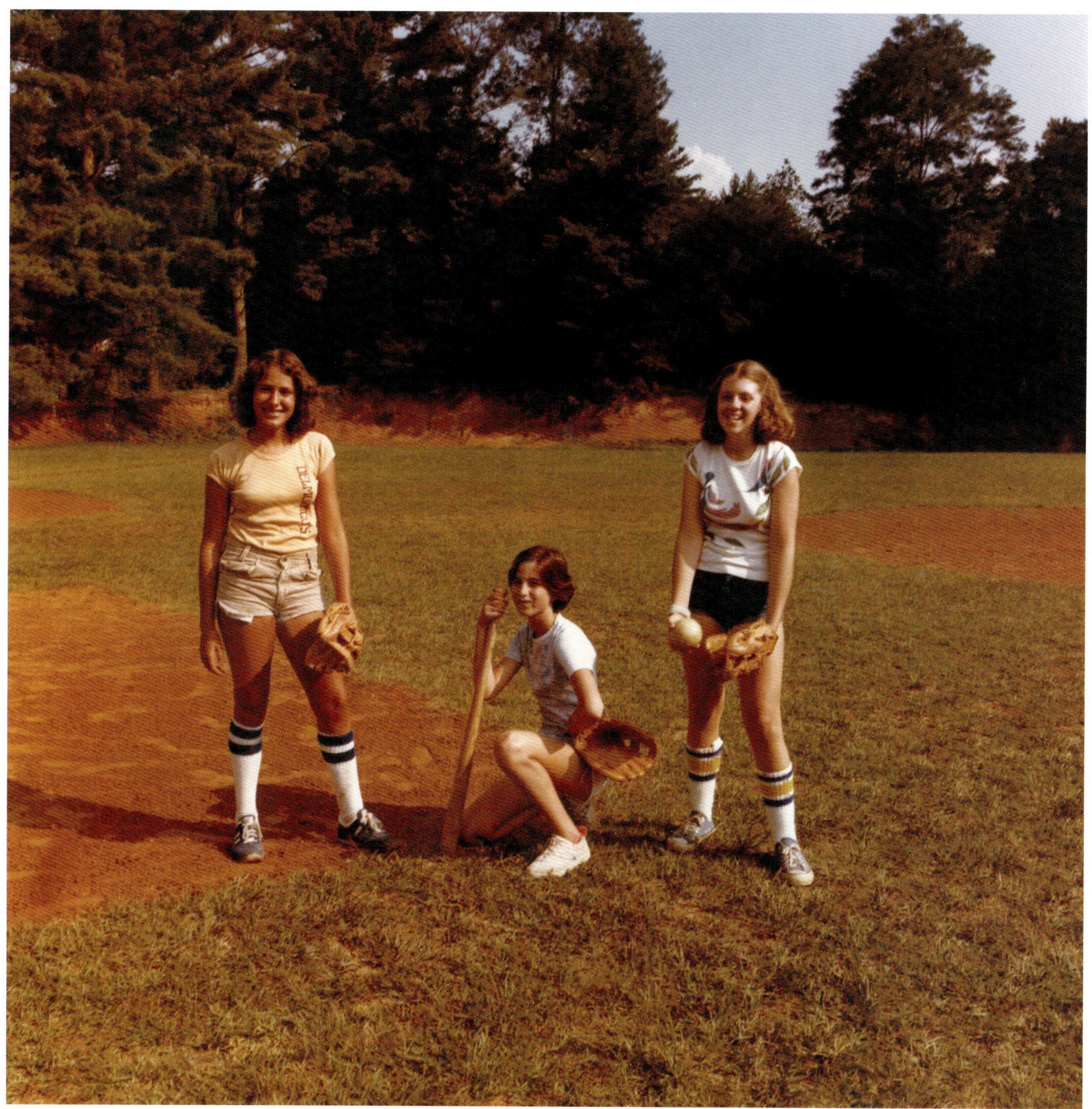

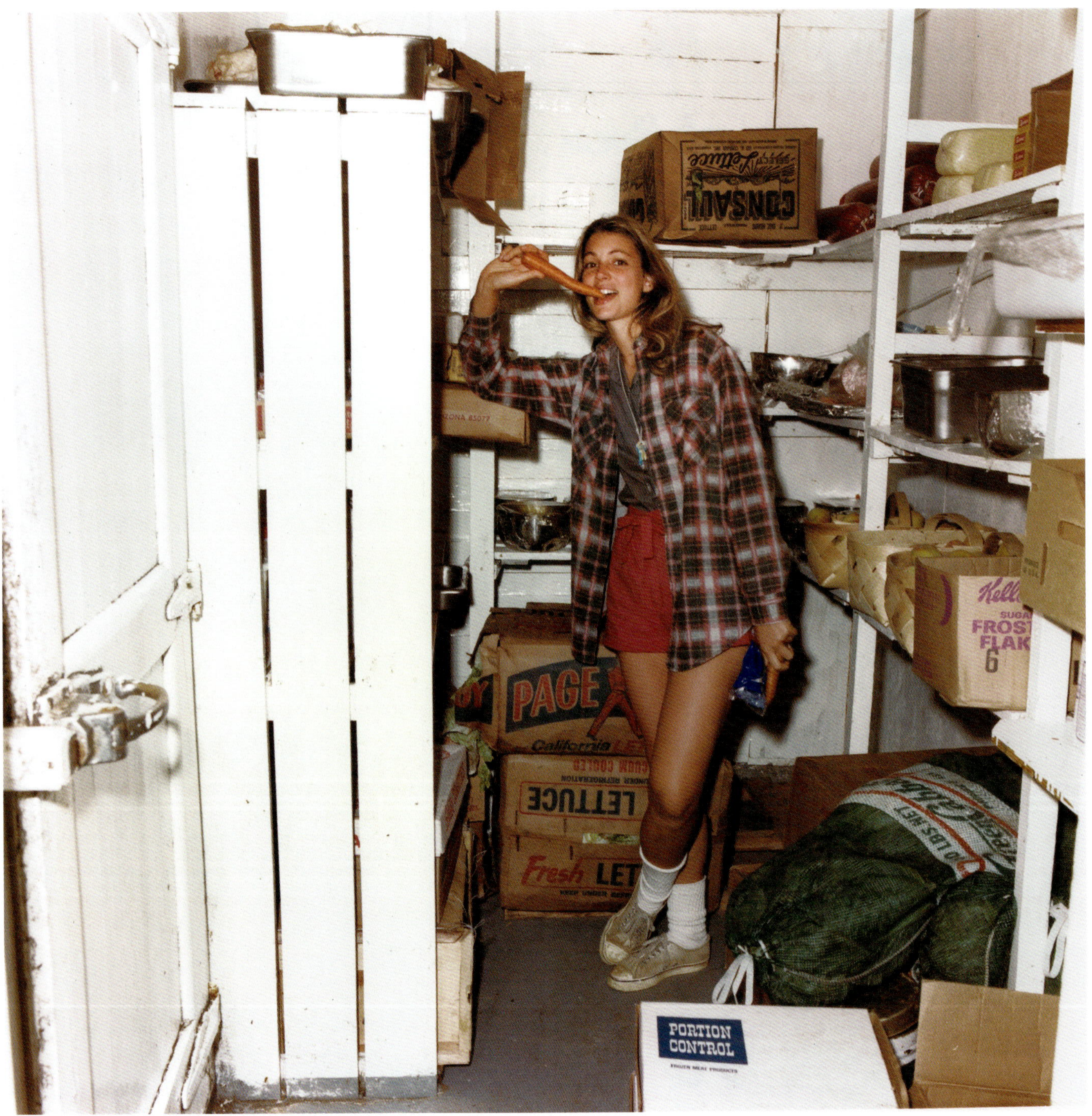

CONSAUL
PAGE
California
LETTUCE
COLOR REFRIGERATION
Fresh LET
Kello
SUGA
FROST
FLAK
6
PORTION
CONTROL
FROZEN MEAT PRODUCTS

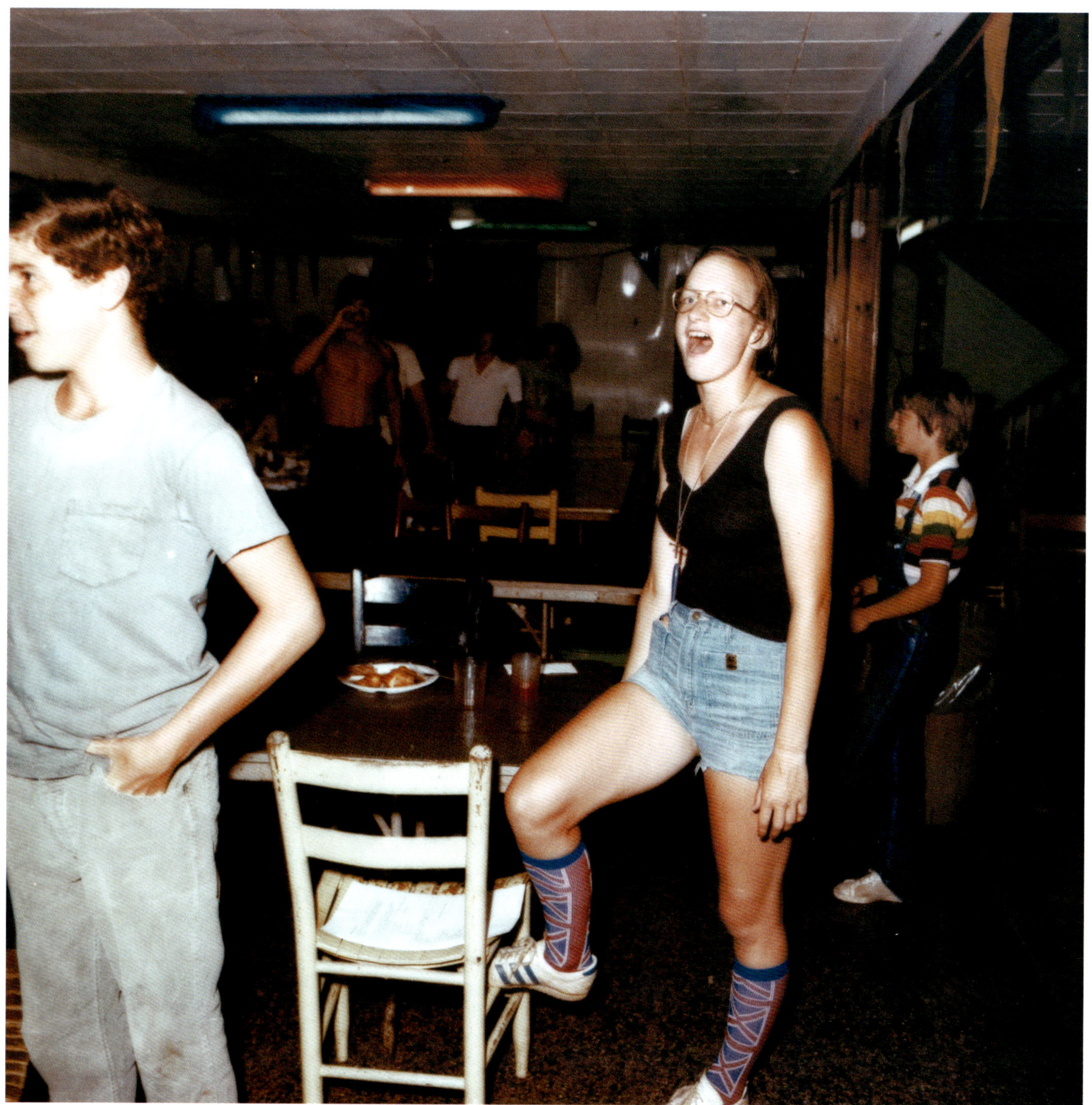

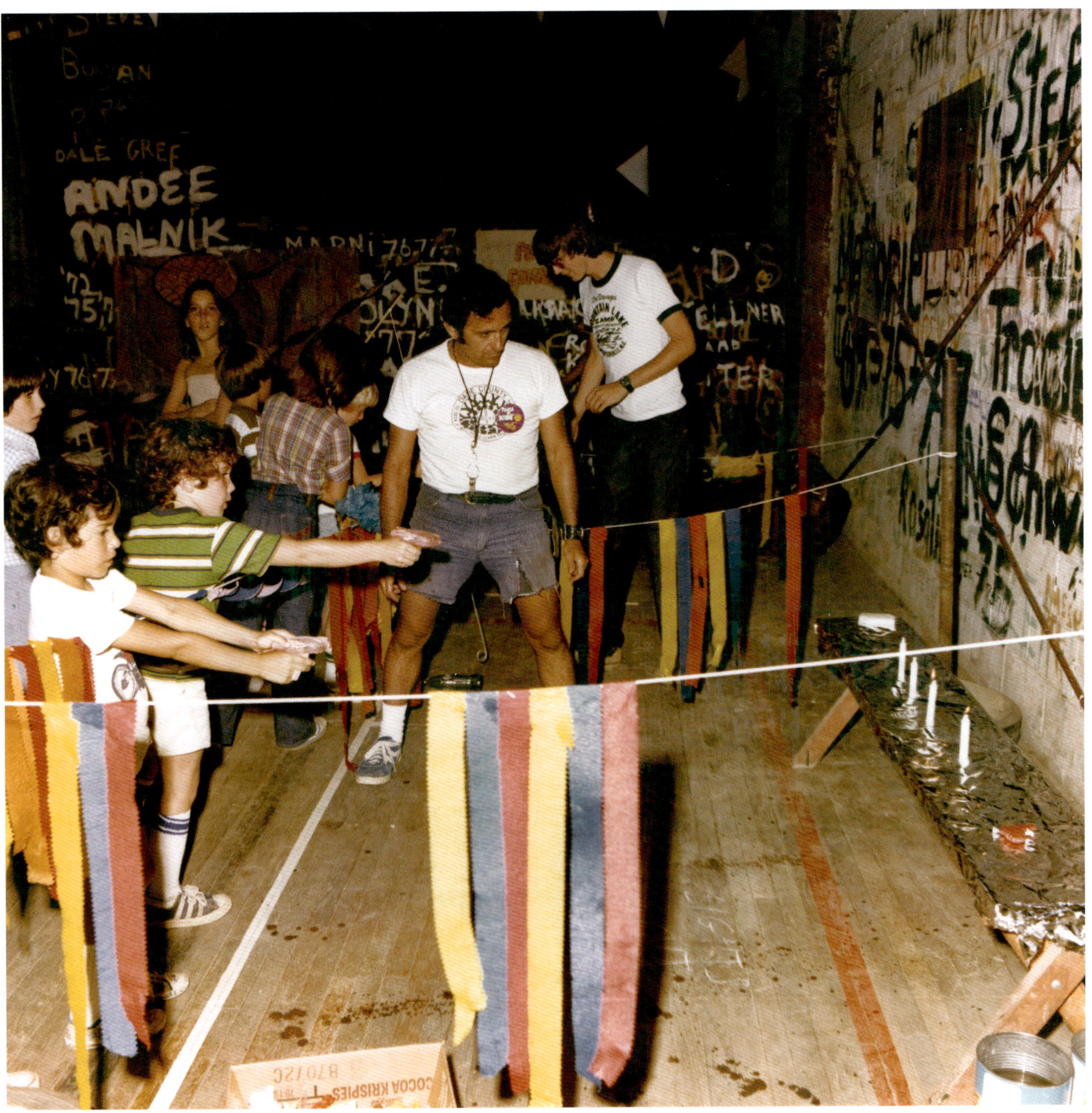

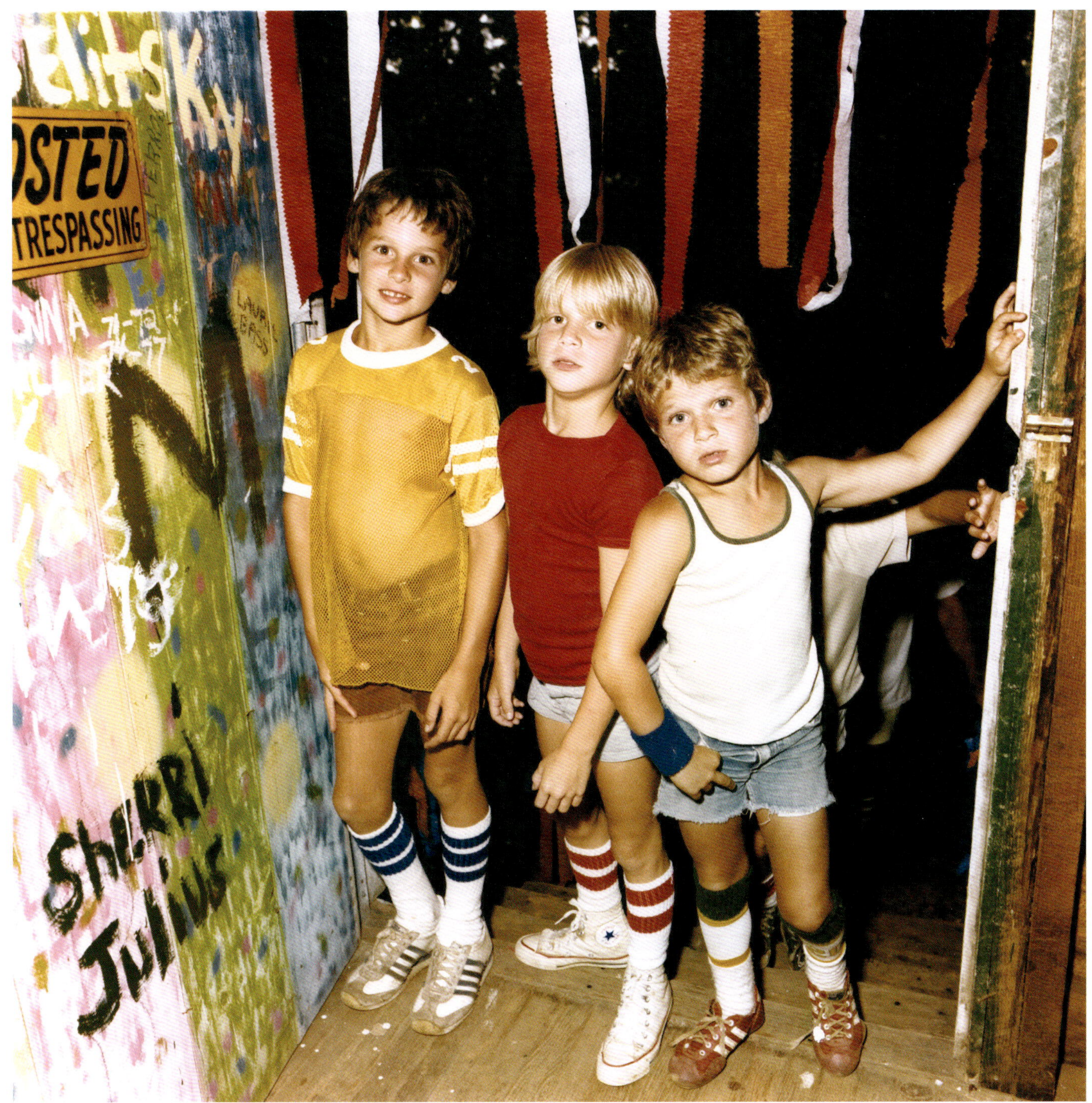
POSTED
NO TRESPASSING
SHERRI
Julius

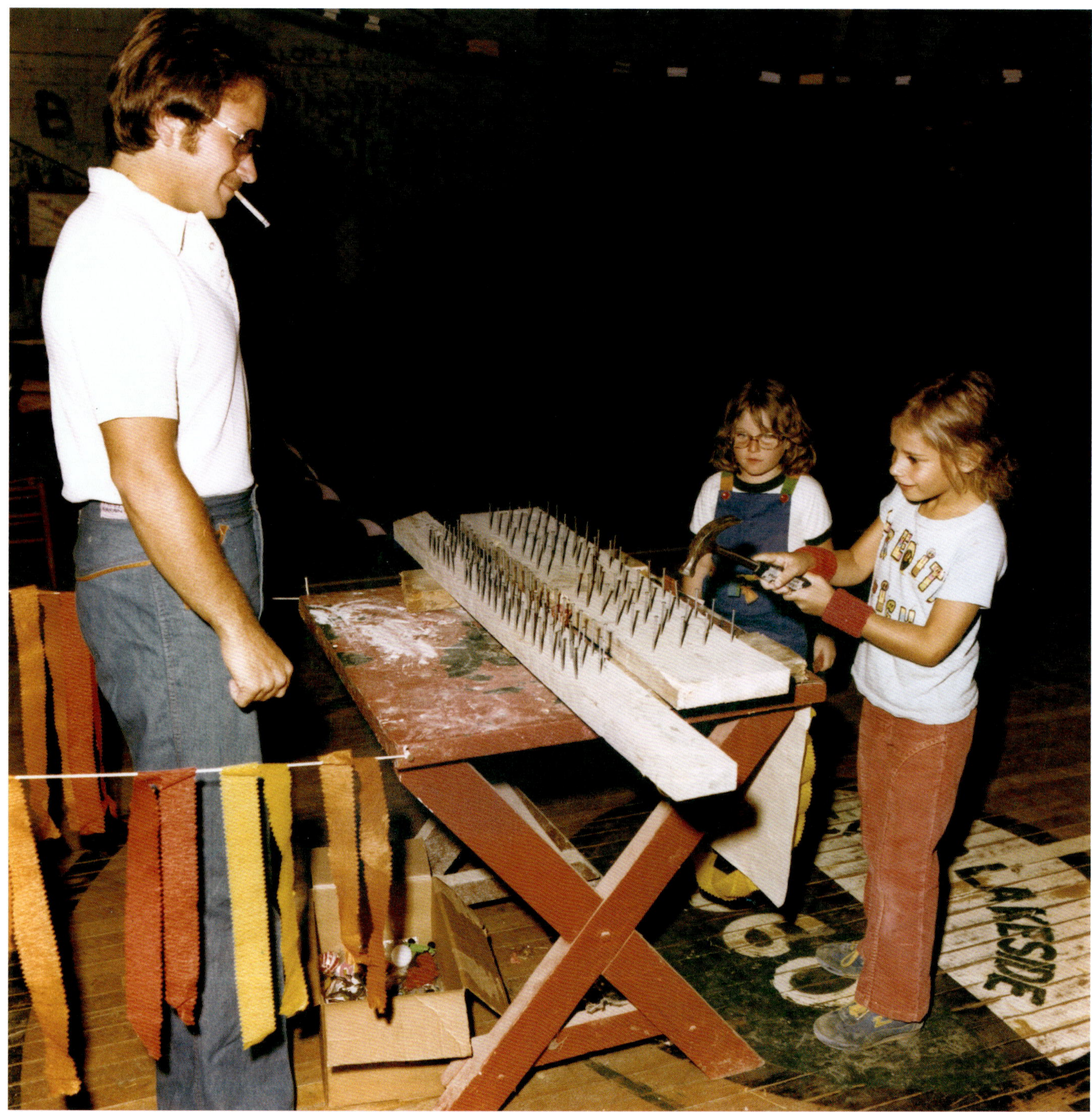

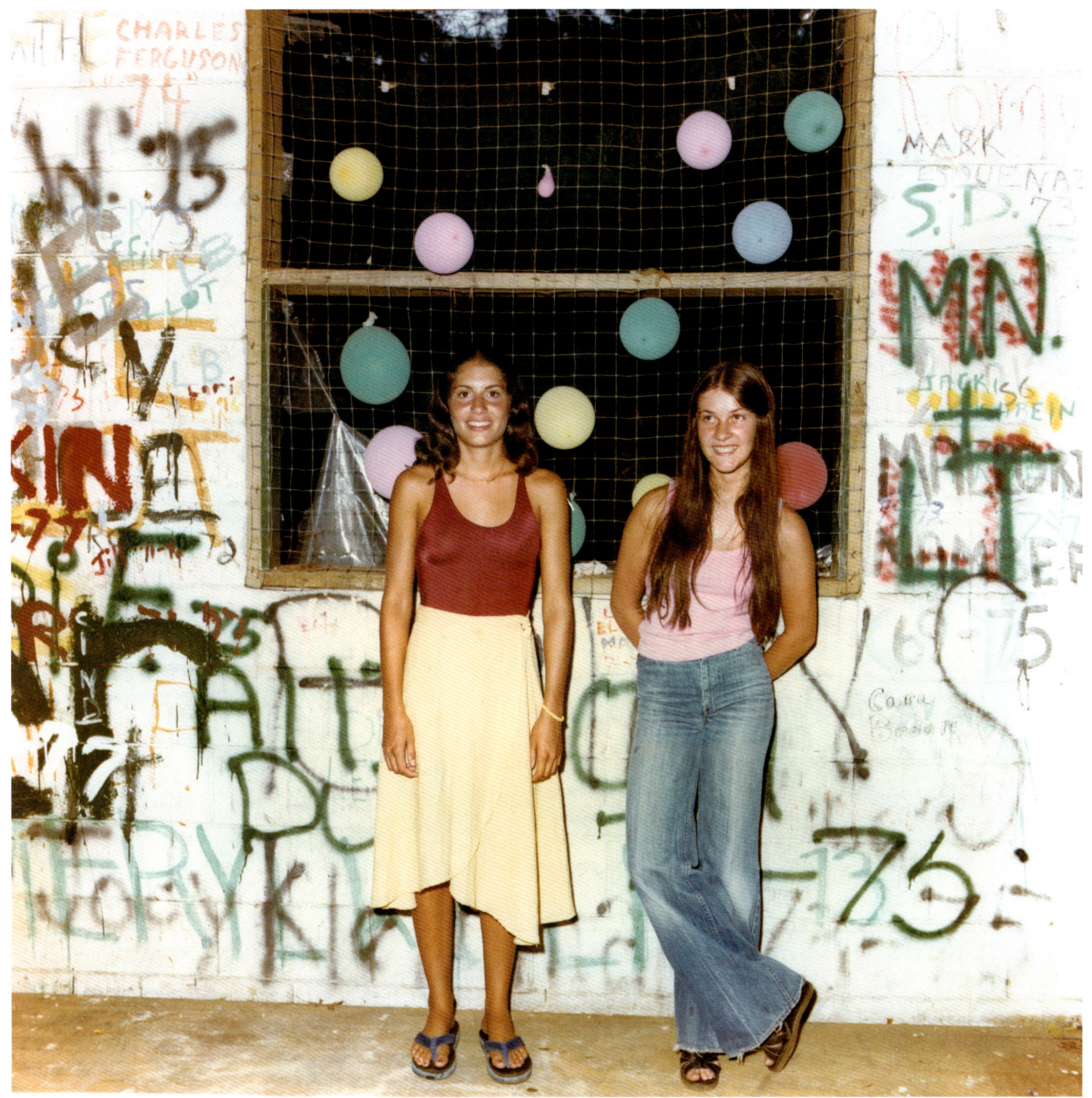

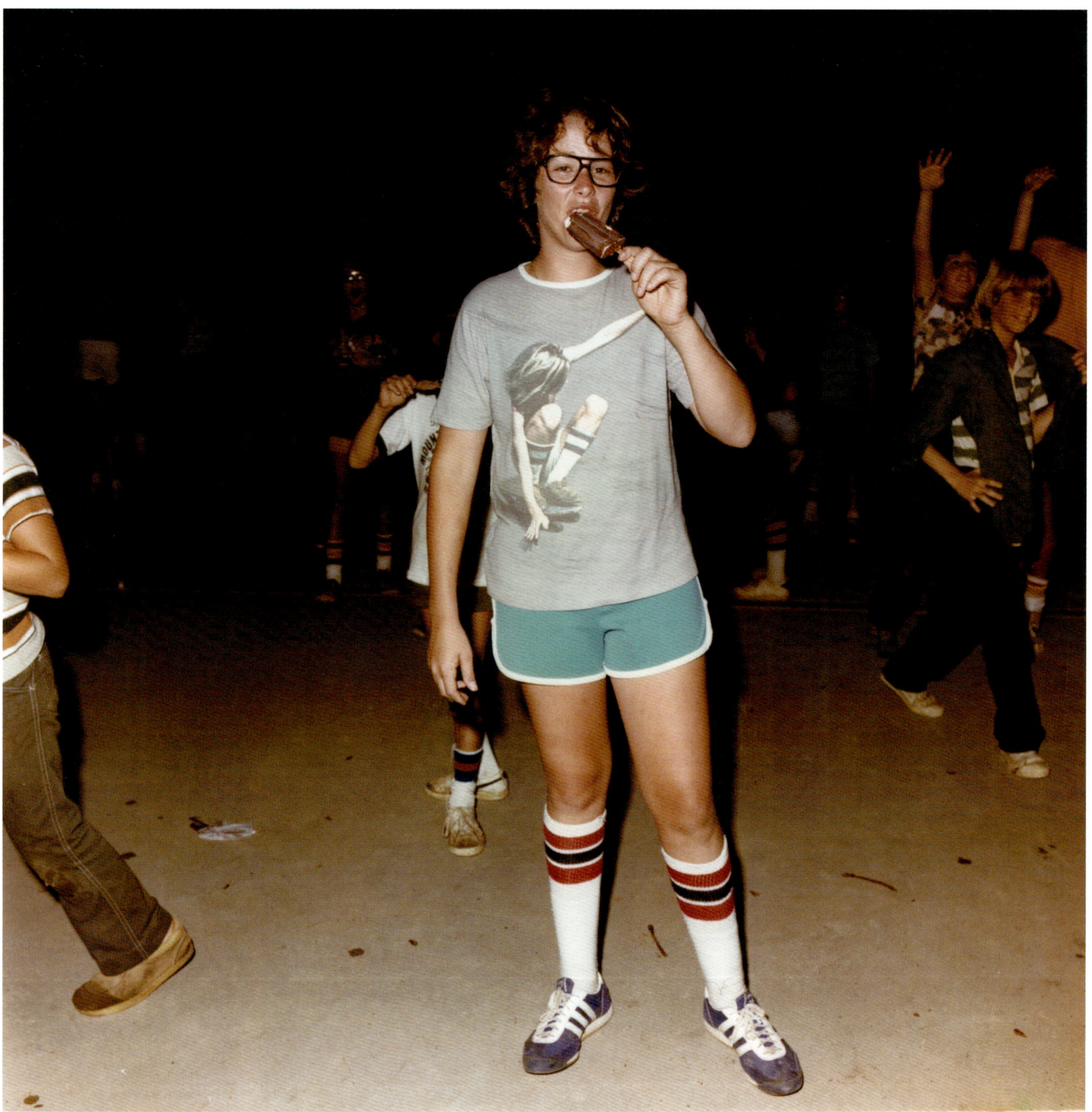

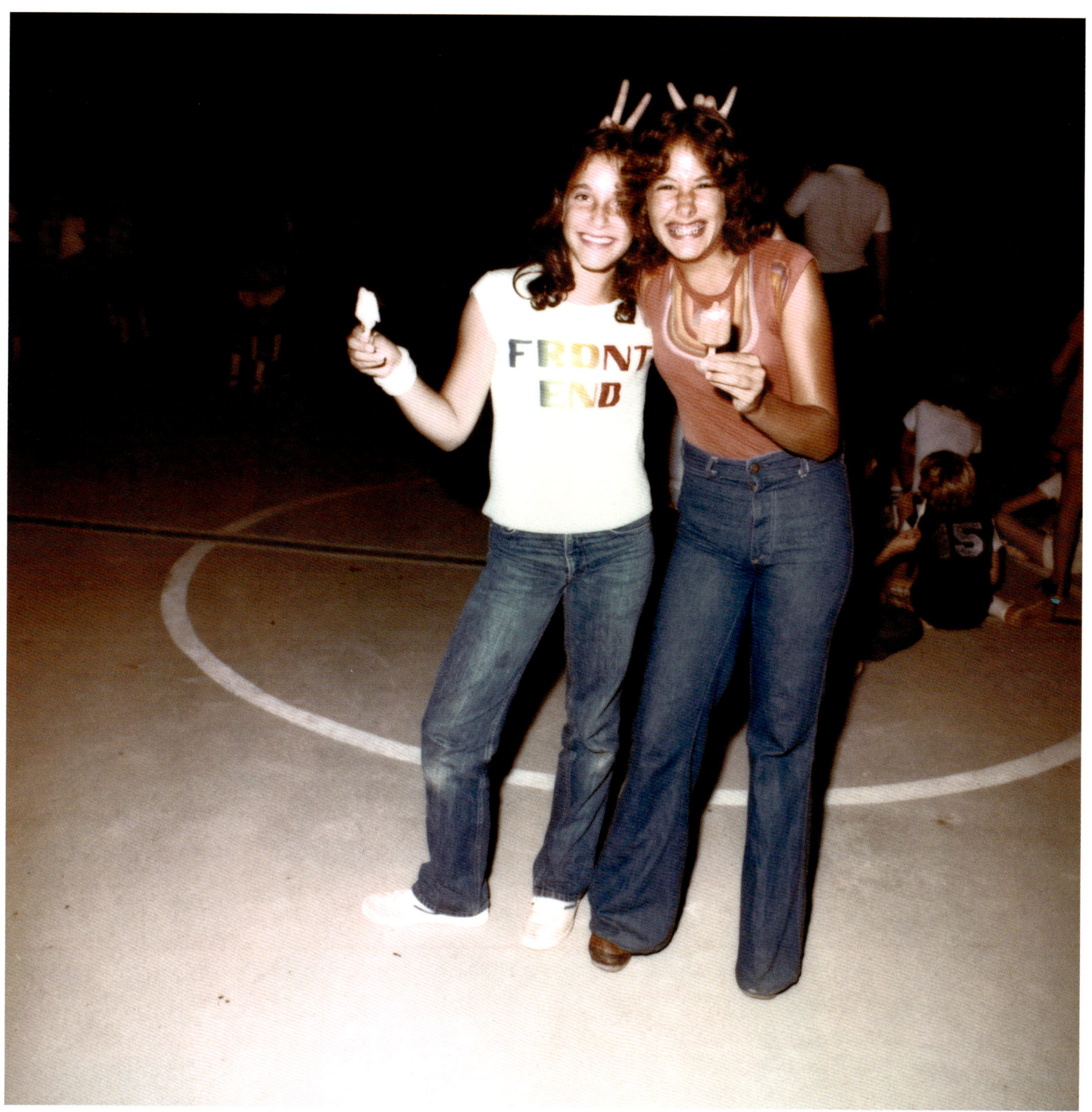

FRONT
END
15

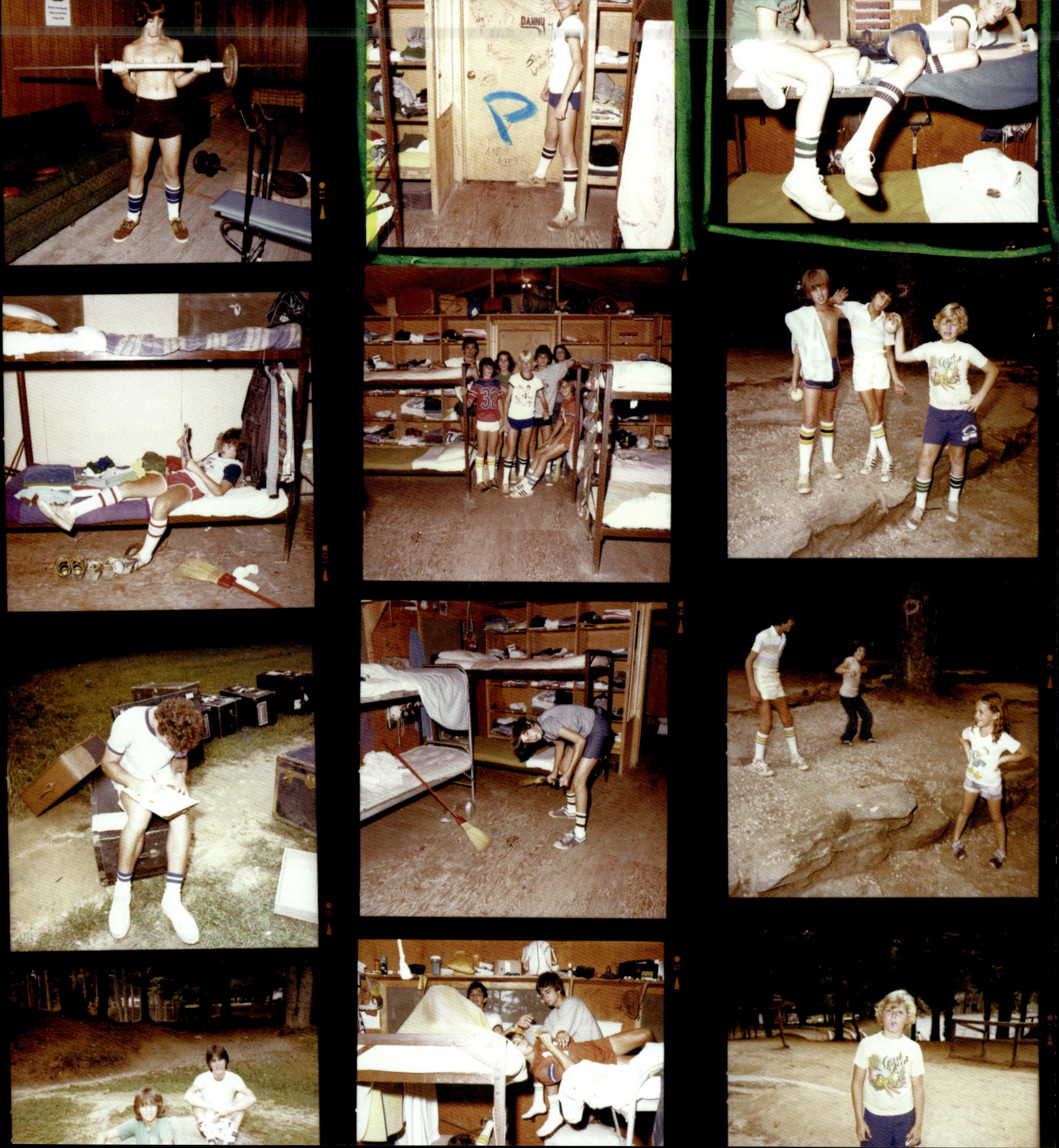

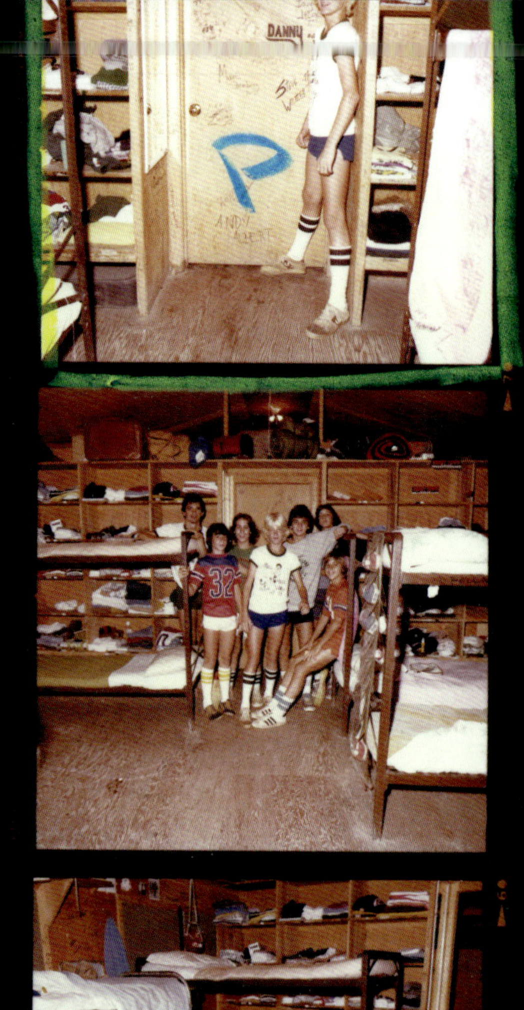
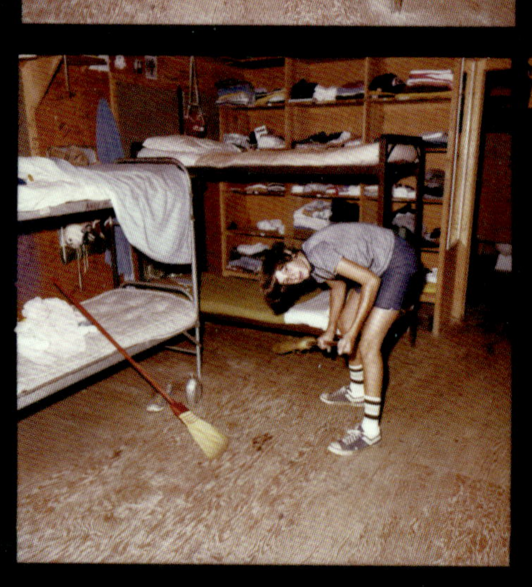
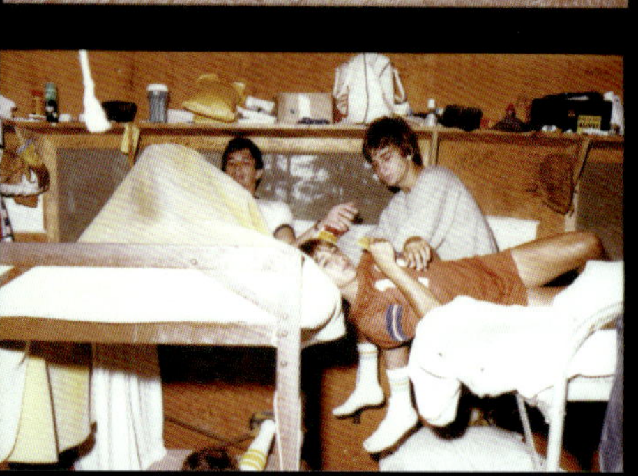
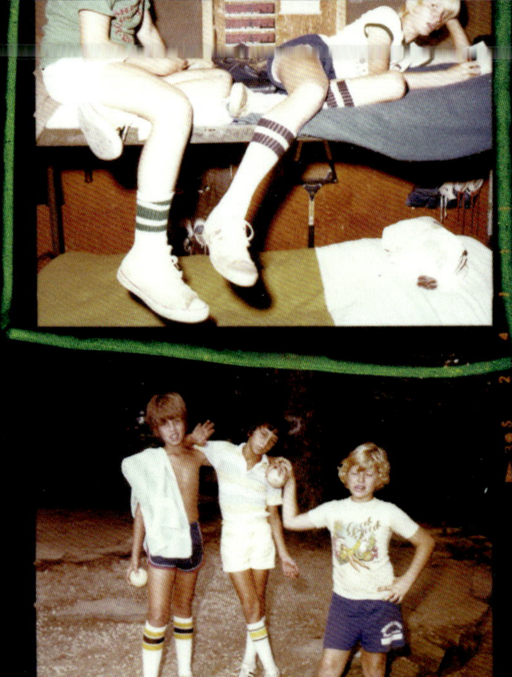
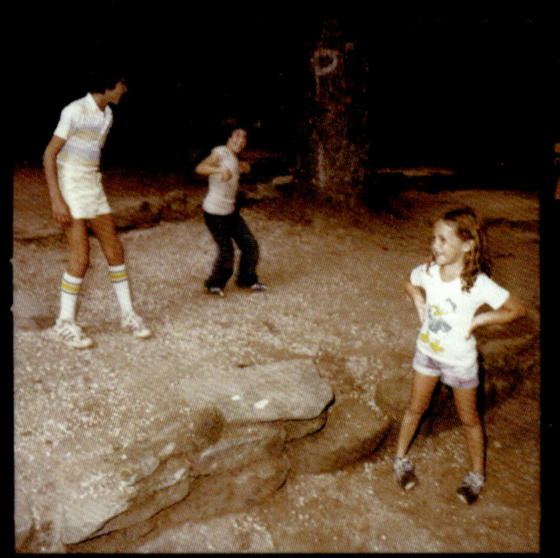
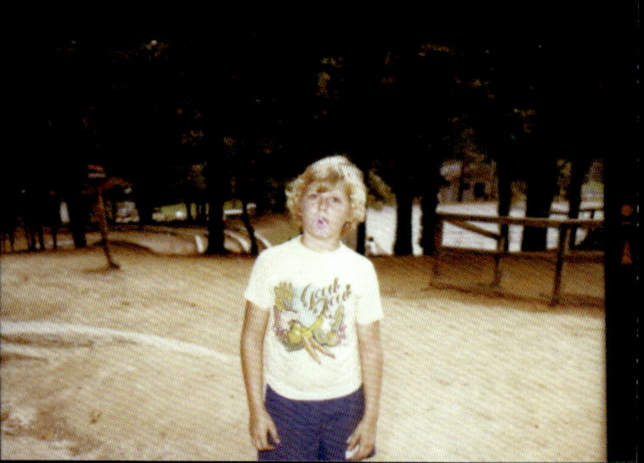

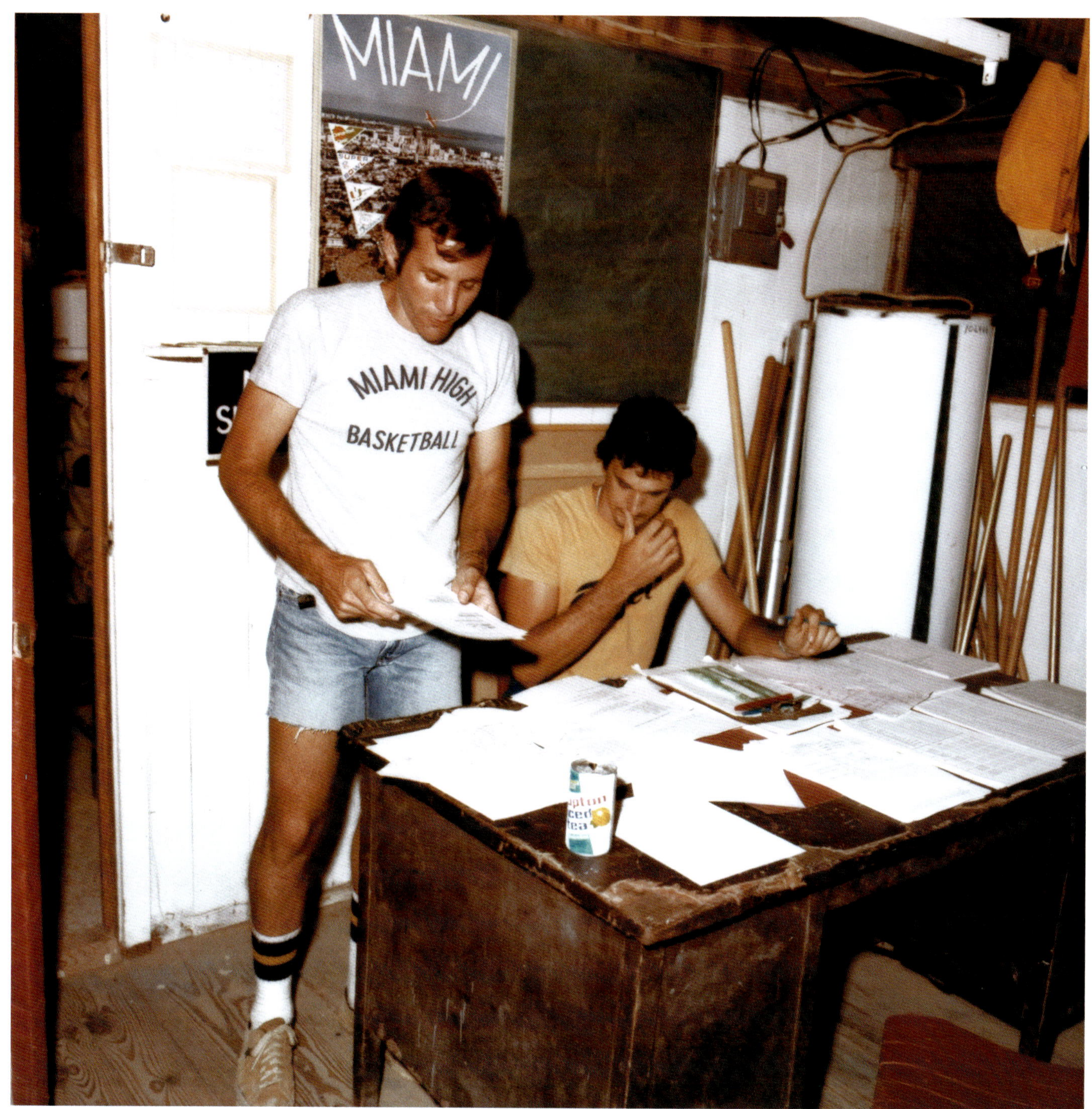

MIAMI
MIAMI HIGH
BASKETBALL

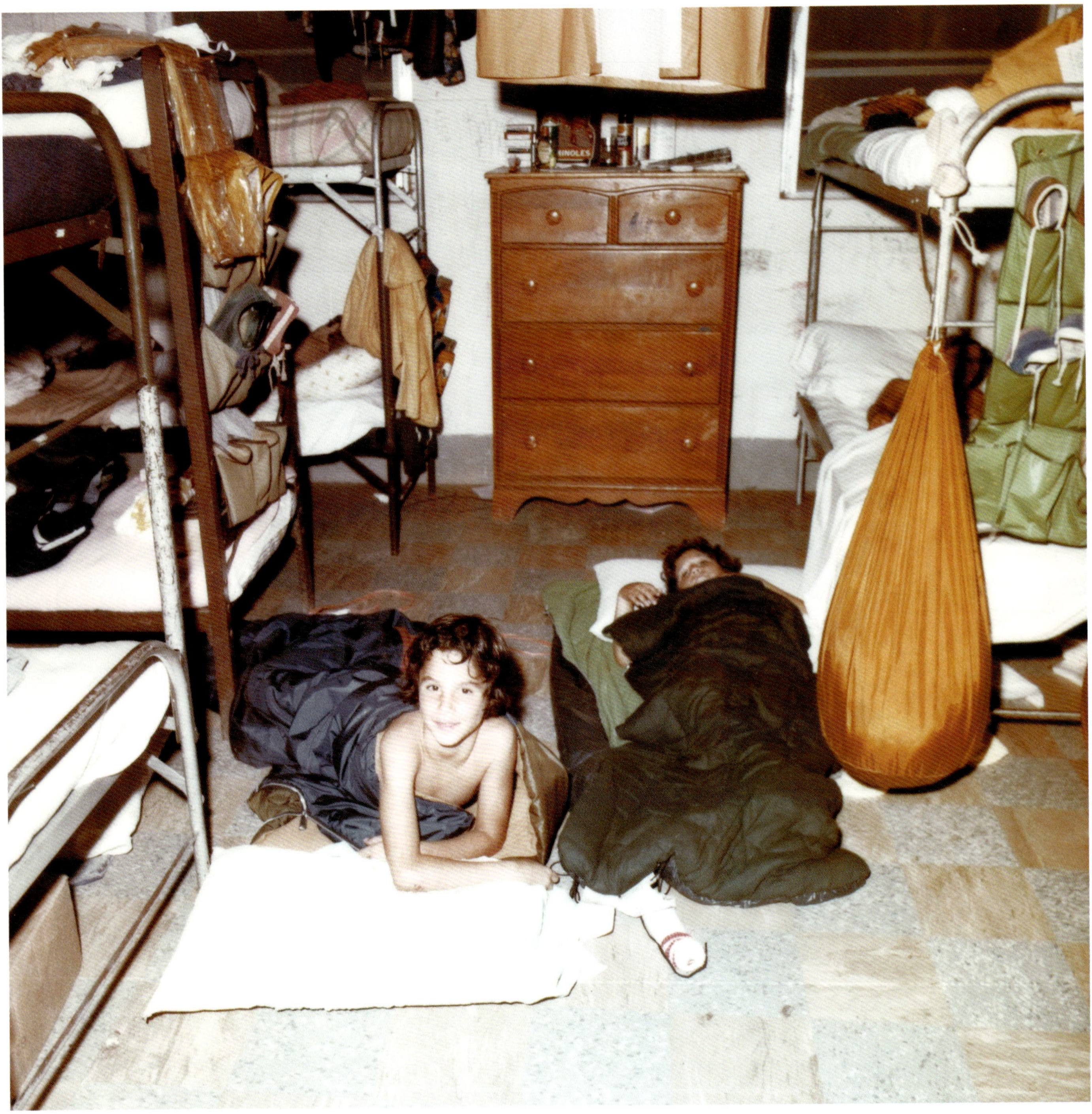

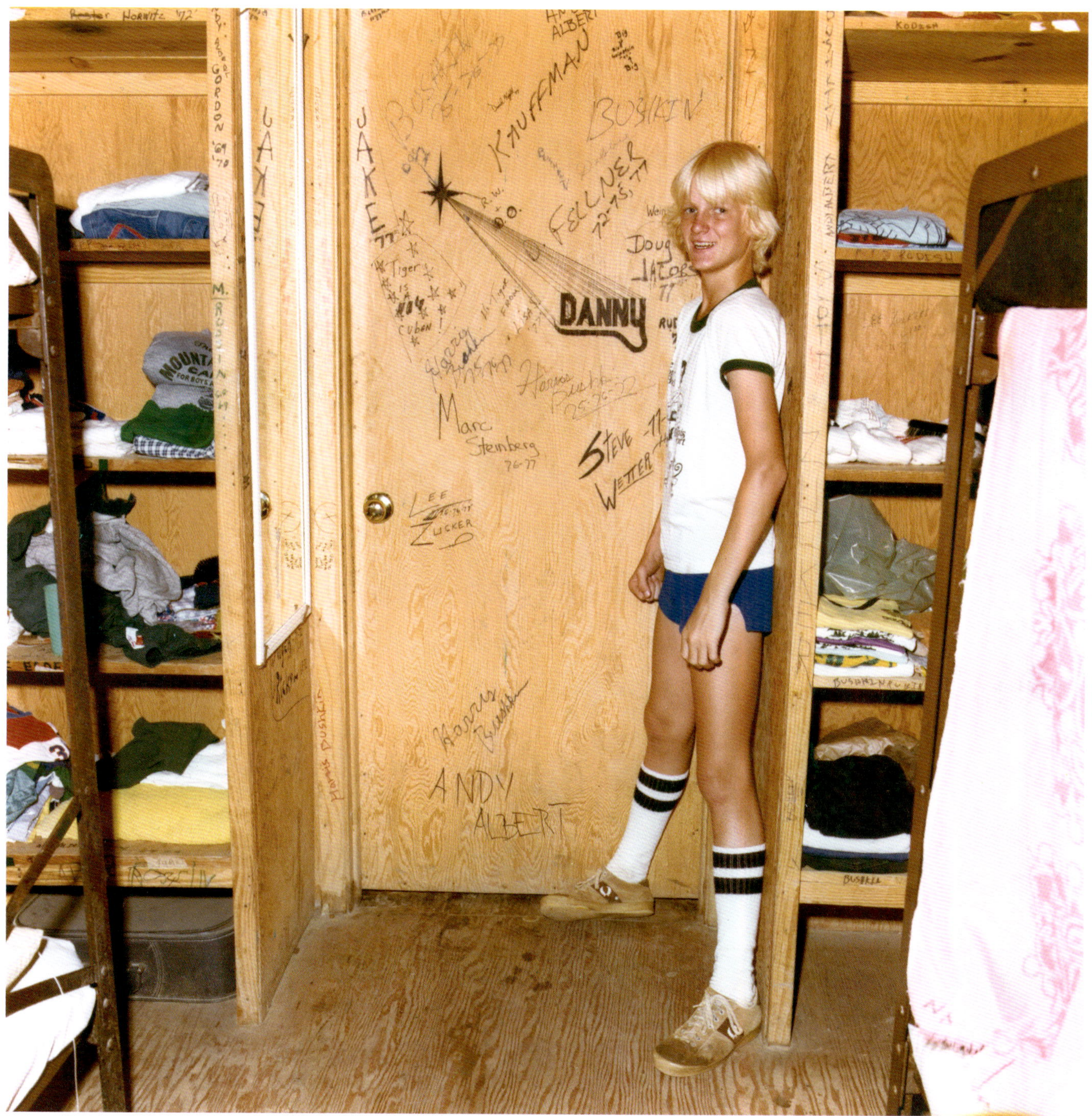
KAUFFMAN
BUSKIN
FELLNER
72-73,77
DOUG
JACOBS
77
DANNY
JAKE
77
Marc
Steinberg
76-77
LEE
ZUCKER
STEVE 77
WETTER
ANDY
ALBERT
GORDON
MOUNTAIN
CAMP
FOR BOYS
ALBERT

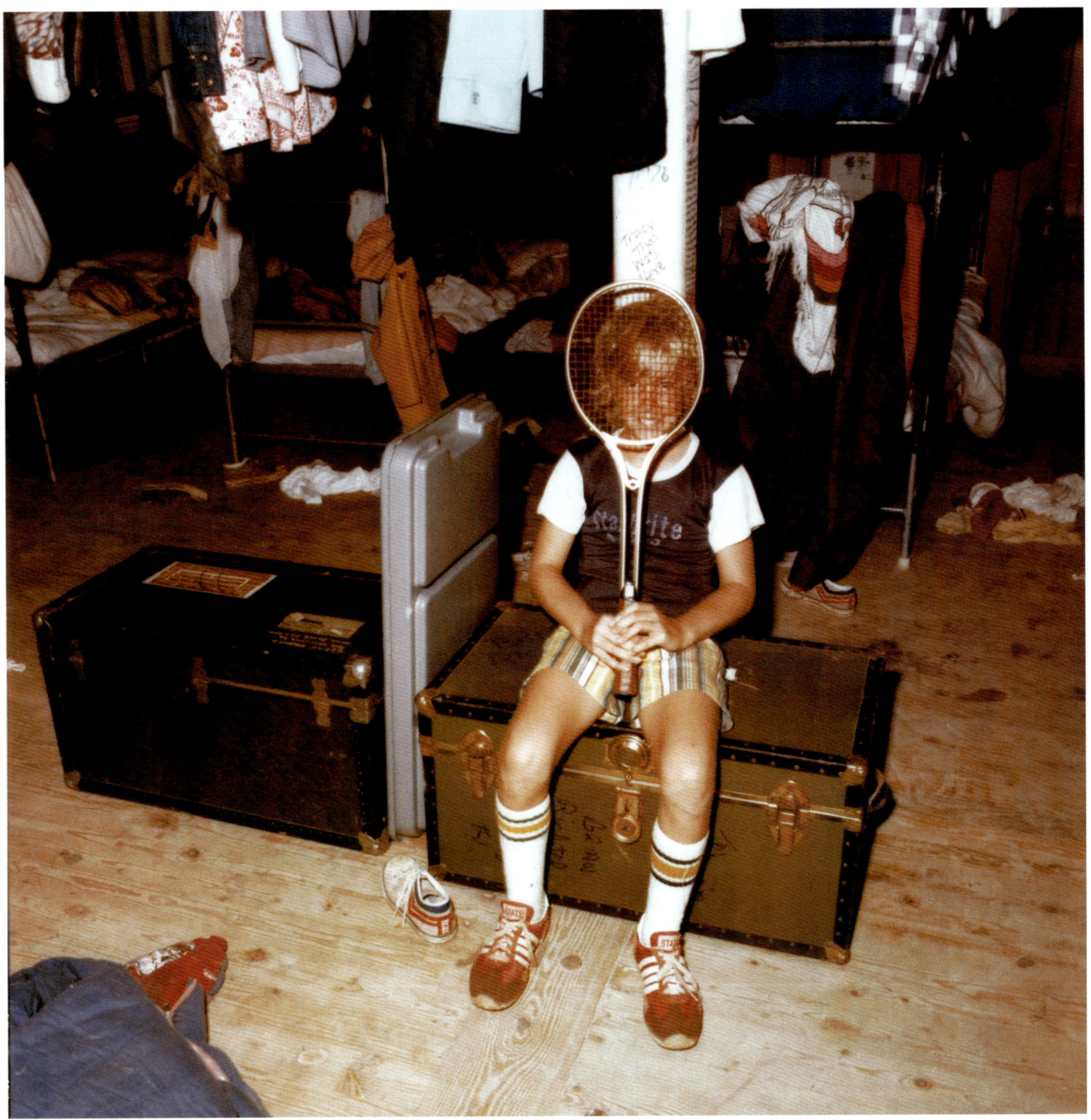

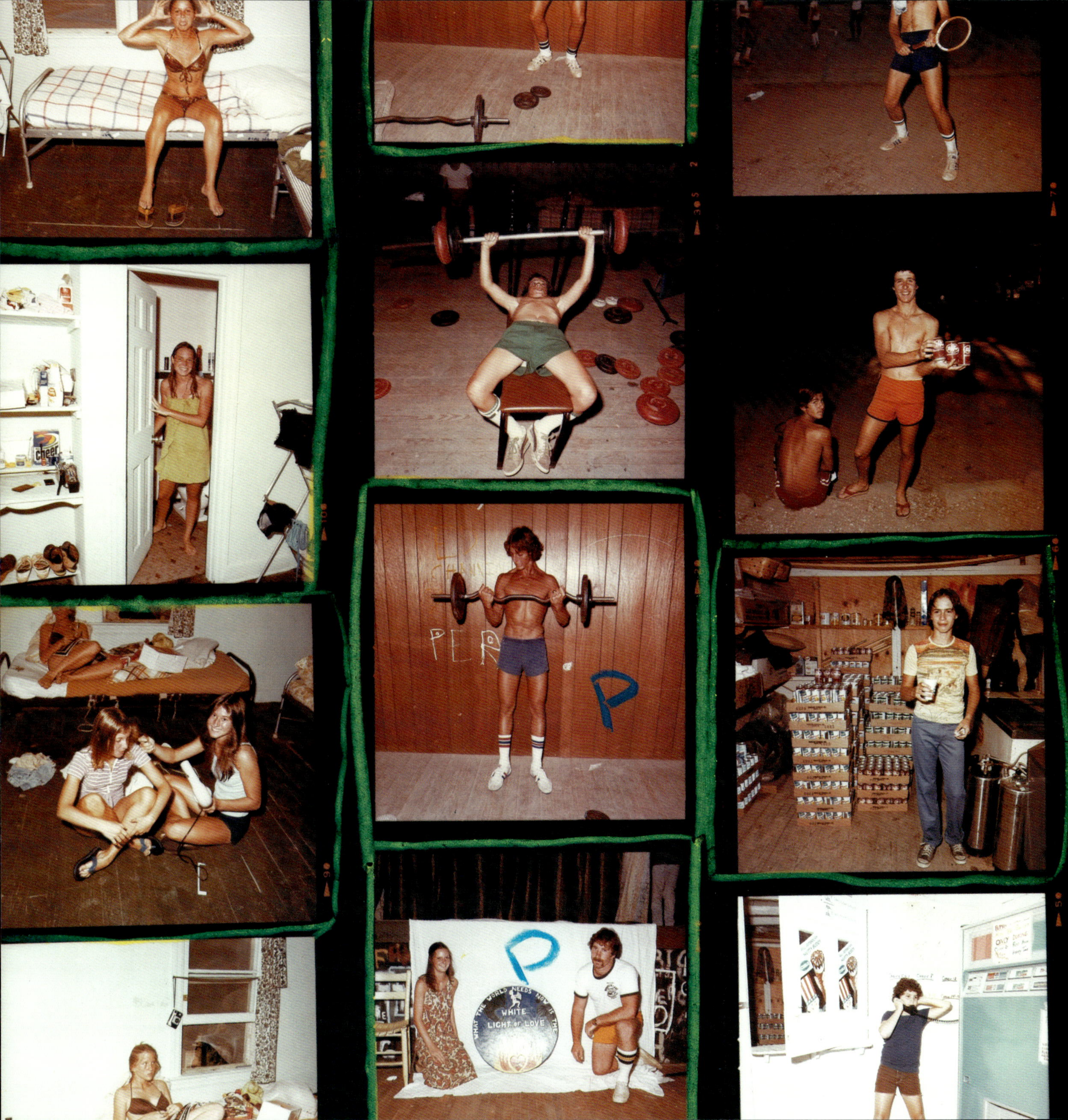
PER
P
P
WHAT THE WORLD NEEDS NOW IS THE
WHITE
LIGHT of LOVE

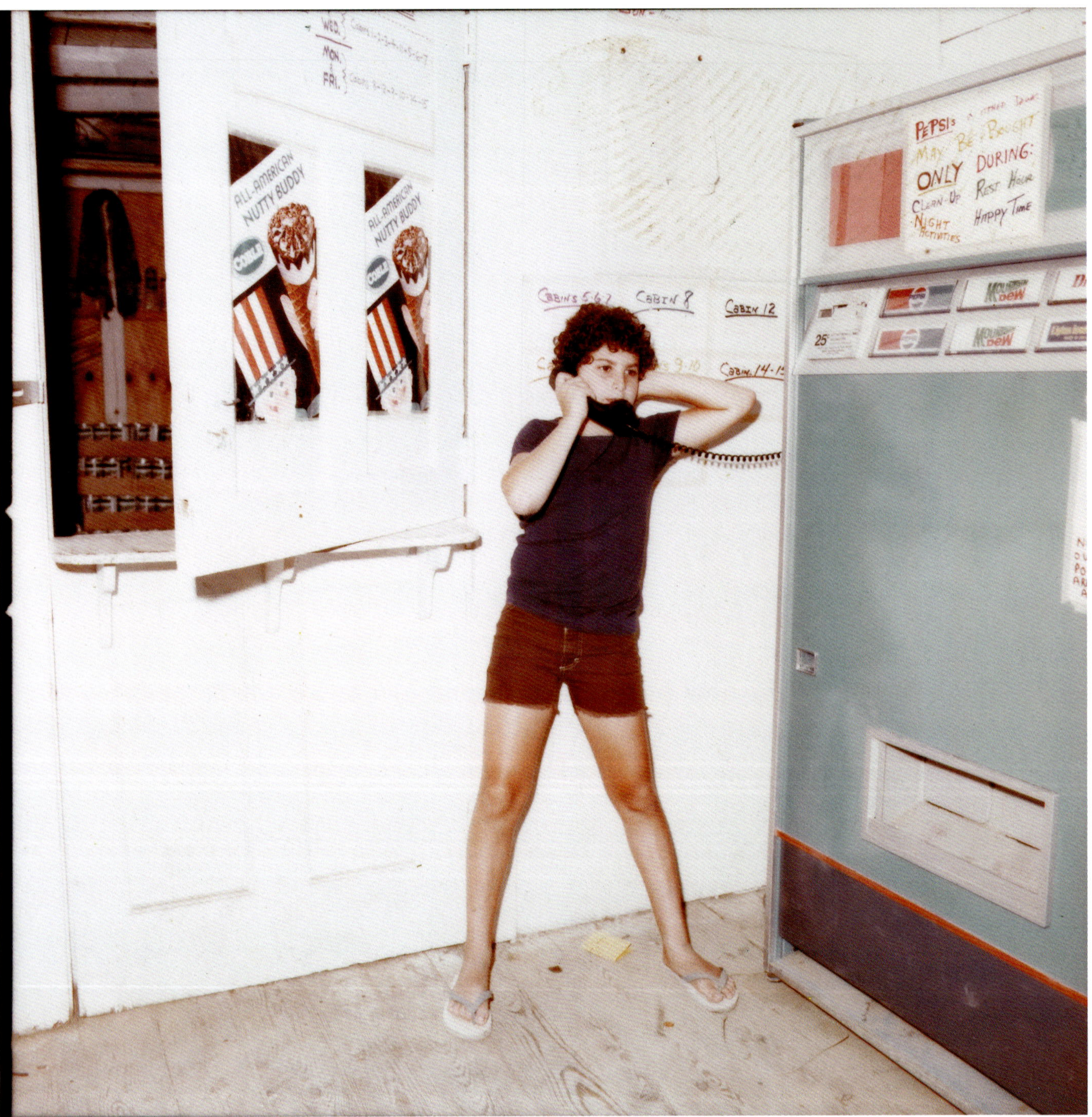
ALL-AMERICAN NUTTY BUDDY
ALL-AMERICAN NUTTY BUDDY
Cabins 5-6-7   Cabin 8   Cabin 12
Cabin 14-15
PEPSIs MAY BE BROUGHT ONLY DURING:
CLEAN-UP   REST HOUR
NIGHT ACTIVITIES   HAPPY TIME
25¢

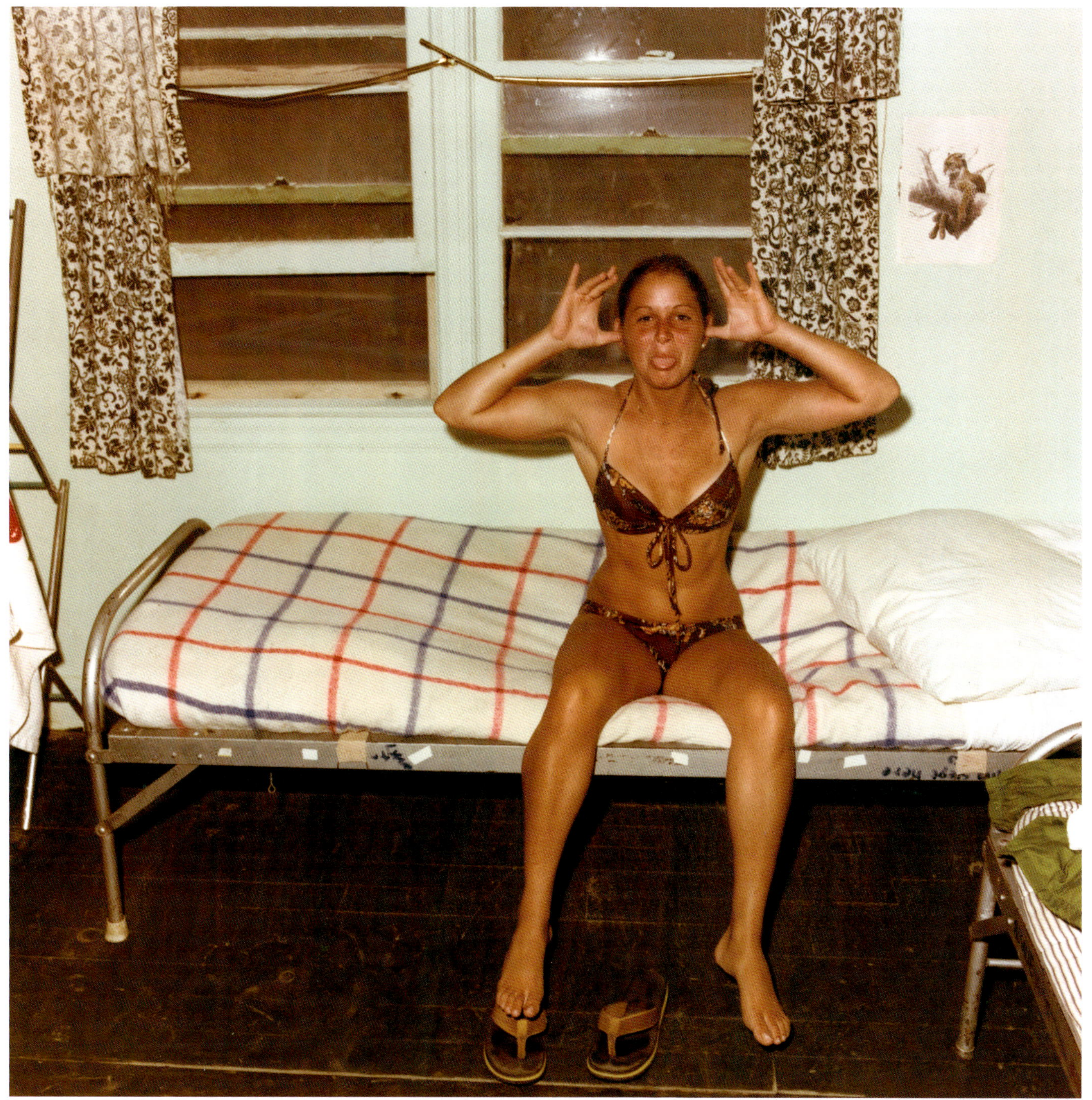

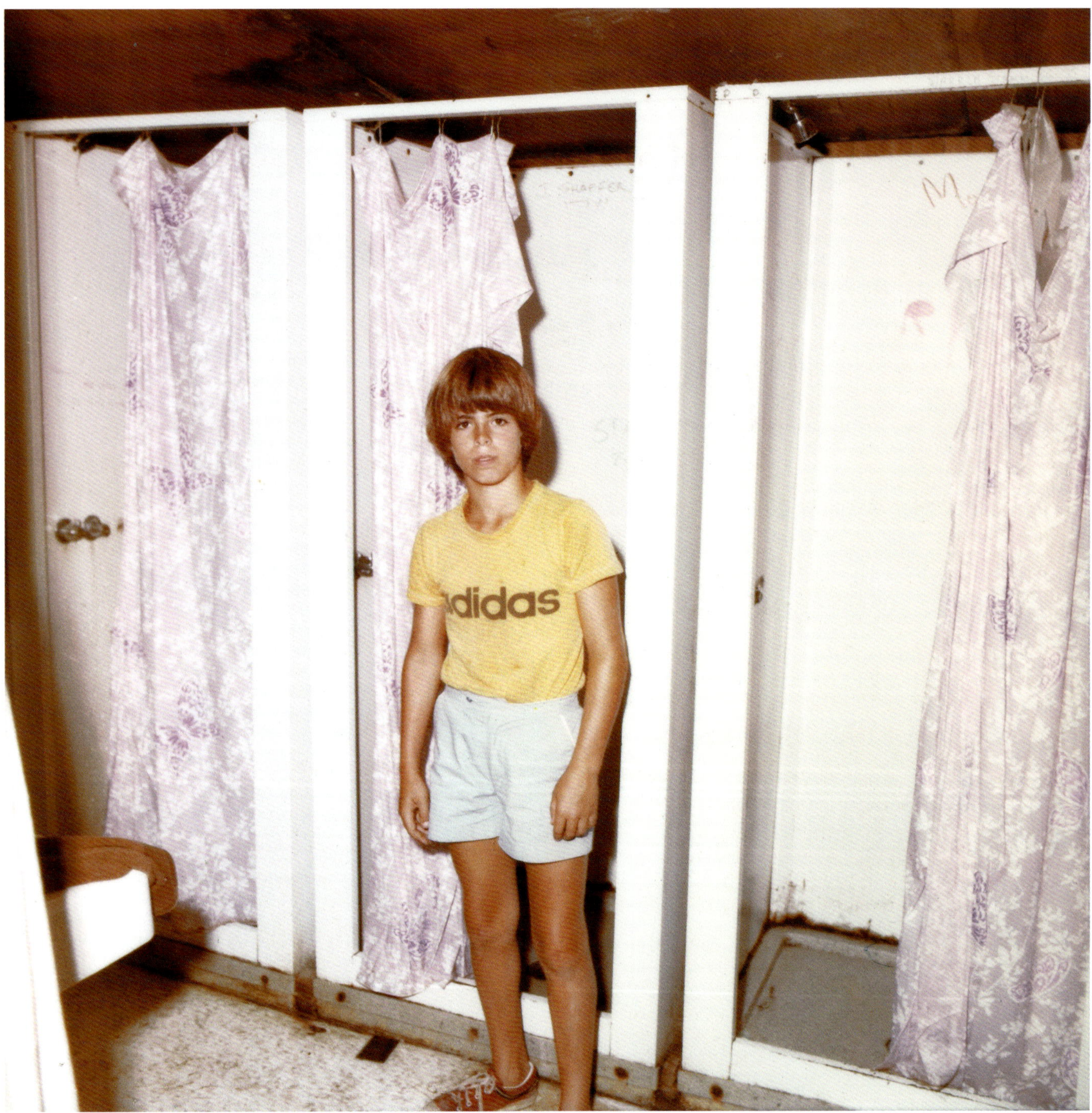

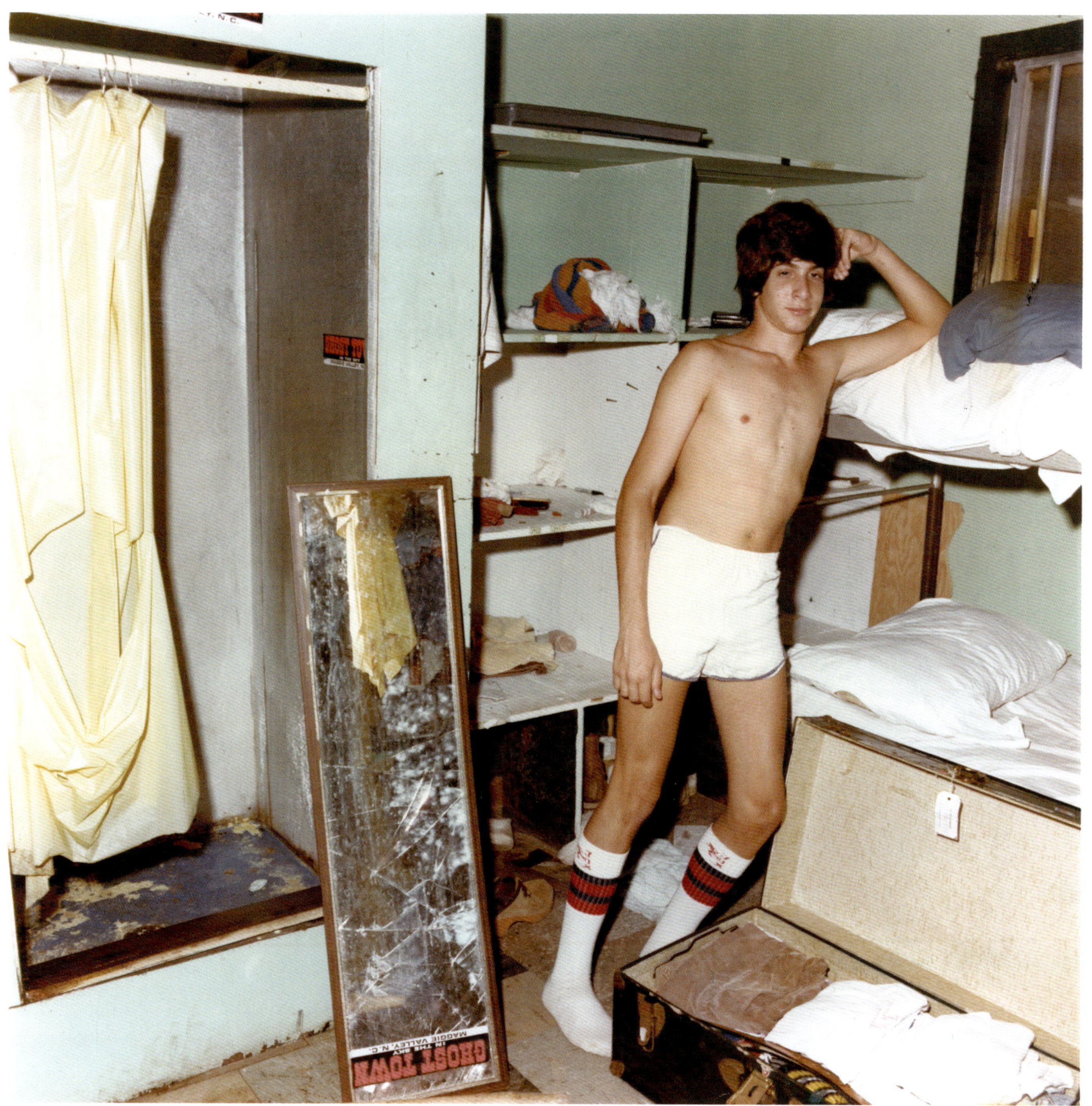

GHOST TOWN
IN THE SKY
MAGGIE VALLEY, N.C.

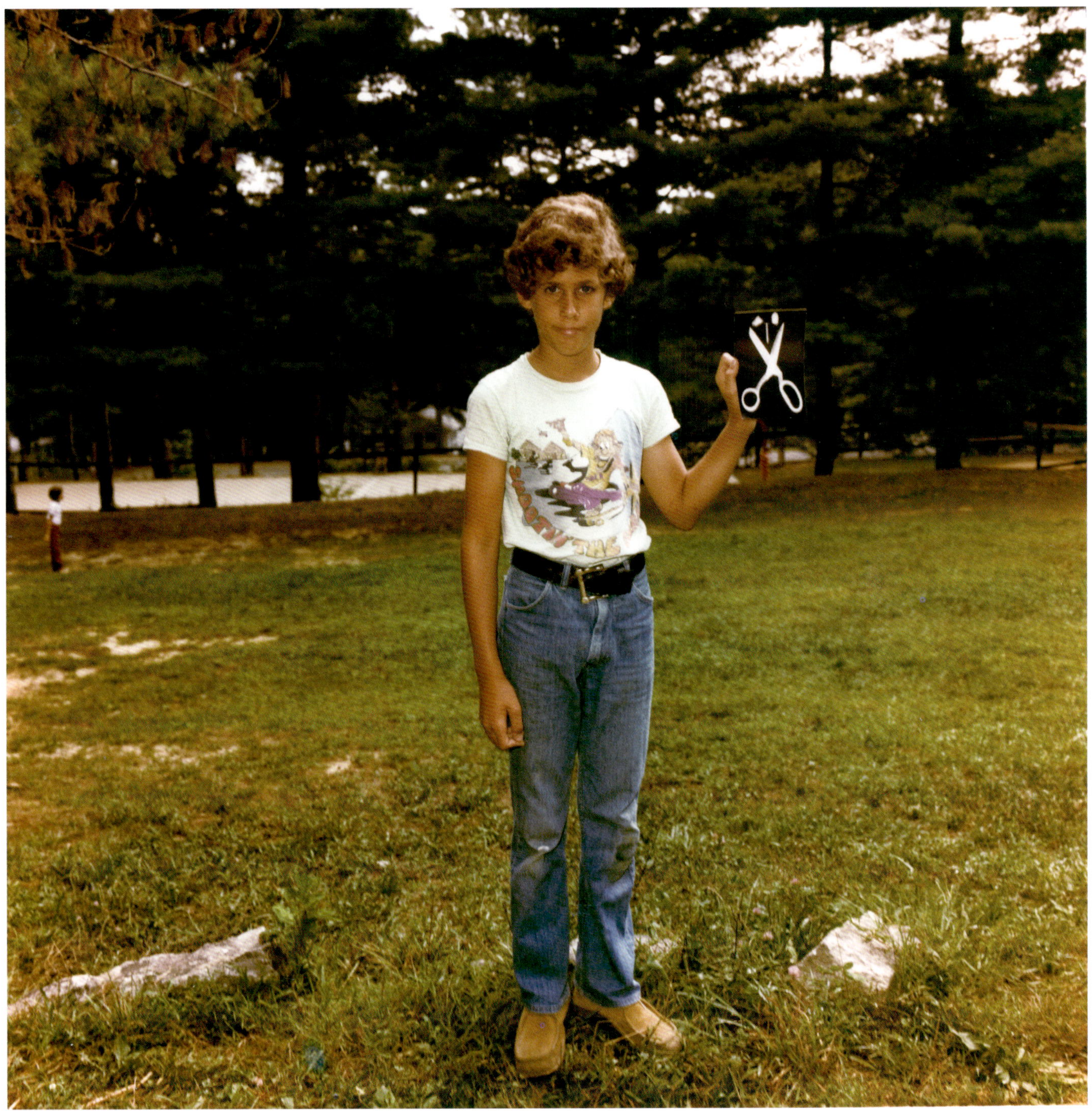

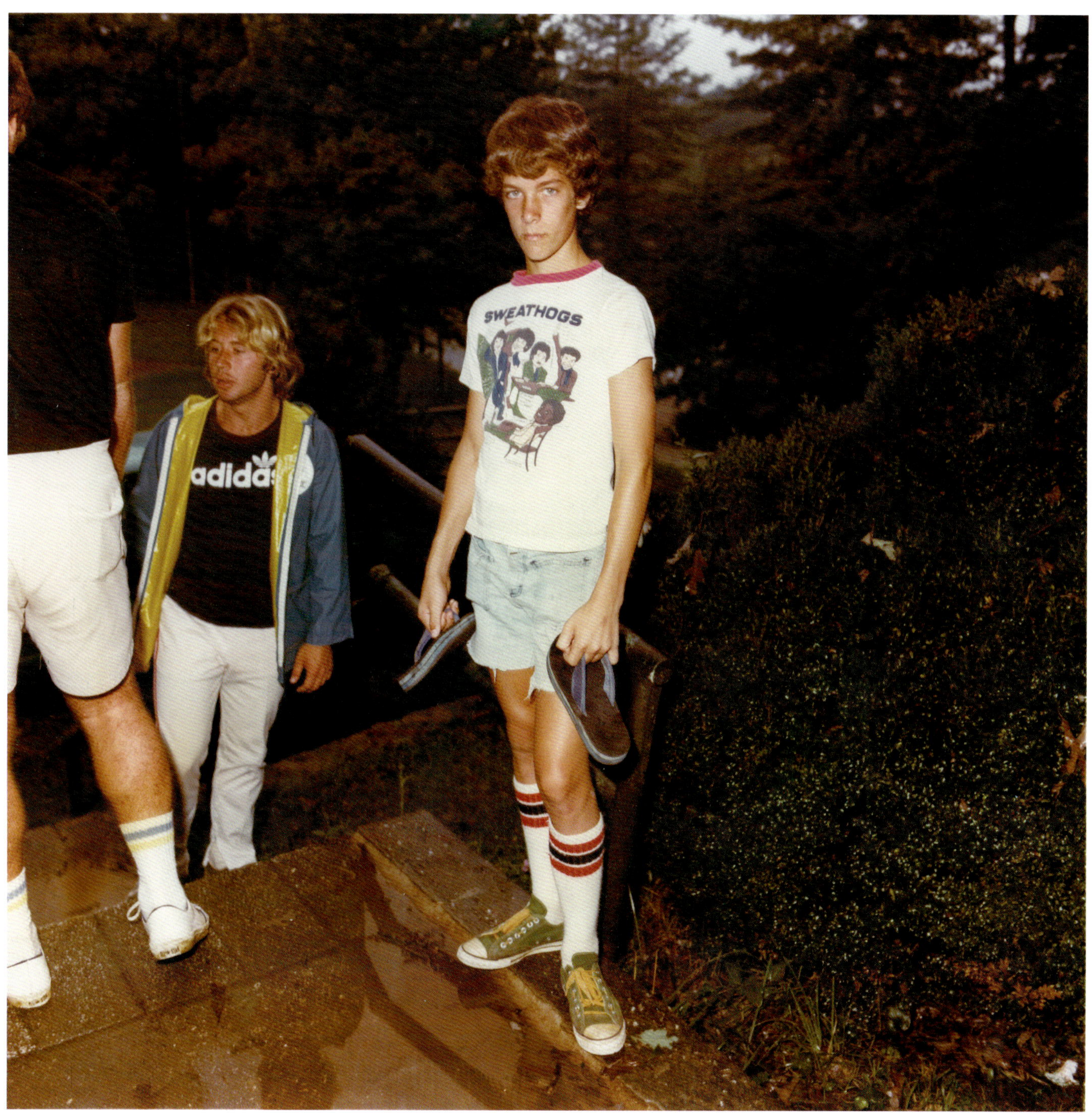

adidas
SWEATHOGS

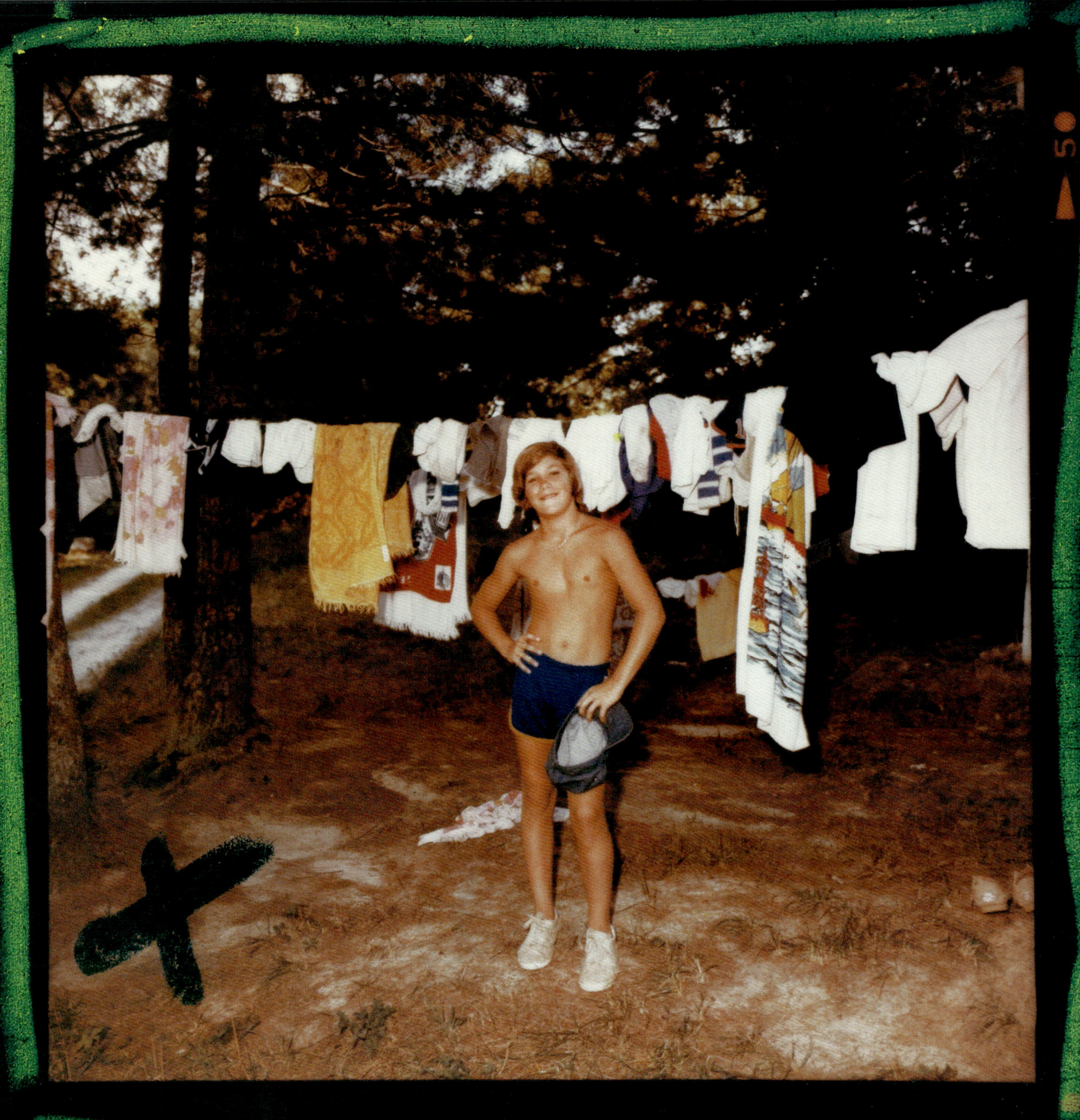

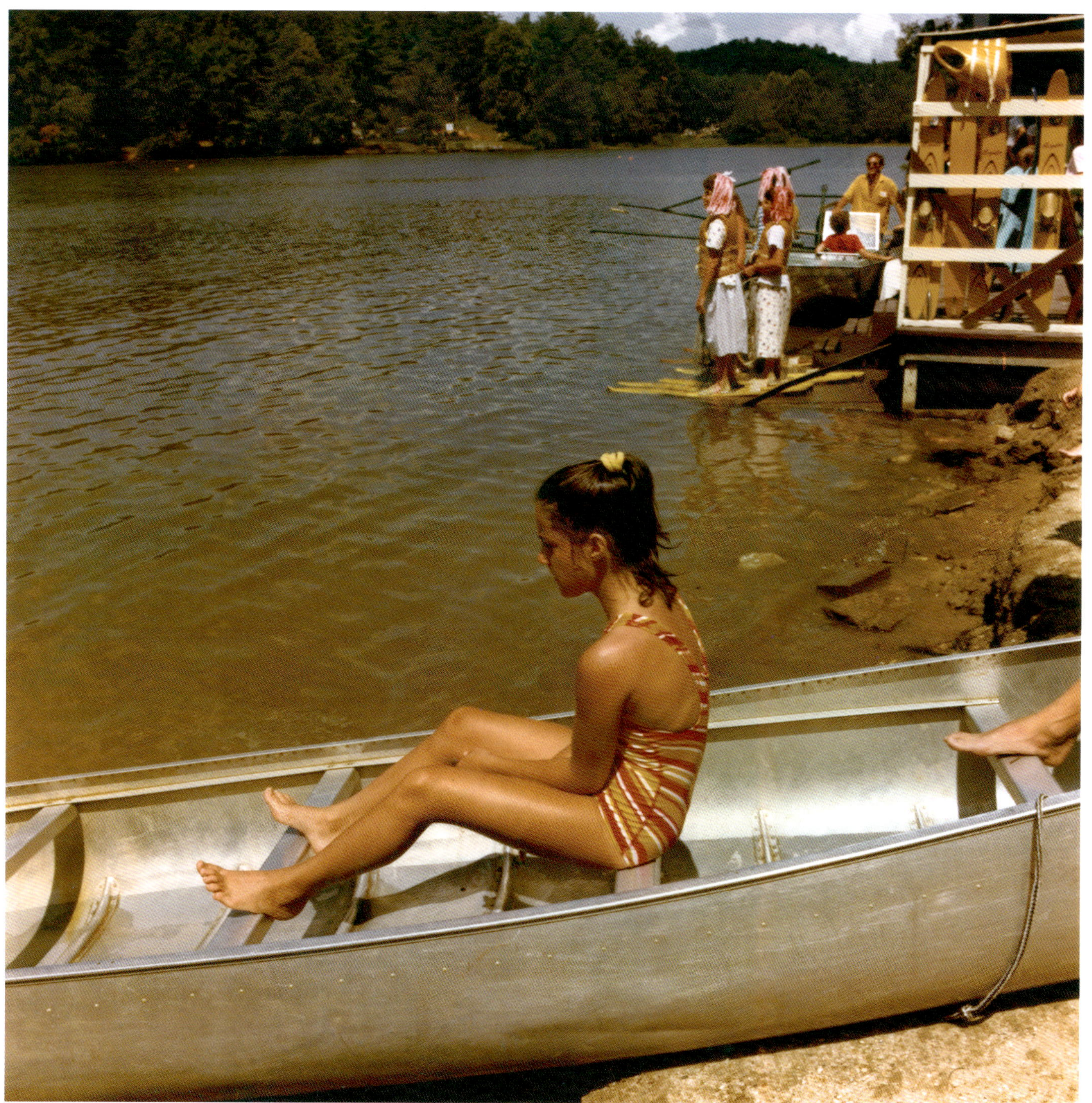

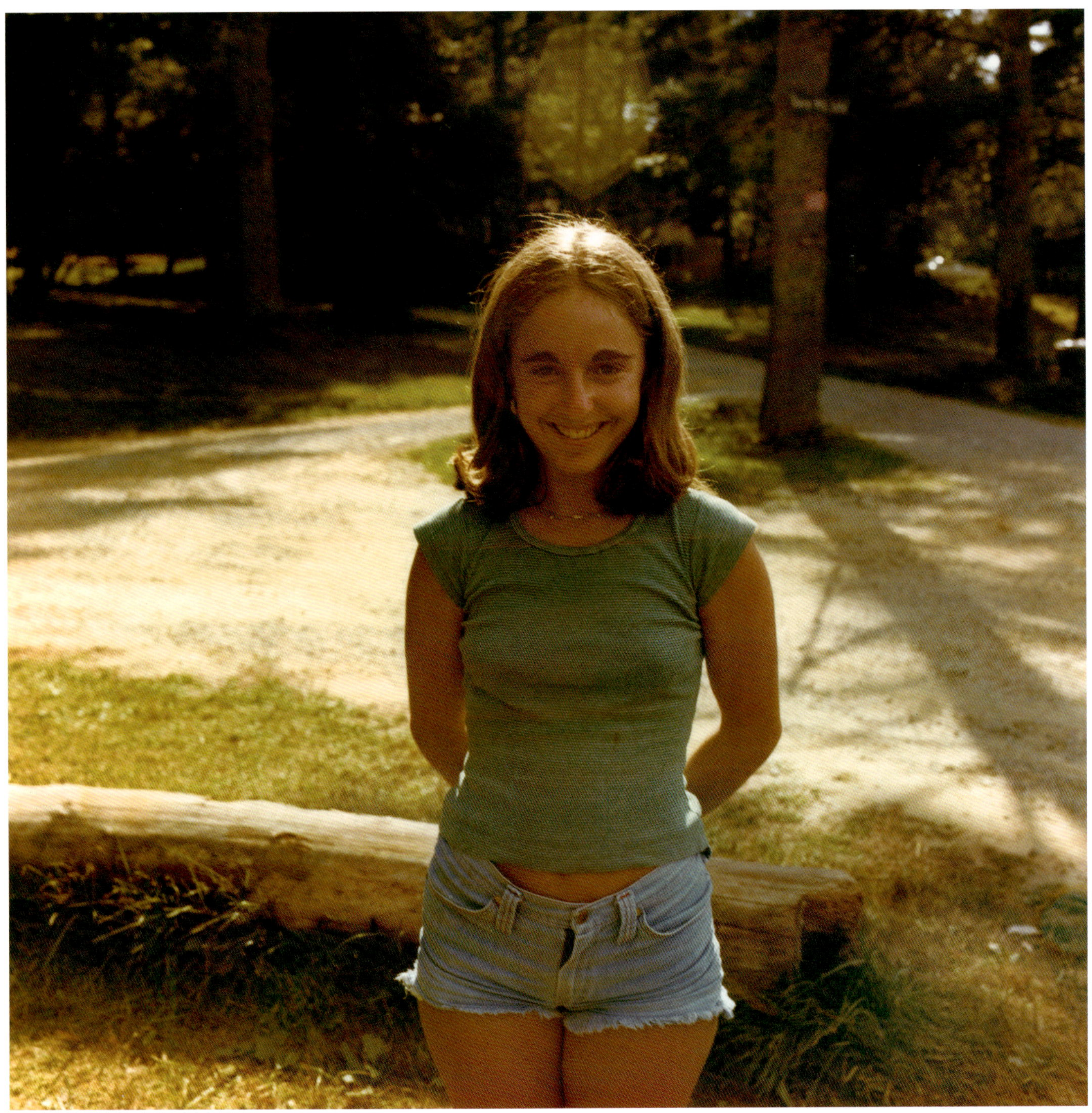

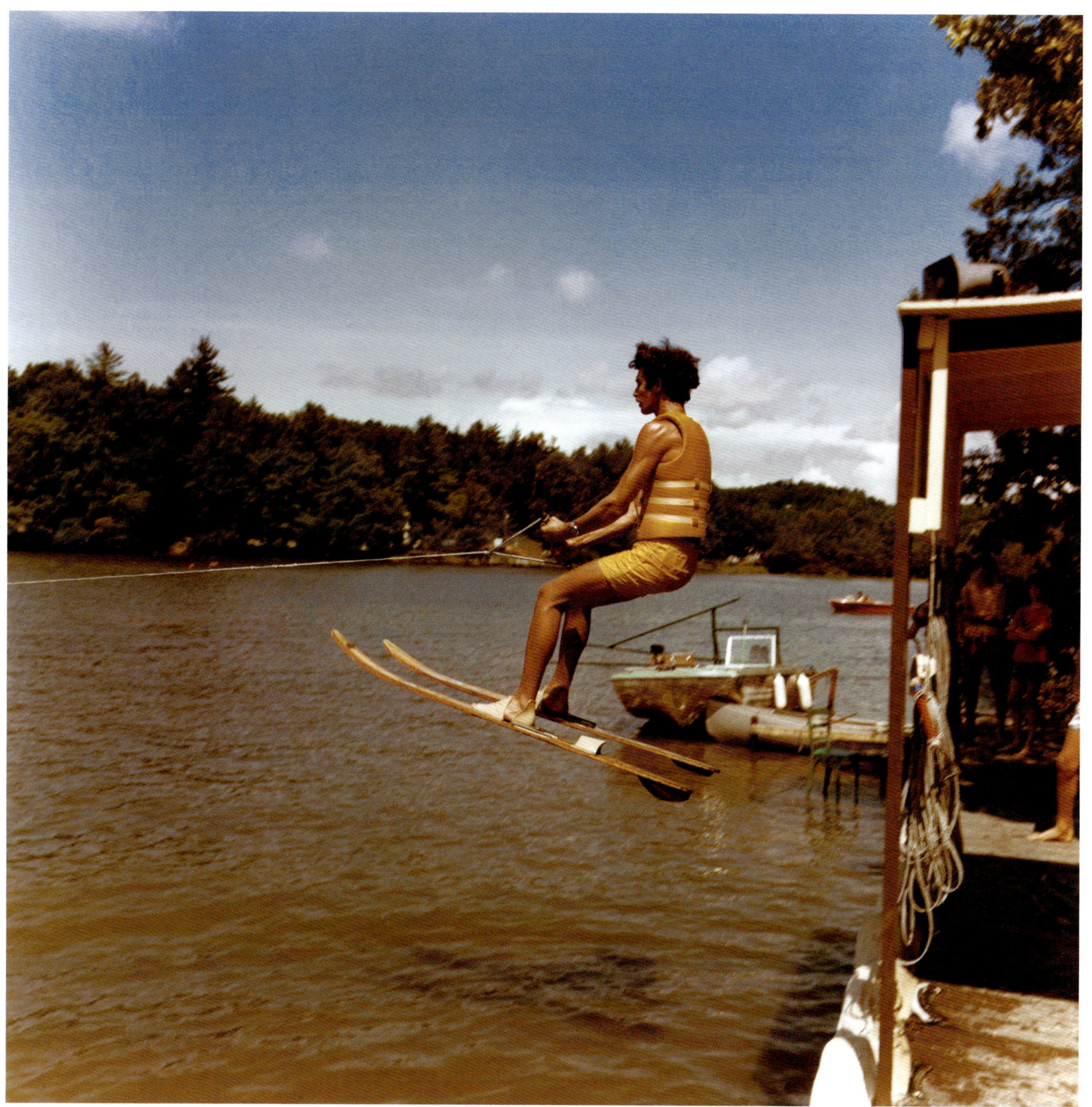

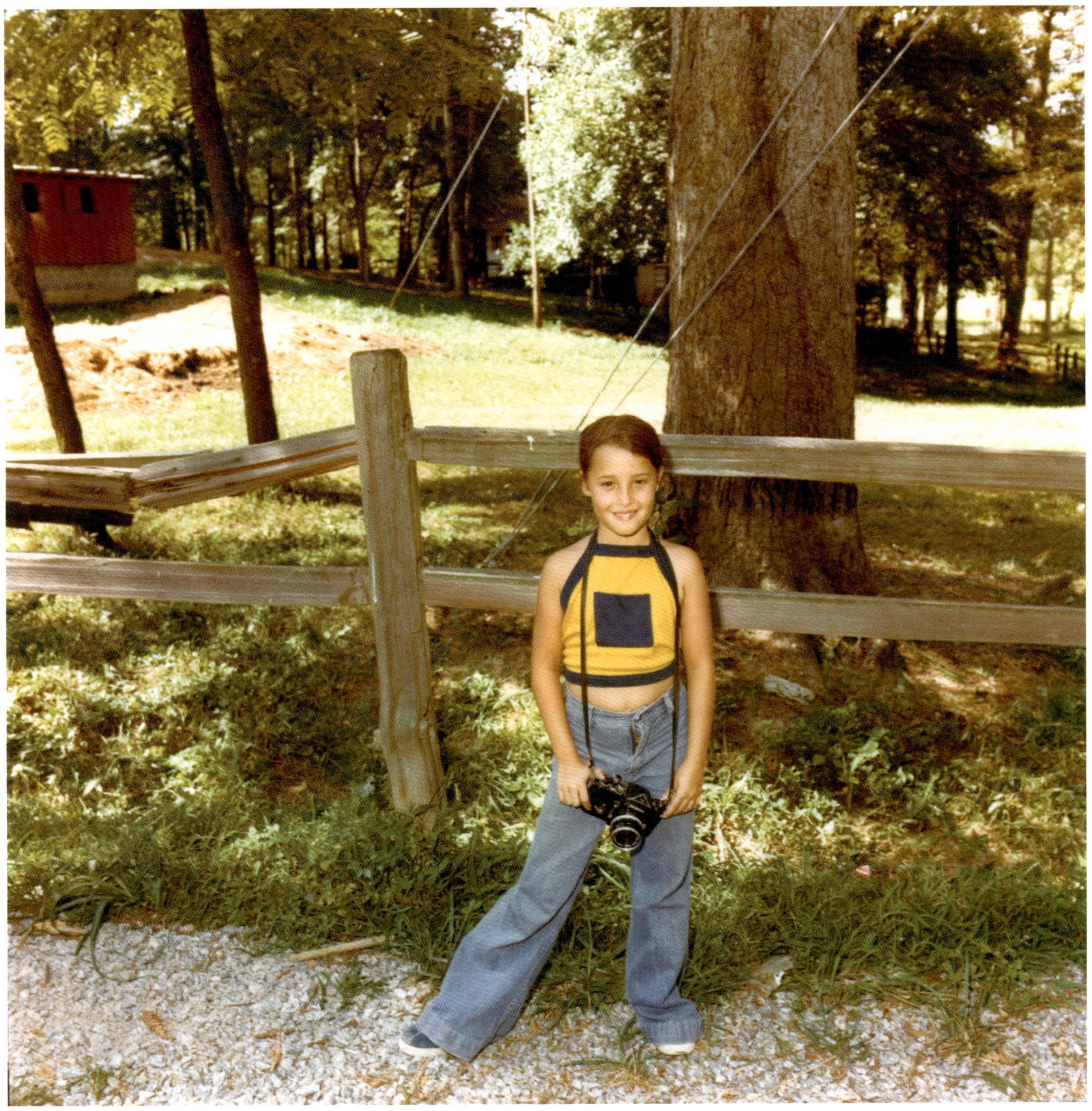

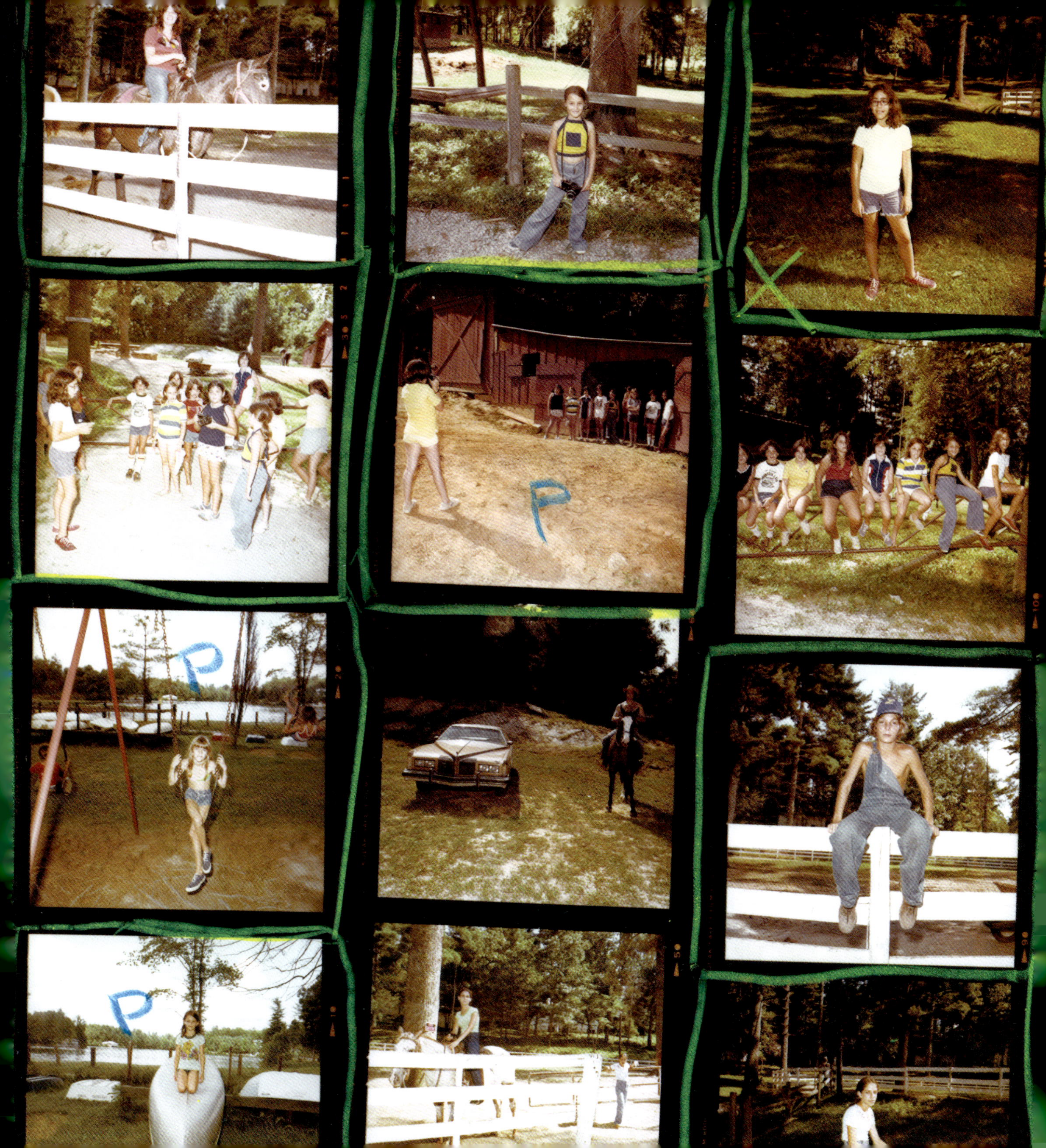

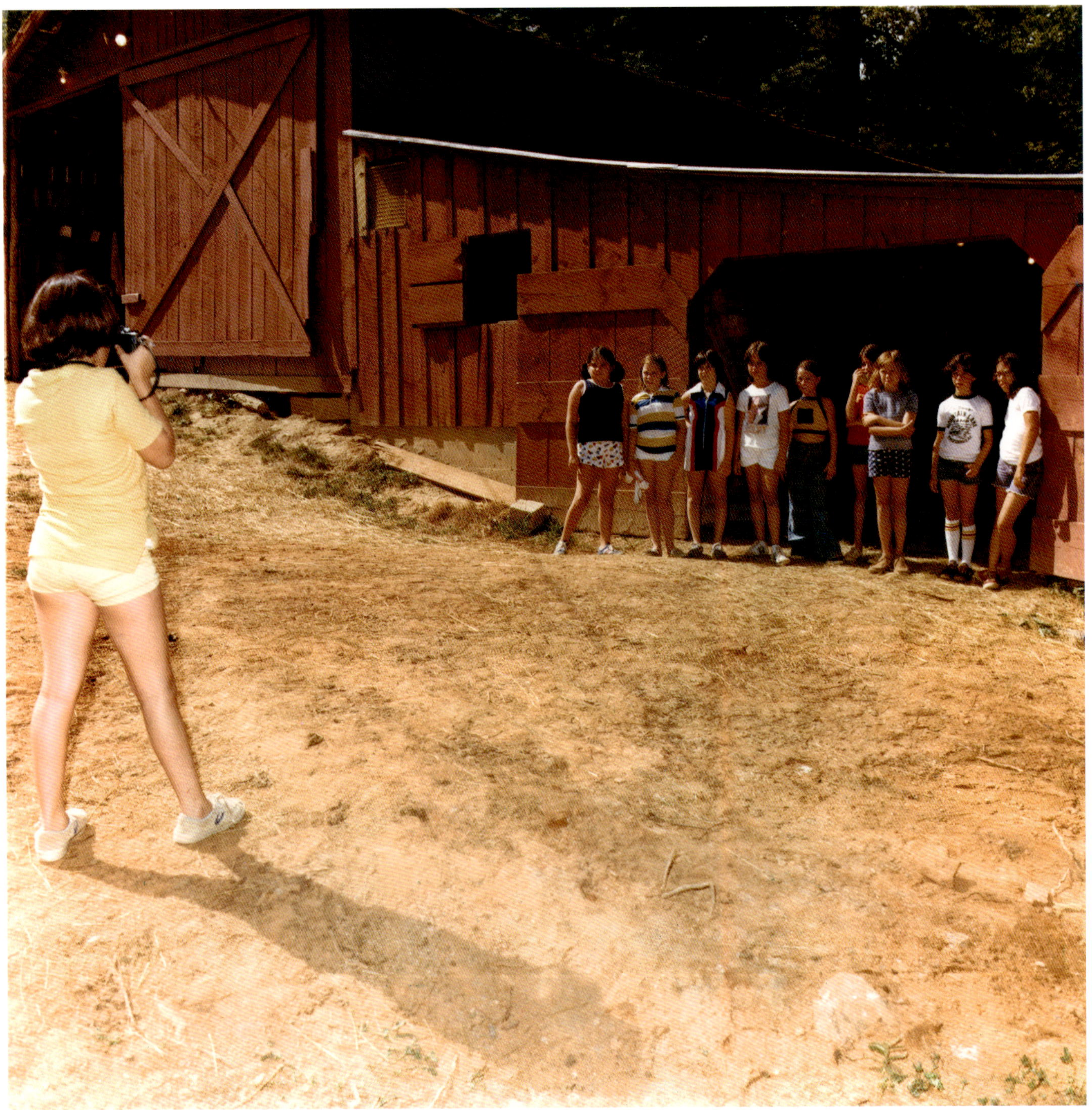

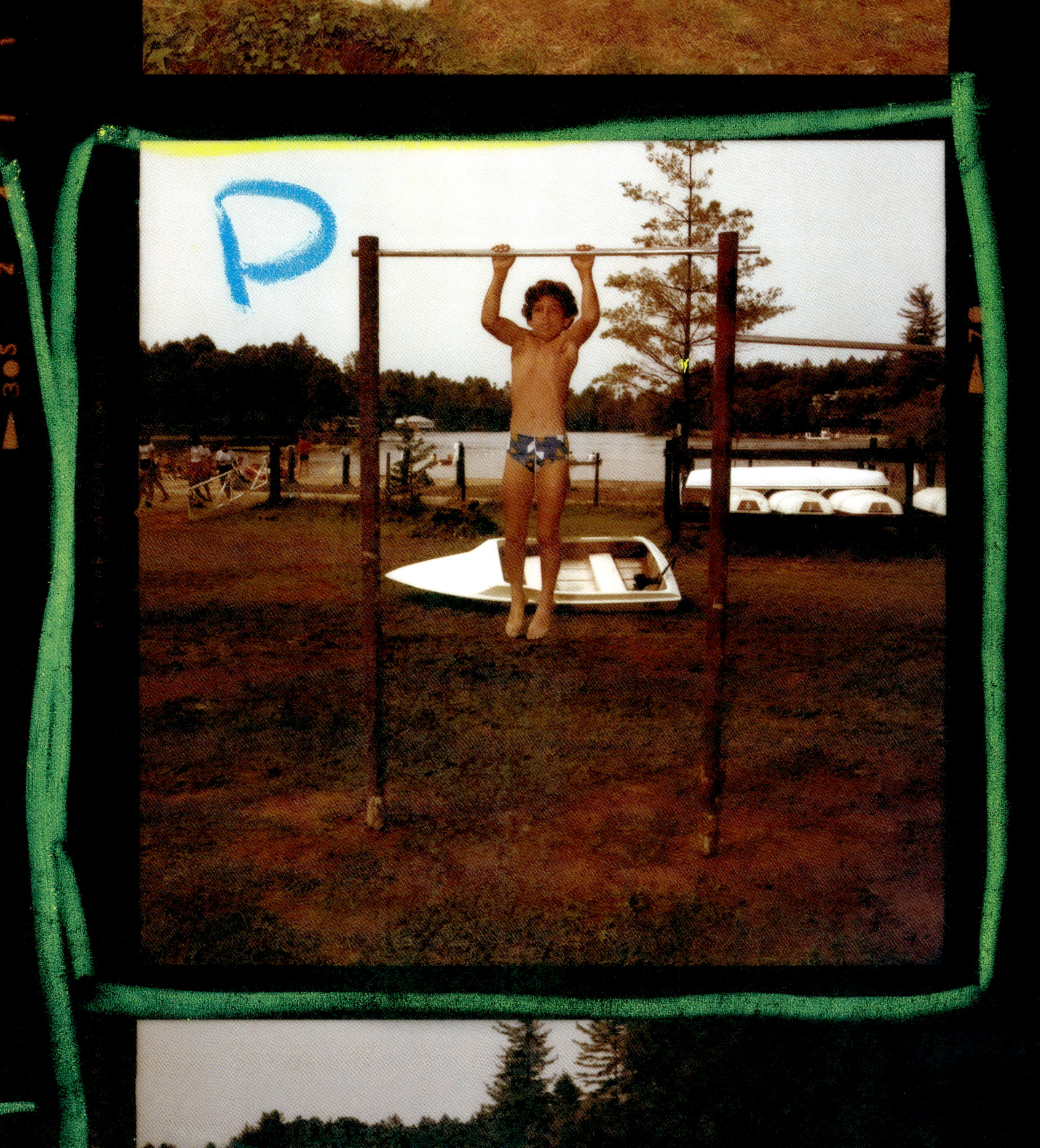
P

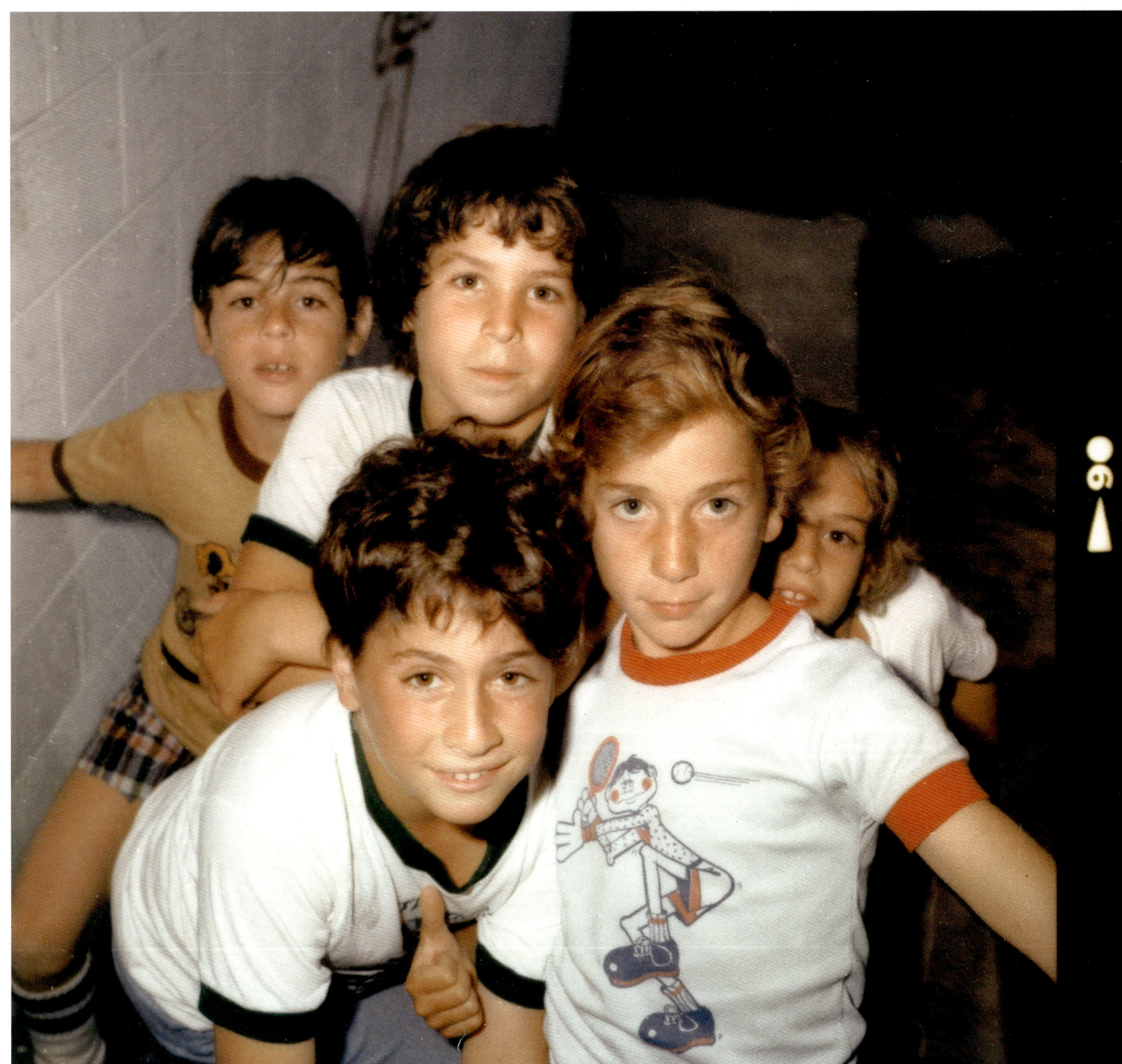

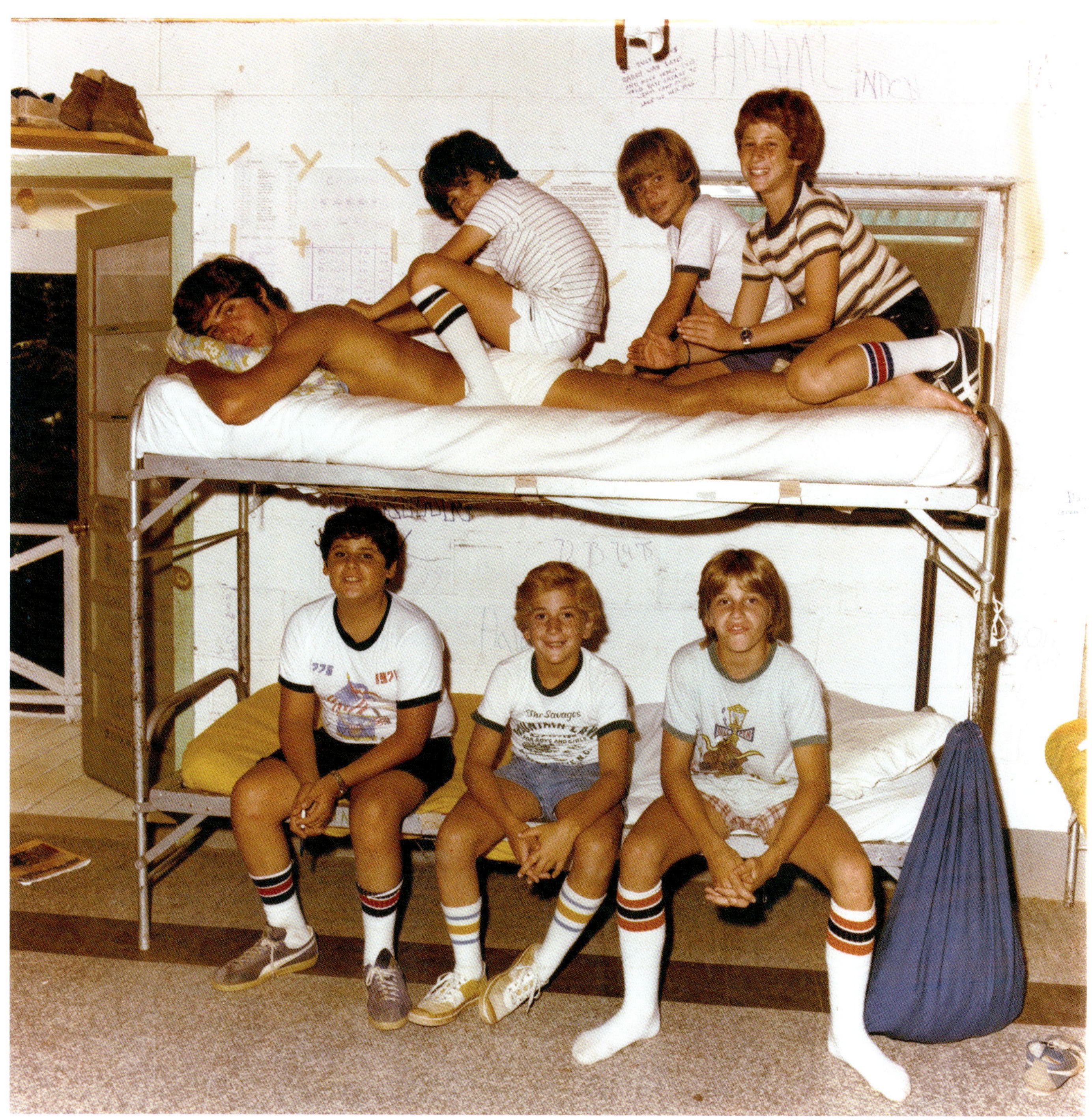

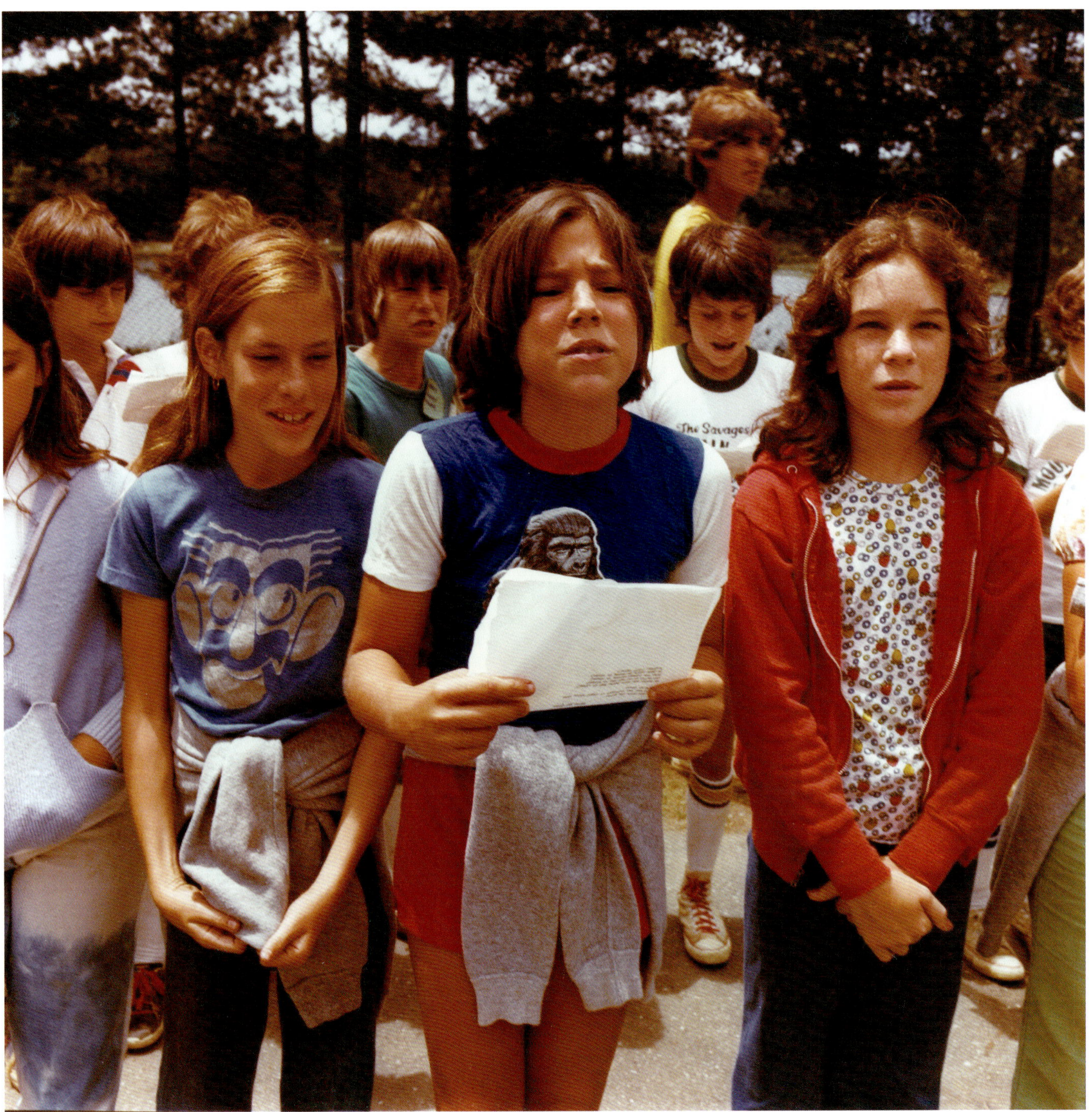

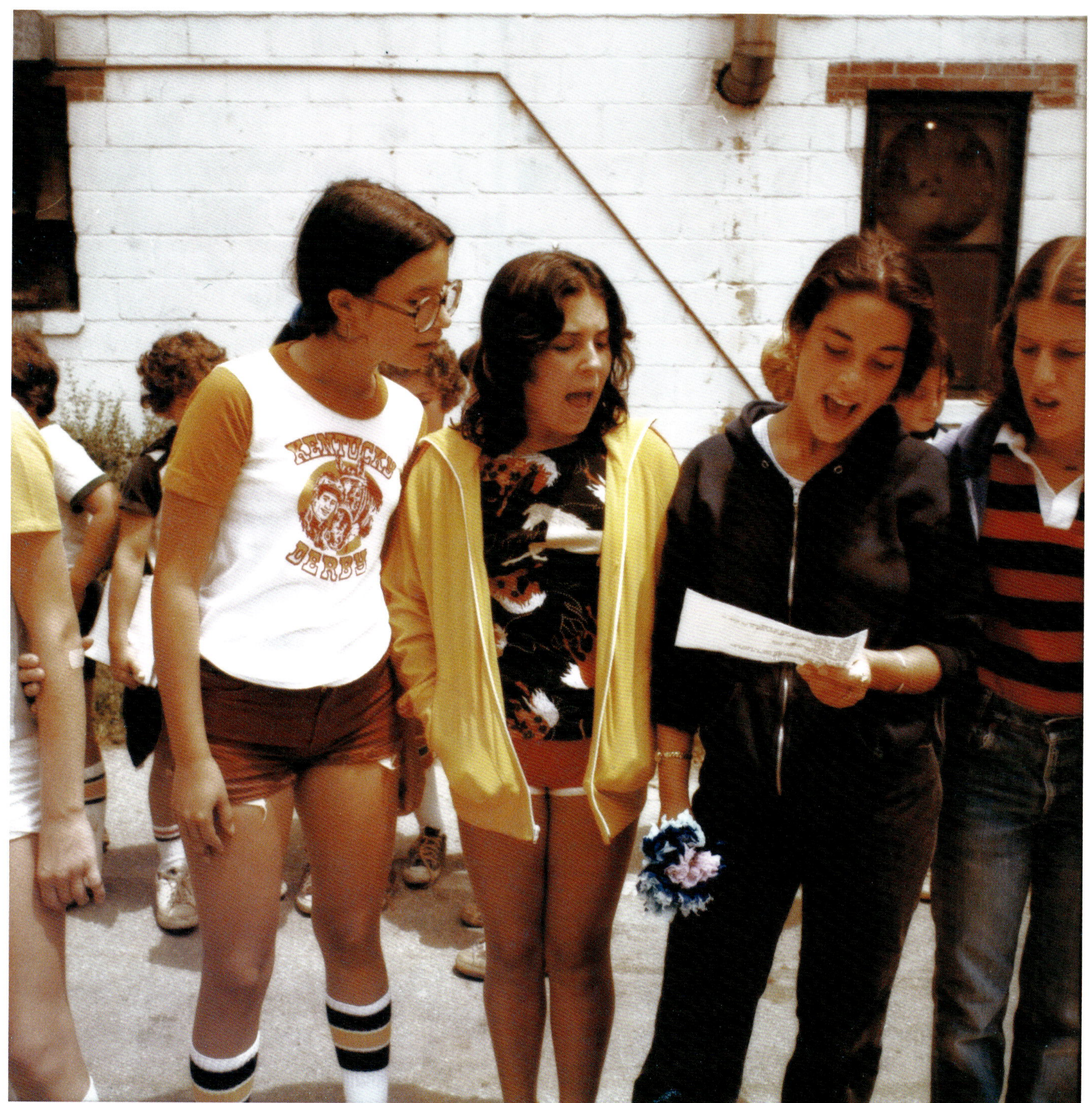

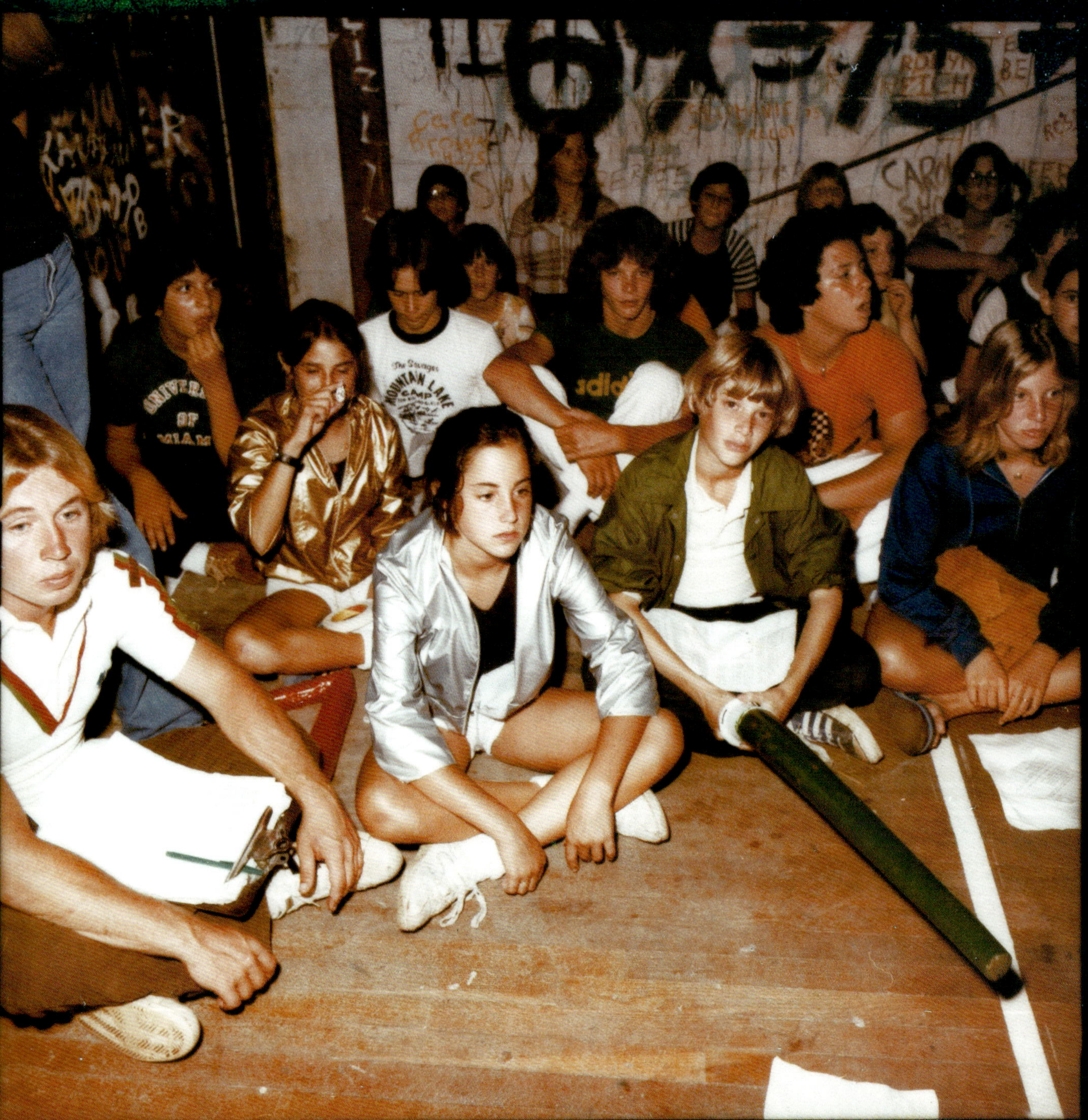

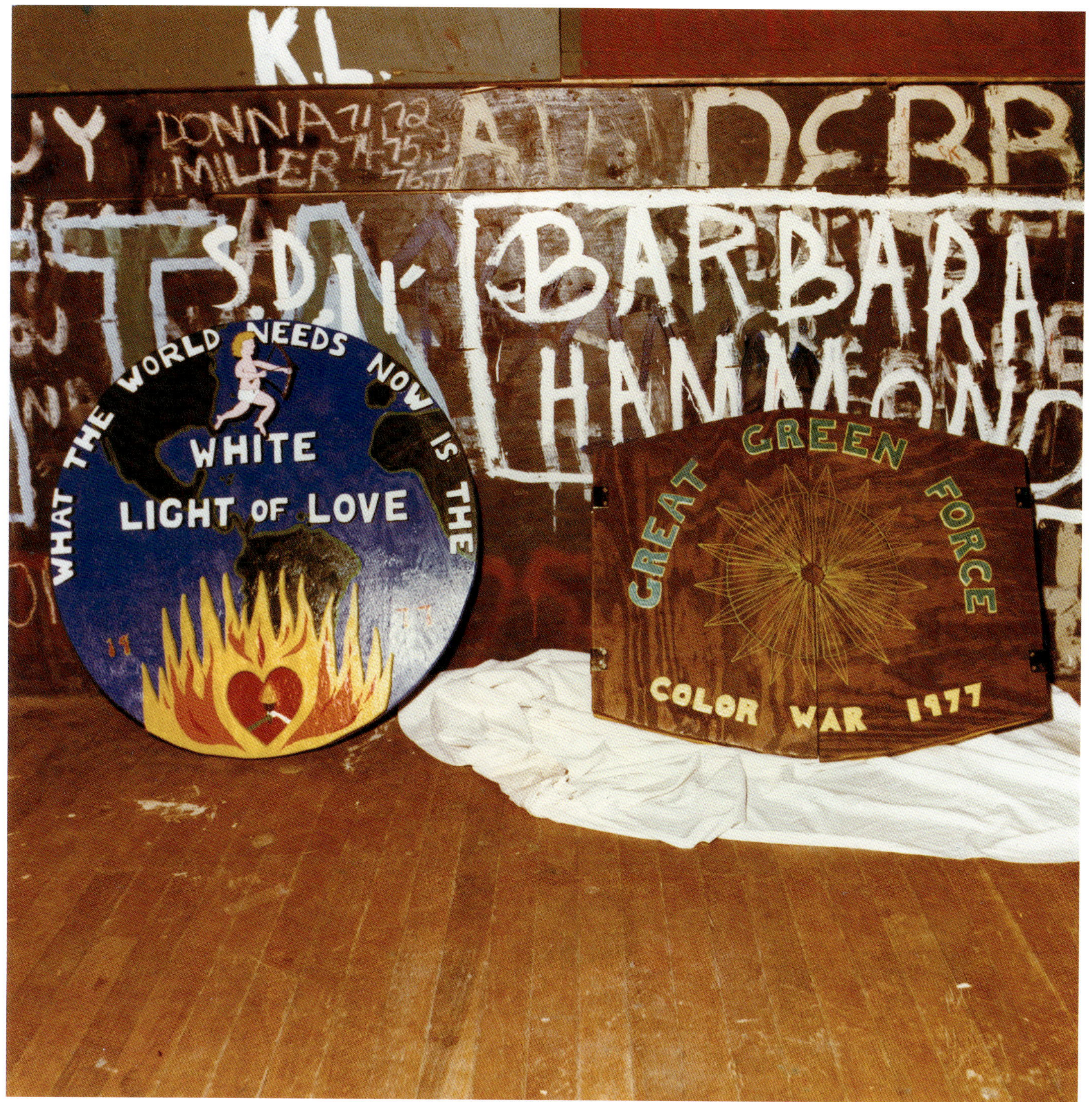
K.L.
DONNA 71 72
MILLER 74 75
76 T
BARBARA
HAMMOND
WHAT THE WORLD NEEDS NOW IS THE
WHITE
LIGHT OF LOVE
GREAT GREEN FORCE
COLOR WAR 1977

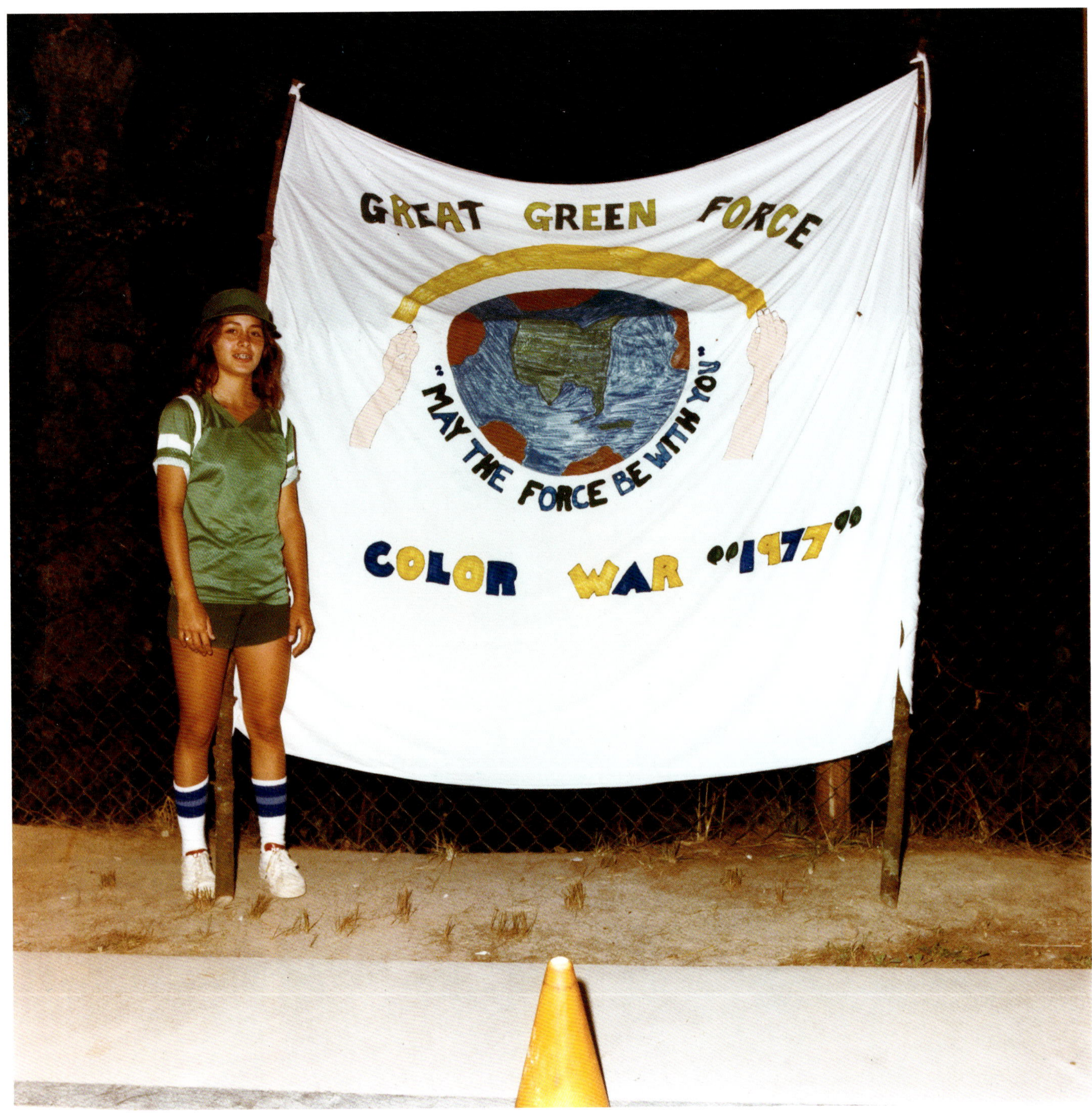

GREAT GREEN FORCE
"MAY THE FORCE BE WITH YOU"
COLOR WAR "1977"

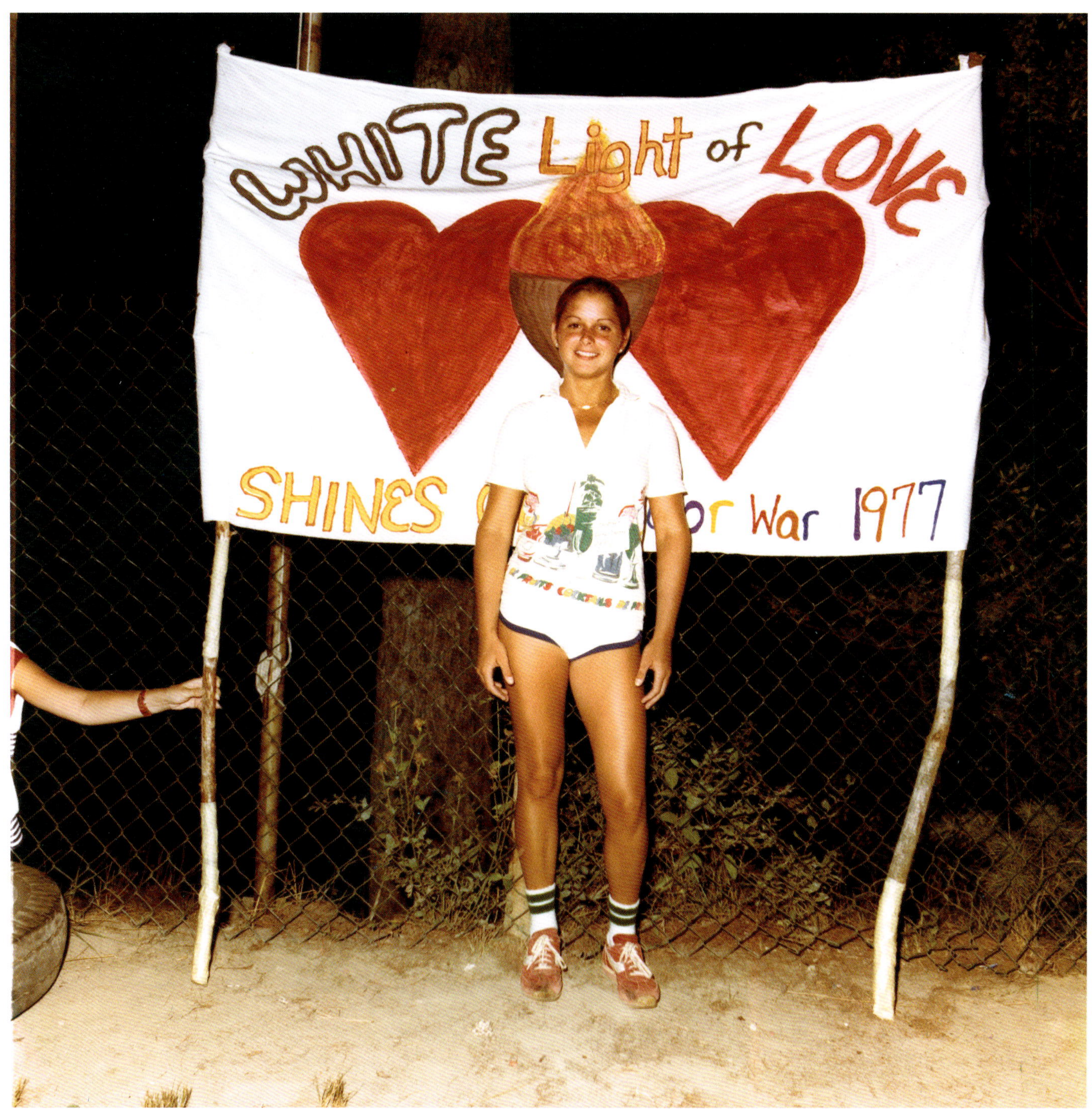
WHITE Light of LOVE
SHINES OVER Color War 1977

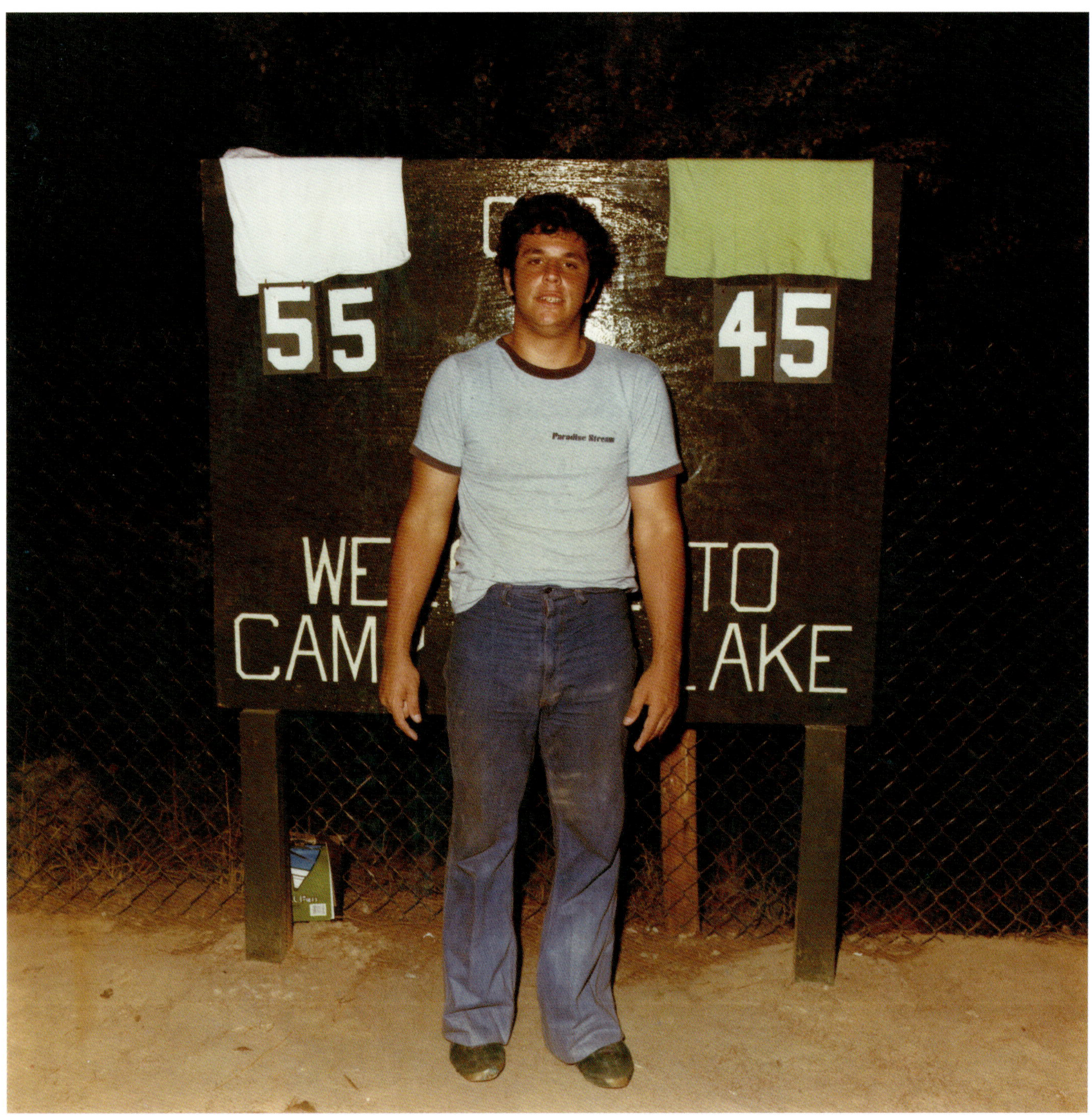

55
45
Paradise Stream
WE   TO
CAM   AKE

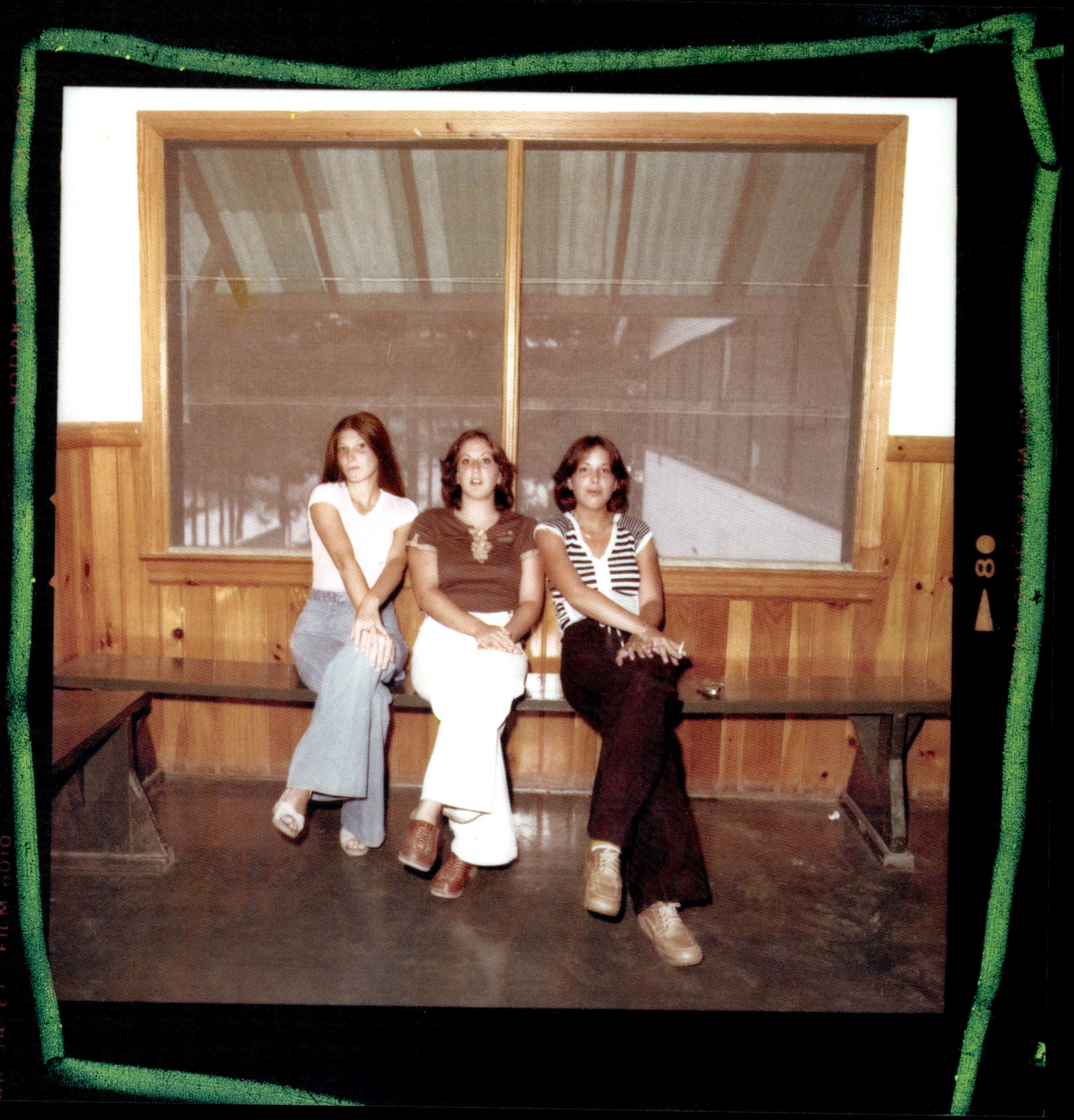

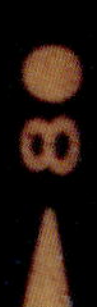

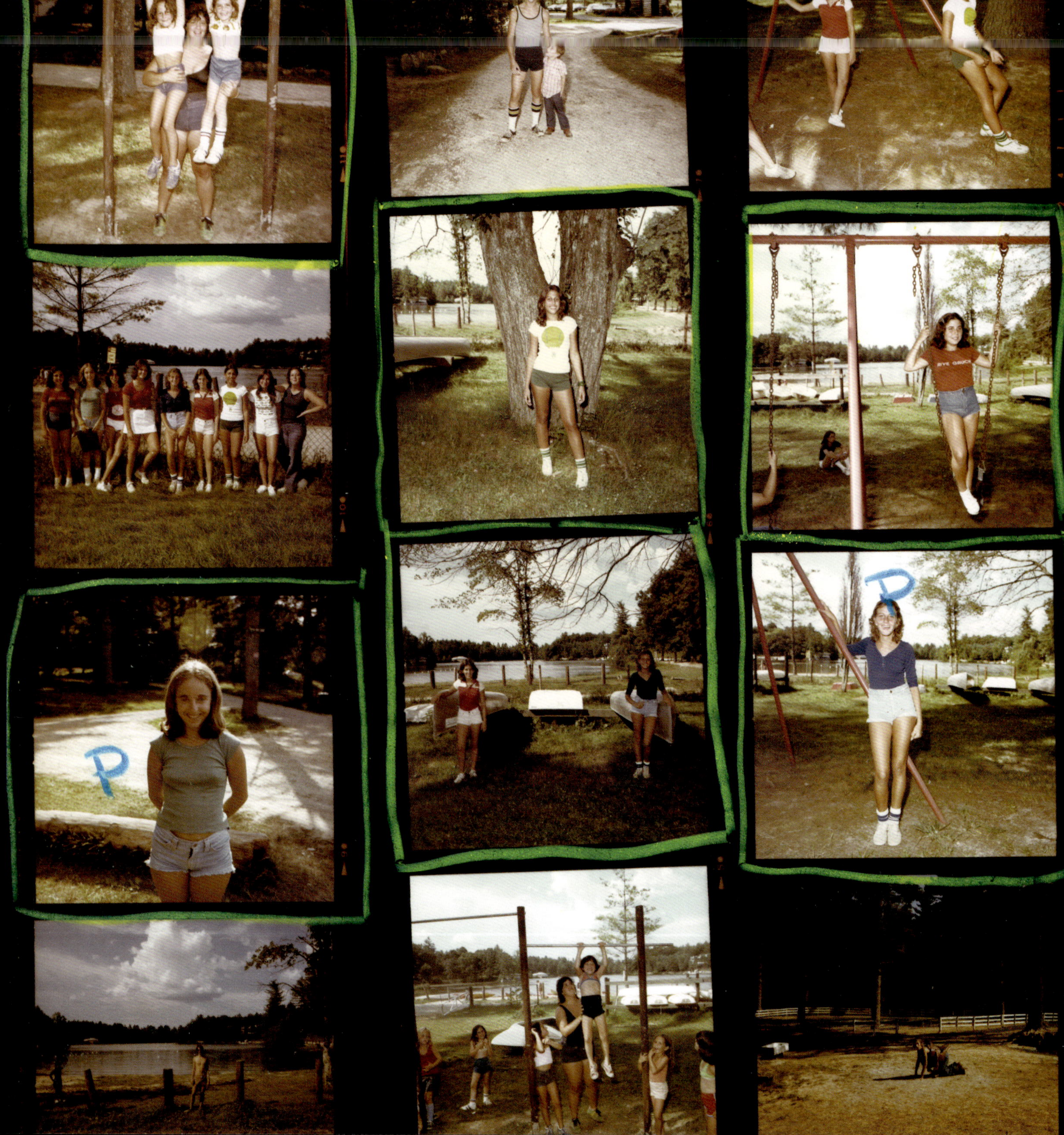

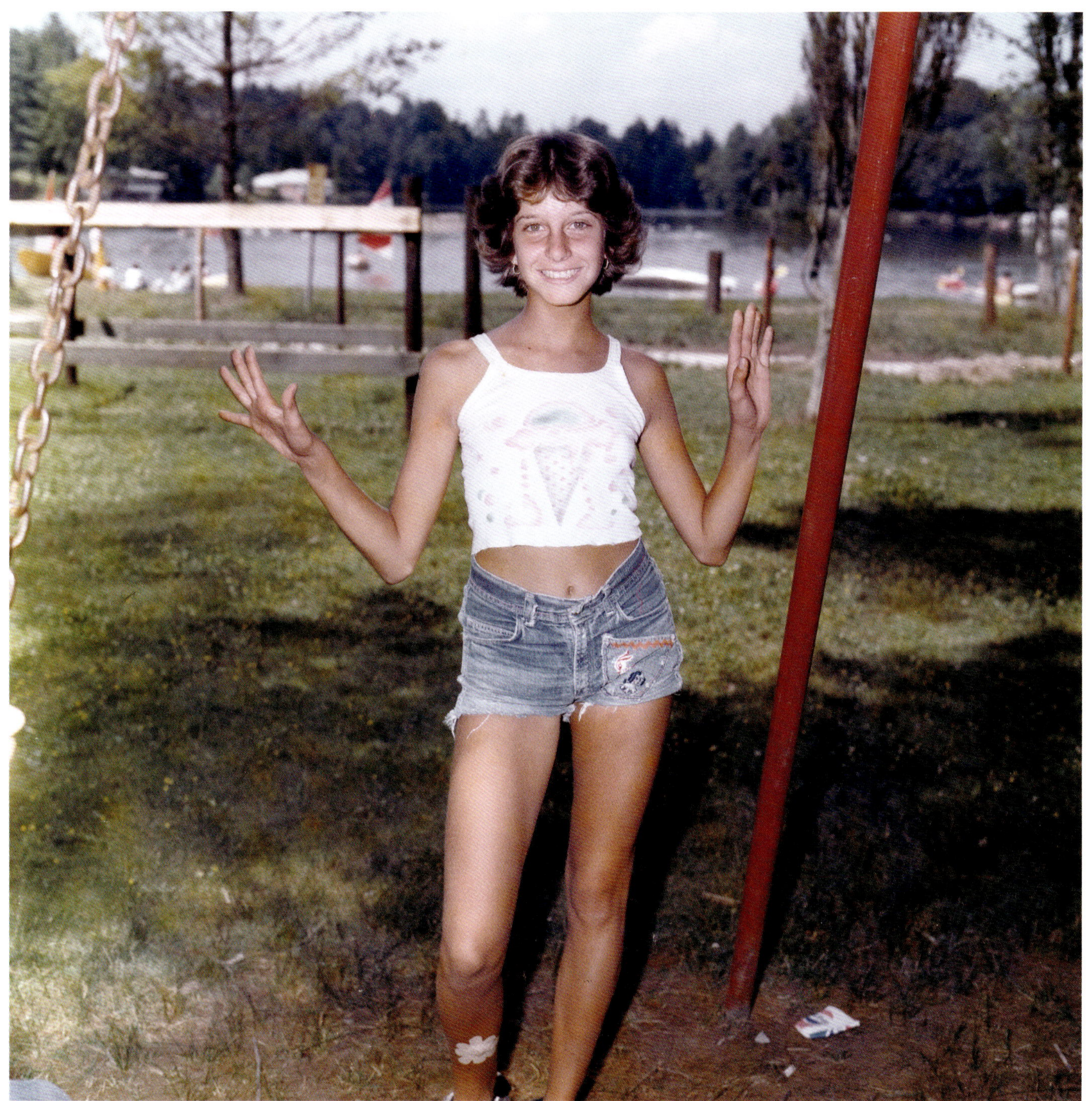

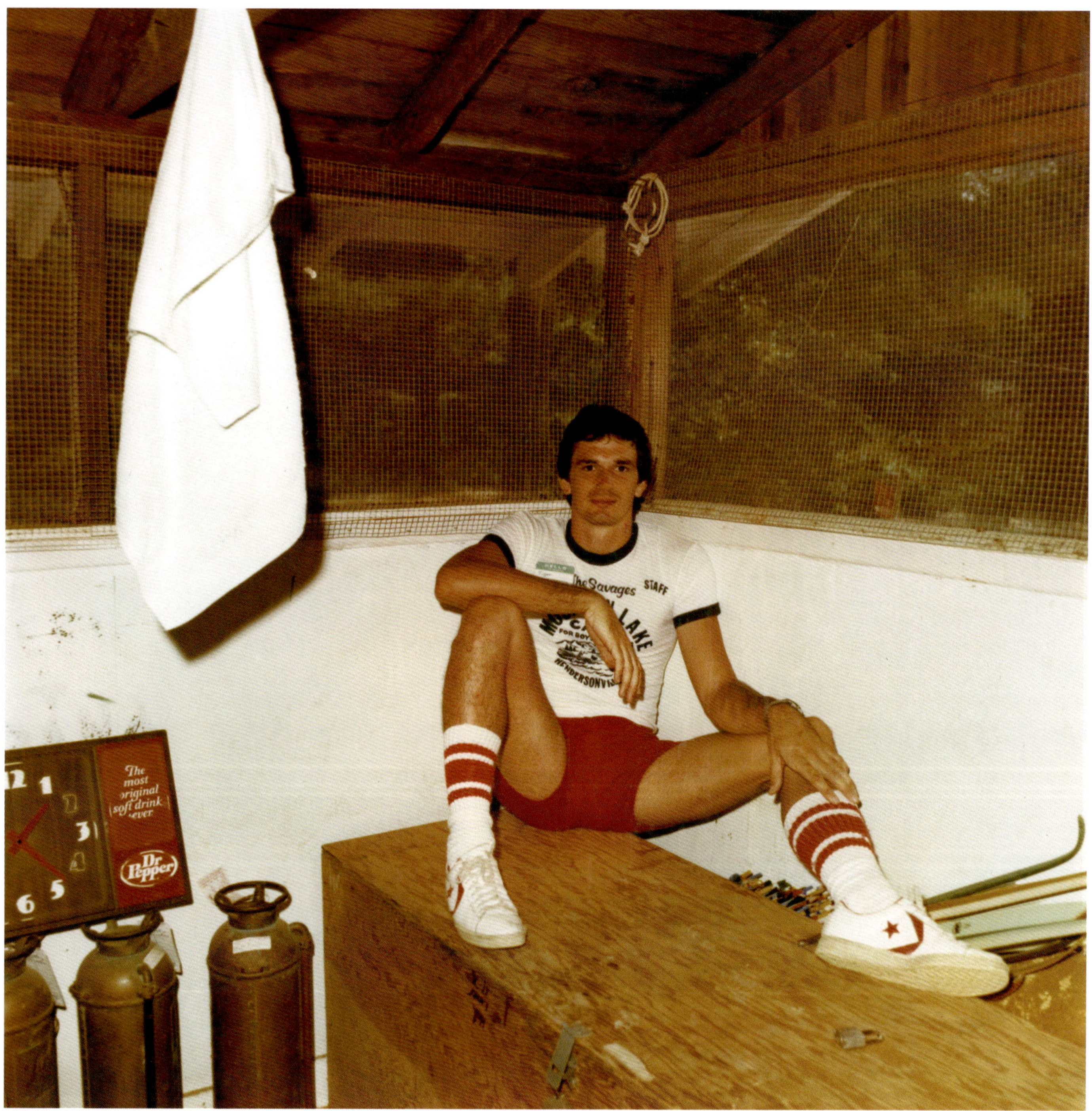

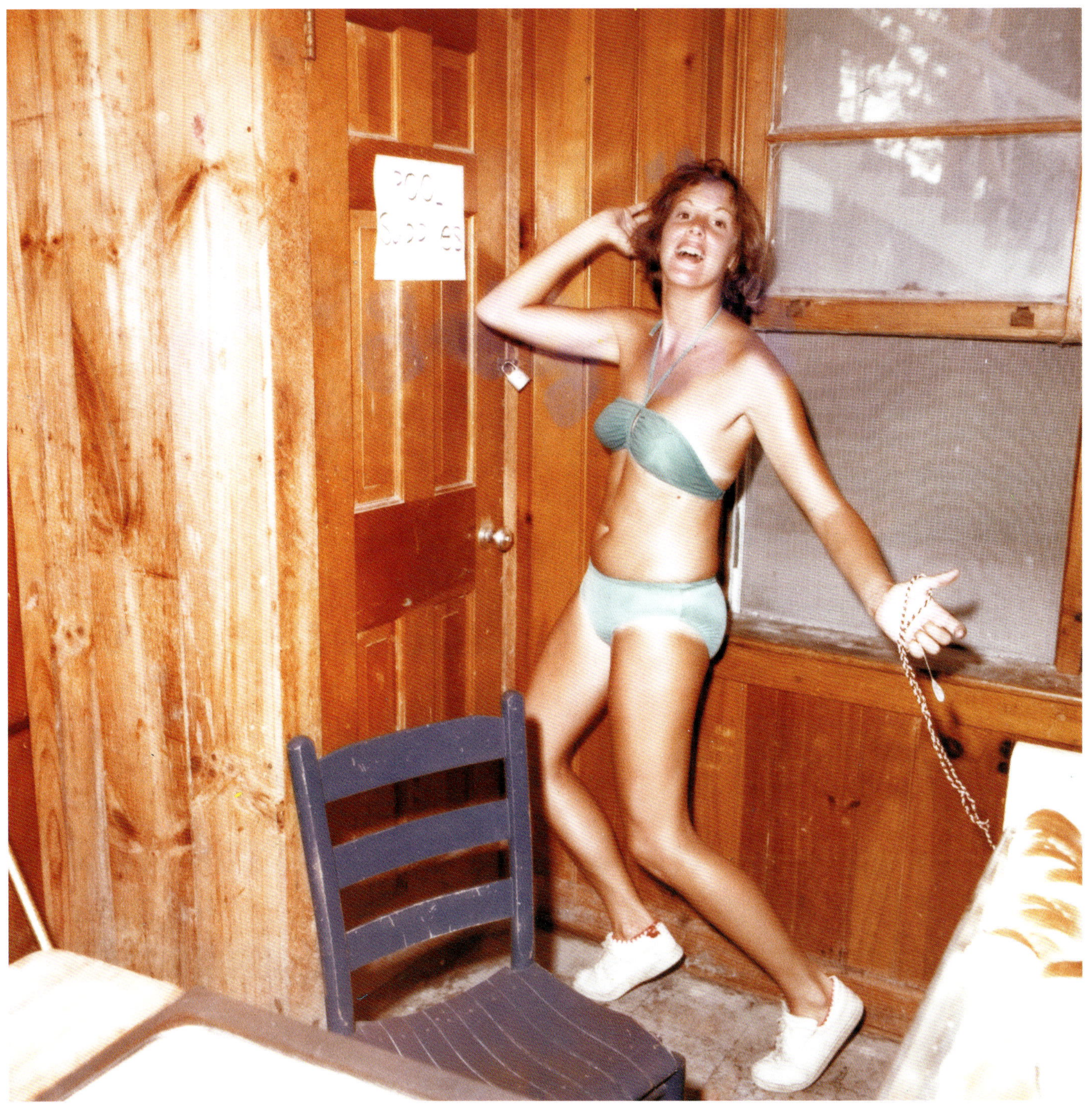
POOL
SUPPLIES

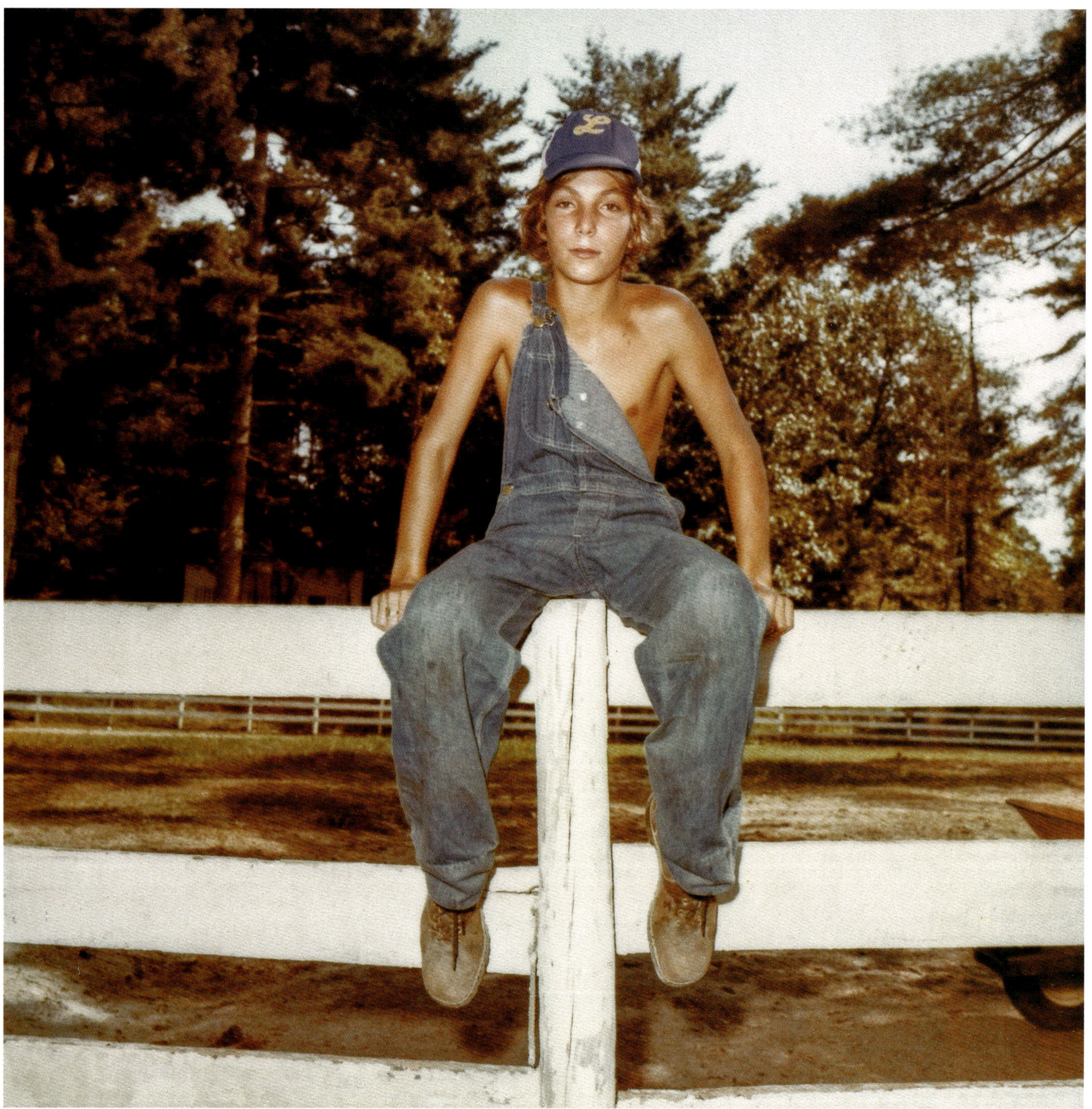

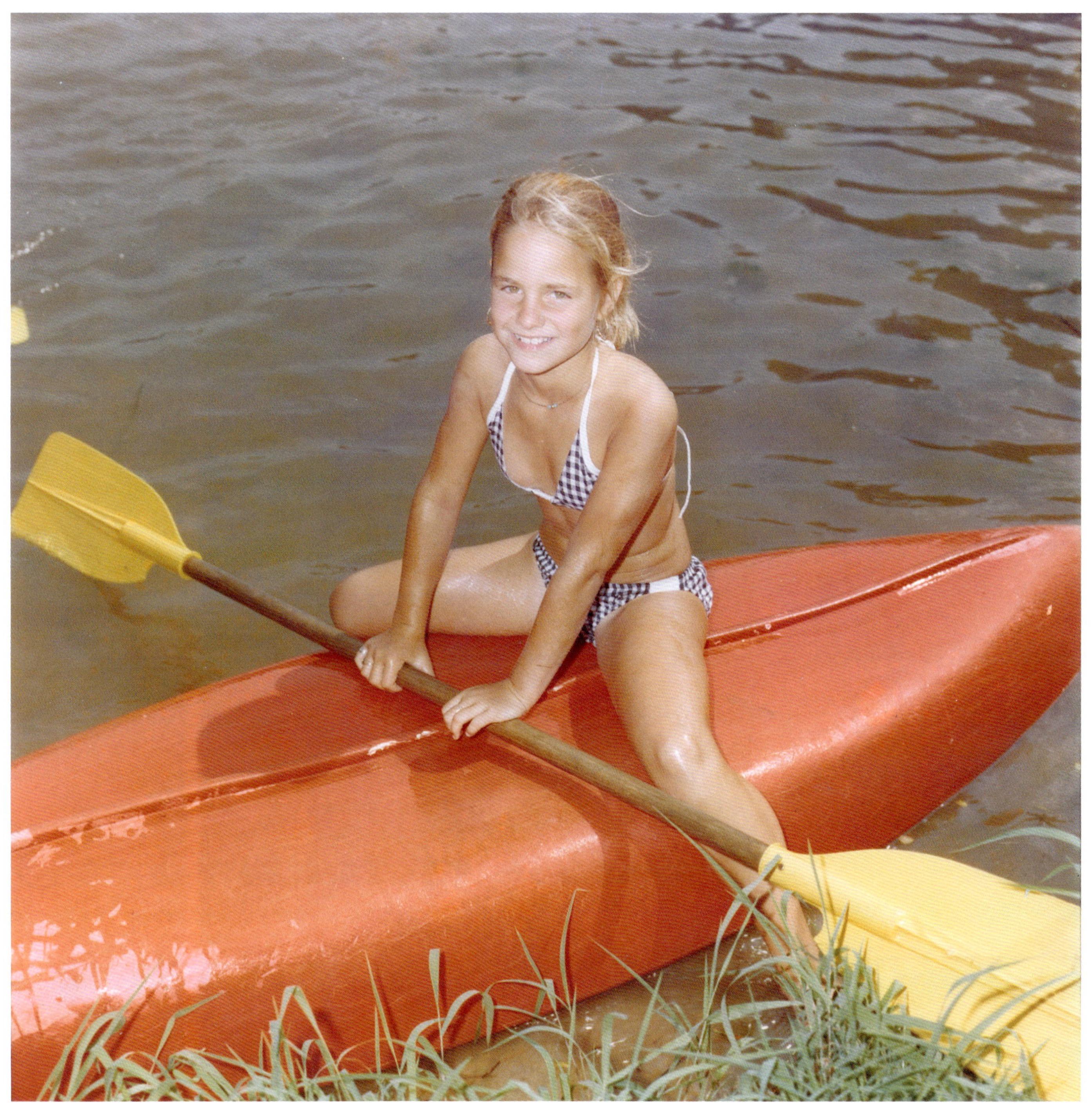

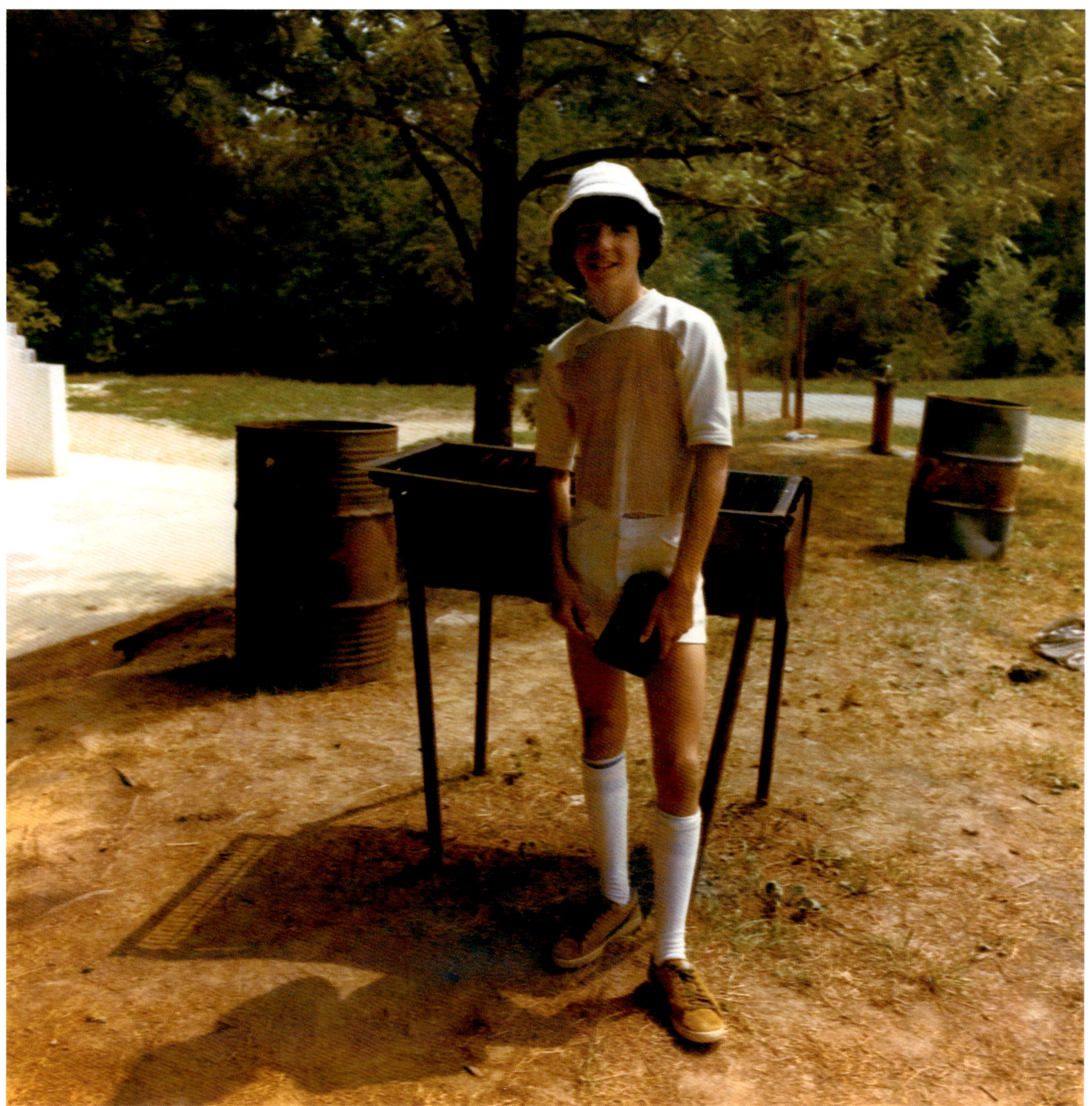

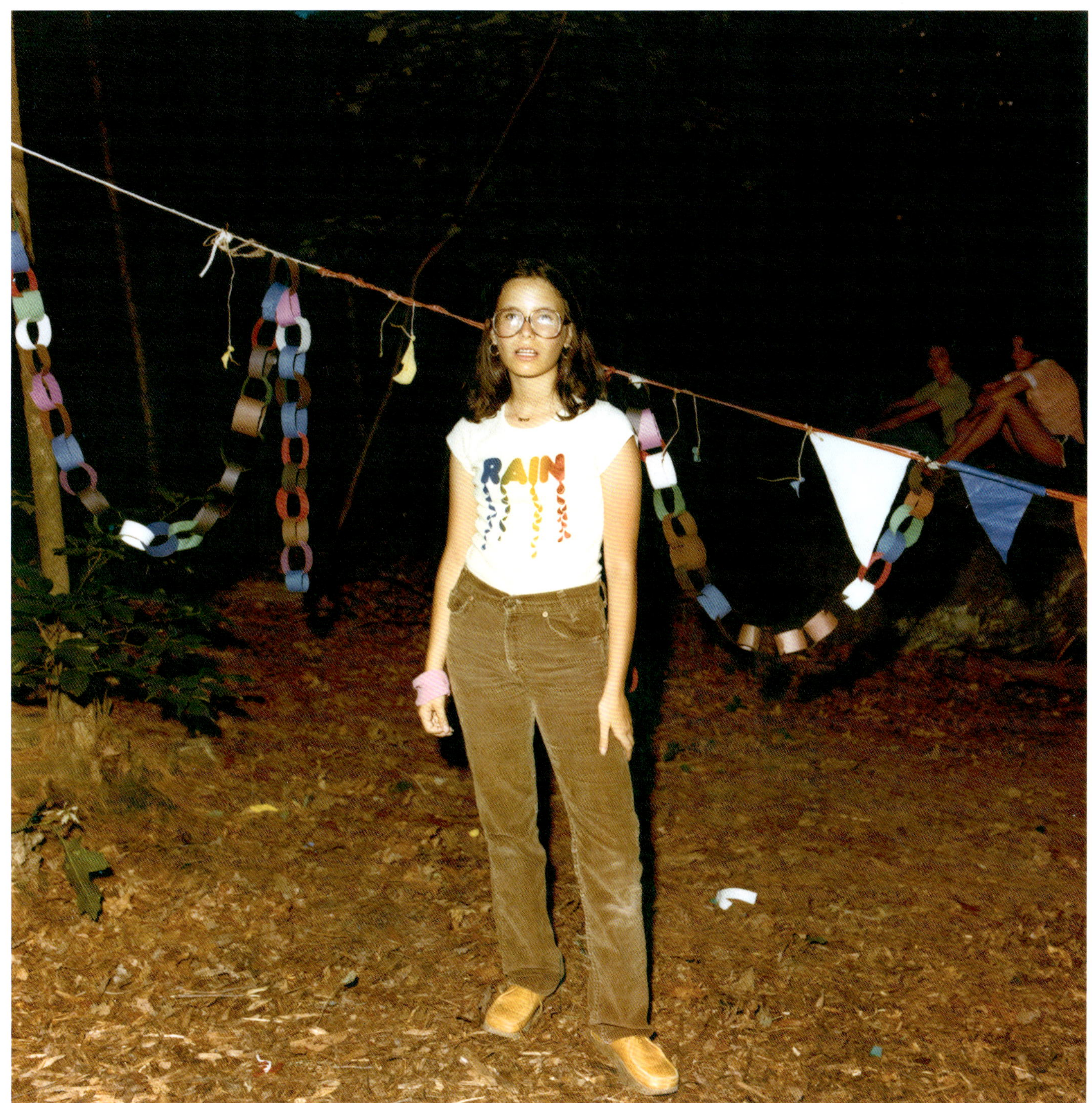
RAIN

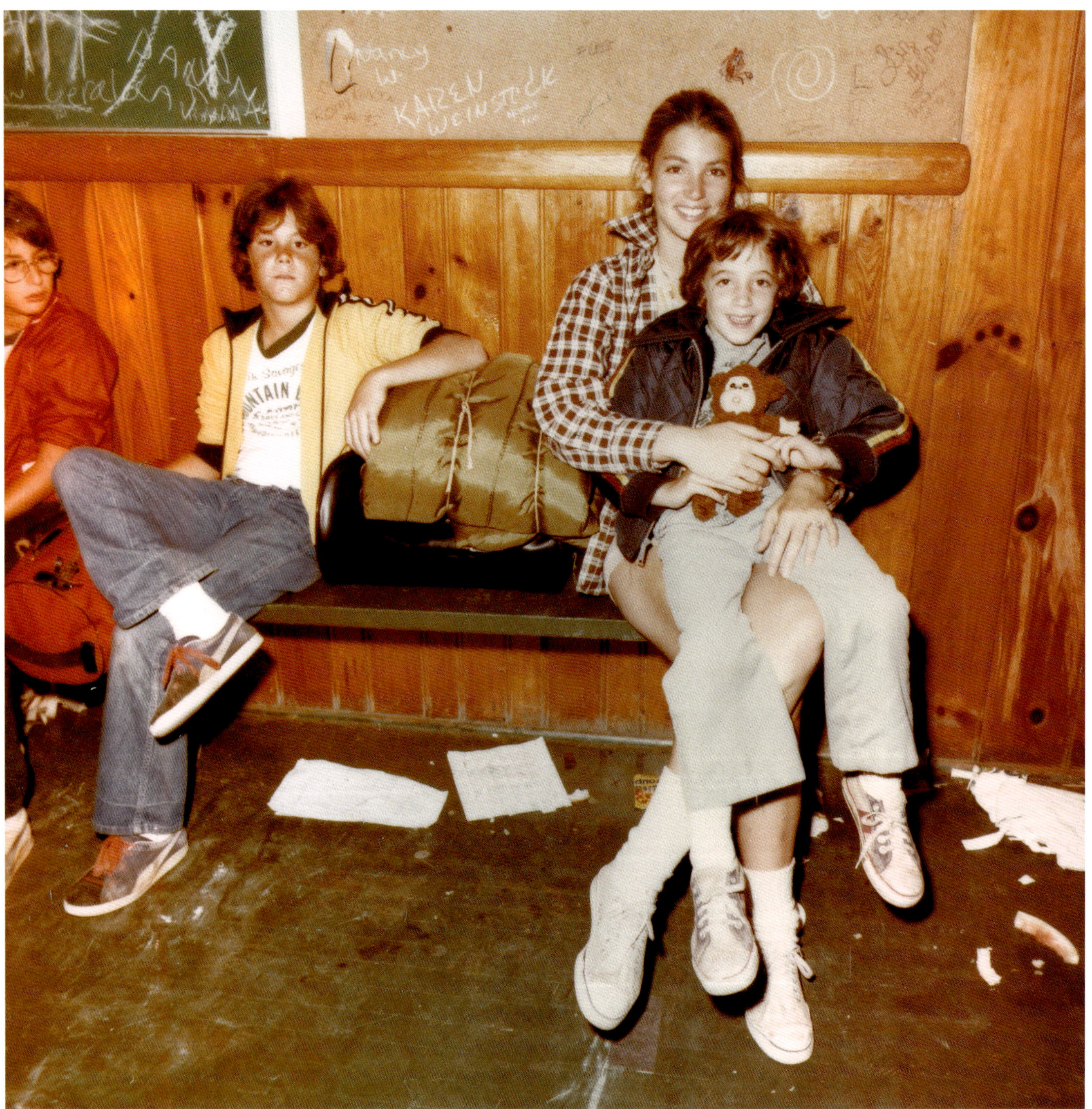

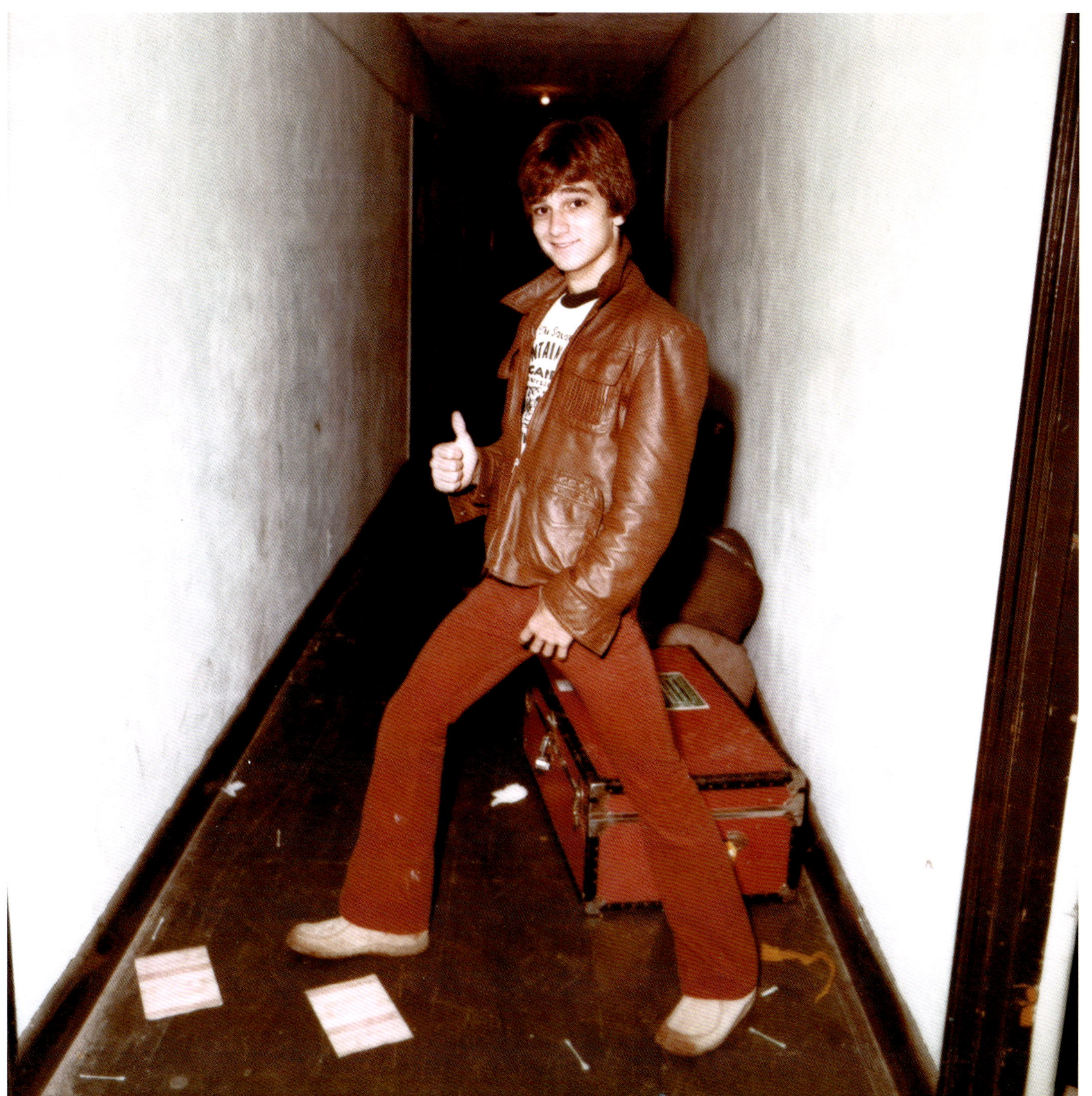

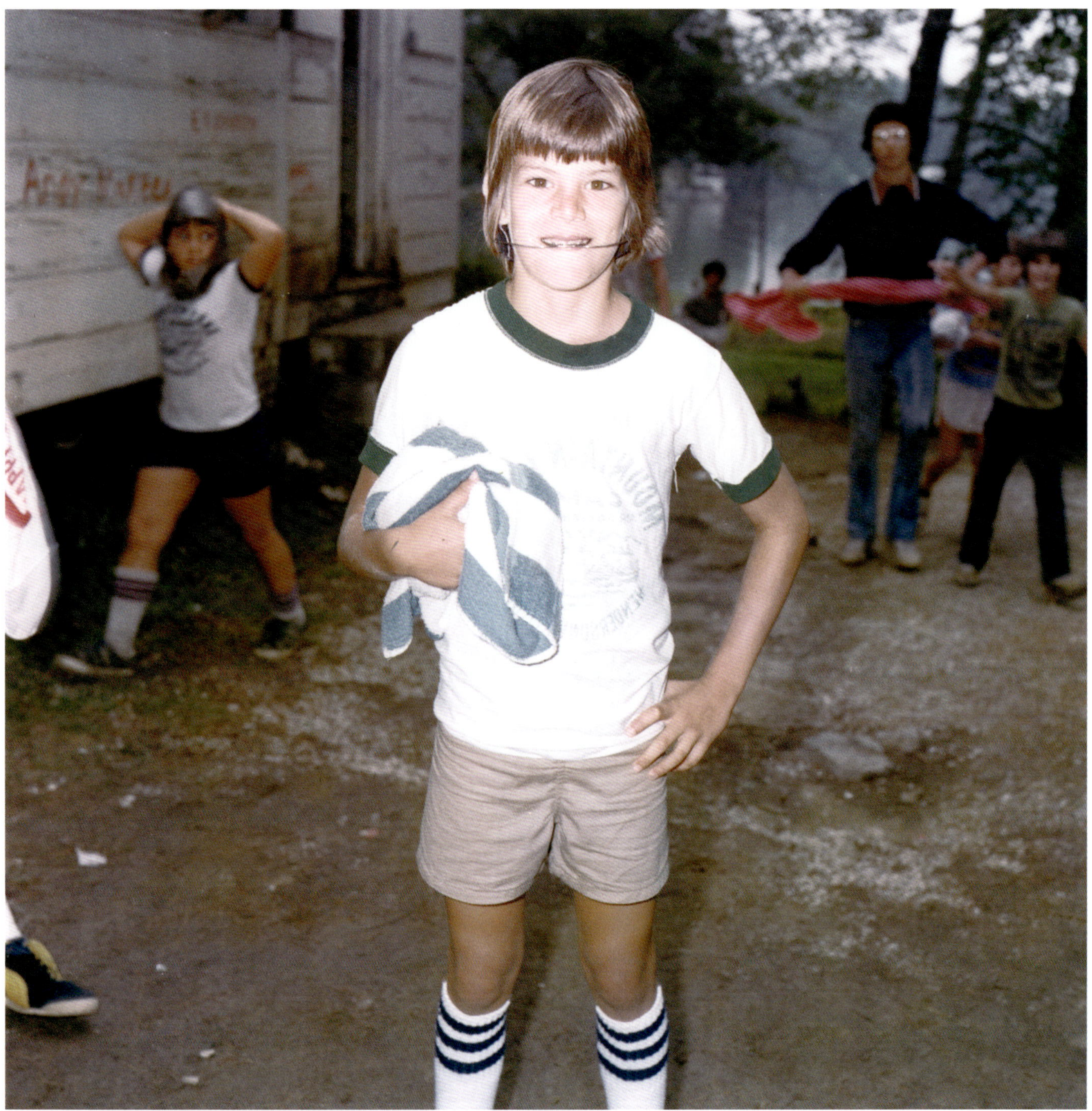

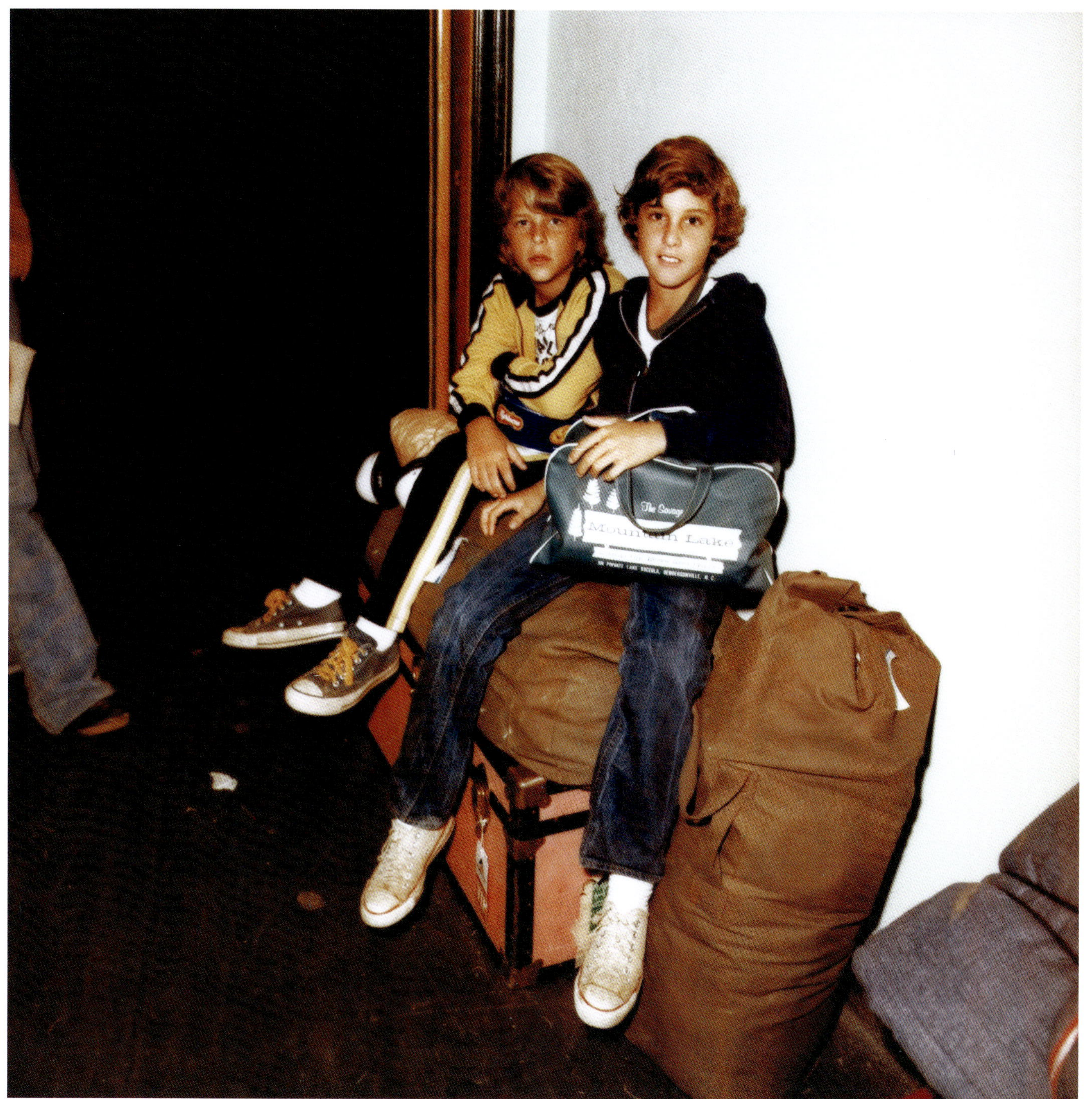

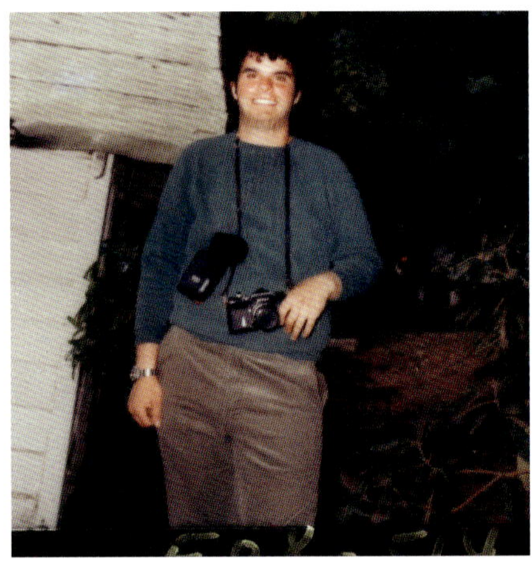

Andy Sweet, Camp Mountain Lake, 1977

Acknowledgments

Our most heartfelt gratitude goes to Ellen Sweet Moss and Stan Hughes for their devotion to restoring the photography of Andy Sweet—and for their faith in our doing justice to his artistic legacy.

Naomi Fry was wonderfully generous with her writing and her enthusiasm for this project was infectious. Mitchell Kaplan offered the kind of guidance that has made him such a beloved figure in the literary world. The Knight Foundation provided key financial aid and encouragement. Augusto Maxwell, our vital partner from the very start, gave invaluable counsel. Beverly Russin and Mary Ann Scarpino helped fill in the historical picture with rich textural details. Barbara Young remains a source of inspiration, not only for us, but for several generations of Miami artists.

Special thanks also to Carlos Betancourt, Susan Gladstone, Jacqueline Goldstein, Barbara Graustark, Carson Hall, Charles Hashim, Luis Hernandez, Bill Kearney, Amanda Keeley, Rebecca Kleinman, Polly Landess, Gady Levy, Avery Lozada, Lissette Mendez, Gary Monroe, Elisa Nadel, Lisa Palley, Chris Remington, Erika Resnick, Dennis Scholl, Kareem Tabsch, Patricia Alfonso Tortolani, Liz Tracy, Anne Tschida, Joseph B. Treaster, and Jane Wooldridge.

Frank is grateful to his three roommates for their ongoing support: Coco, Mama Cat, and Orange Julius. Brett is equally grateful to his Timber Lake Camp counselors, who imparted vital life lessons as true today as at the dawn of the 1980s. Namely: Rush is cooler than REO Speedwagon, but the Ramones are the coolest of all; if there's drool on your chin, you're not French kissing correctly; and you don't need to waste the summer worrying about being popular, you just need to try and make one good friend. (They may have borrowed that last bit of wisdom from Bill Murray's head counselor in "Meatballs," but it's still excellent advice.)

Francesco Casale and Brett Sokol